CONIFERS

CONTRIBUTORS

ALLEN J. COOMBES
*Hardy Trees, Magnolias
and Guide to Tree Care*

KENNETH A. BECKETT
Tender Trees

KEITH RUSHFORTH
Conifers and Dwarf Conifers

SUSYN ANDREWS
Hollies

HOW TO USE THIS BOOK

THIS BOOK PROVIDES the ideal quick reference guide to selecting and identifying trees for the garden.

The **Trees in the Garden** section is a helpful introduction to trees and gives advice on choosing a suitable tree for a particular site or purpose, such as for a container, as a screen, or simply as a specimen plant.

To choose or identify your tree, turn to the **Catalogue of Garden Trees,** where photographs are accompanied by concise plant descriptions. The entries are grouped by size and season of interest. In addition, if you have a colour preference, the trees are also grouped by colour (see the Colour Wheel below) for easy selection. Clear descriptions and cultivation requirements are to be found under each plant entry.

For additional information on tree cultivation, routine care, and propagation, turn to the **Guide to Tree Care,** where comprehensive information on all aspects of caring for your tree can be found.

The Colour Wheel

All the trees featured in the book are grouped according to the colour of their main feature of interest.

They are always arranged in the same order, indicated by the Colour Wheel below, from white through reds and blues, to yellows and oranges.

Variegated trees are categorized by the colour of their variegation, that is, white or yellow.

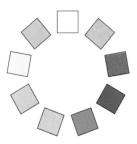

THE SYMBOLS

The symbols below are used throughout the **Catalogue of Garden Trees** to indicate a tree's preferred growing conditions and hardiness. However, both the climate and soil conditions of your particular site should also be taken into account, as they may affect a tree's growth.

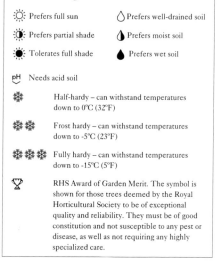

☼ Prefers full sun   ◊ Prefers well-drained soil

☼ Prefers partial shade   ◊ Prefers moist soil

☀ Tolerates full shade   ◊ Prefers wet soil

pH   Needs acid soil

❄   Half-hardy – can withstand temperatures down to 0°C (32°F)

❄ ❄   Frost hardy – can withstand temperatures down to -5°C (23°F)

❄ ❄ ❄   Fully hardy – can withstand temperatures down to -15°C (5°F)

♢   RHS Award of Garden Merit. The symbol is shown for those trees deemed by the Royal Horticultural Society to be of exceptional quality and reliability. They must be of good constitution and not susceptible to any pest or disease, as well as not requiring any highly specialized care.

Tree size categories

The trees featured in the Catalogue are divided according to the average height they attain. However, heights may vary from the ones given, according to site, climate, and age.

The categories are as follows:

LARGE
Over 15m (50ft)
MEDIUM
10–15m (30–50ft)
SMALL
Up to 10m (30ft)

How to use the Catalogue of Trees

HEADINGS
Each chapter is subdivided into sections, according to the average size of the trees and their main season of interest.

The tree's *family name* appears here.

The tree's *common name(s)* appear here.

The tree's *botanical name* appears here.

TREE PORTRAITS
The colour photographs show the main features of the tree (see THE COLOUR WHEEL on previous page).

ENTRIES
Each tree's growing habit, flowers, fruits, and leaves are described. Details of the tree's native habitat, cultivation, and propagation, together with any other botanical names, are also provided.

SYMBOLS
The symbols indicate the sun, soil, and temperature requirements (see THE SYMBOLS on previous page). Ideal temperatures are given for trees that cannot withstand below 0°C (32°F).

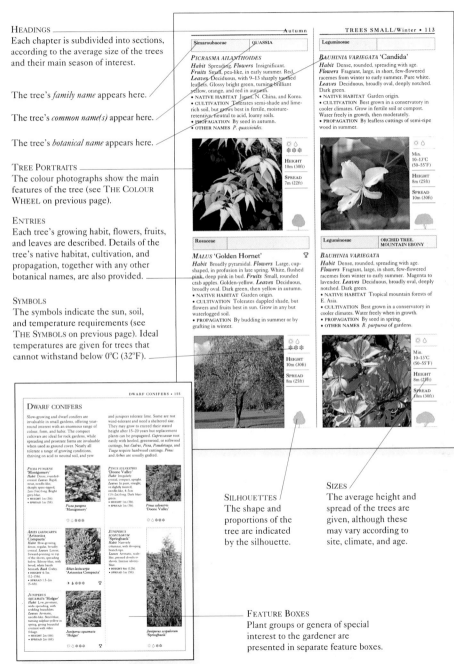

SILHOUETTES
The shape and proportions of the tree are indicated by the silhouette.

SIZES
The average height and spread of the trees are given, although these may vary according to site, climate, and age.

FEATURE BOXES
Plant groups or genera of special interest to the gardener are presented in separate feature boxes.

TREES IN THE GARDEN

MORE THAN ANY other feature in the garden, trees form the structural framework of a design, with their distinctive silhouettes providing a foil of contrasting elements against the softer lines of other plantings.

Trees offer an enormous diversity of shape and form, as well as colour and texture of foliage, flowers, and bark. They may be grown in many ways: informally in a woodland setting, under-planted with bulbs and shade-loving perennials, or formally in avenues or as pleached (interlaced) hedging. Some are so beautiful in bloom that, if sited alone, they make a beautiful, eye-catching garden feature.

Choosing trees

Trees are generally the largest, longest-lived and most expensive of plants in the garden, so selecting and siting them are primary design decisions. In smaller gardens or in a 'one-tree garden', careful choice and siting are vital. Although a tree's overall appearance and special features are important, it is also essential to consider its suitability for the garden's soil, climate, and aspect, and to take account of its rate of growth and final height and spread.

Garden centres usually carry a limited range of the most popular ornamental trees, but specialist nurseries and mail-order services offer a much wider choice.

Trees as design elements

Trees are the living equivalent of hard landscaping features, creating a strong visual impact in much the same way as walls and paving. If used structurally, trees can define or enclose space: they can mark boundaries or separate one part of the garden from another. If used as hedging, they can create effective screens; when used in pairs they can frame a distant view; or when in rows, may be used to create an arch.

Long-lasting designs
Grouped together in a planned design, trees create a strong impact, developing over the years, with their varied colours and forms.

Shape and form

A tree's form and shape are important to the style of a garden. Many trees can be used in formal or informal settings, but some, especially those that are cone-shaped, such as *Carpinus betulus* 'Fastigiata', almost demand formal use. Trees with a strong architectural form fit well in small, paved gardens. In contrast, rowans (*Sorbus aucuparia*) and crab apples (*Malus*) are typical 'English cottage garden' trees. For gardens with an oriental theme, Japanese maples (*Acer palmatum*) and *Salix babylonica* var. *pekinensis* 'Tortuosa' are ideal.

While round-headed or spreading trees often have an informal appearance, they cast shade and rain shadow, making

TREE SHAPES

SPREADING
Prunus x *yedoensis*
(Yoshino cherry)

WEEPING
Prunus x *subhirtella* 'Pendula Rubra'

PYRAMIDAL
Carpinus betulus
'Fastigiata'

ROUND–HEADED
Fagus sylvatica
(Common beech,
European beech)

CONICAL
Pseudotsuga menziesii
var. *glauca*
(Blue Douglas fir)

ARCHING
Archontophoenix alexandrae
(Alexandra palm)

COLUMNAR
Acer rubrum
'Columnare'

Planning garden colour
Although most gardens look their best in summer, successional planting can create year-round interest. Spring and autumn-flowering trees, as well as those grown for their foliage, bark, berries, and winter outline, provide colour and variety throughout the year.

underplanting difficult. Trees with an irregular, open-branch framework cast little shade, and may be underplanted with bulbs and small perennials.

Successional interest
In many gardens, the glorious but short-lived flowers of spring and summer leave little to lift the spirits in the dark days of winter. But with planning and careful selection from a palette of flowers, foliage, berries, and bark, colour and interest can be maintained throughout the year. Choose trees with successive flowering, such as *Cercis siliquastrum* for spring, *Eucryphia* x *nymansensis* for early autumn, and *Magnolia campbellii* and its forms which flower from late winter. The beautiful silvery foliage of *Sorbus aria* 'Lutescens' appears in spring, while in autumn the maples (*Acer*) give displays of brilliant golds and reds. Autumn highlights are provided by berrying species of *Sorbus*, *Cotoneaster*, *Crataegus*, and *Malus*, some persisting well into winter, which is the best time to appreciate the bark of species of *Acer*, *Betula*, *Eucalyptus*, and *Prunus*.

Specimen trees
A specimen tree is grown on its own and so can develop its full natural beauty without competition from other trees. It is important to select a specimen that is in scale with its setting – small trees look lost in wide, open areas and, conversely, large trees overwhelm confined spaces.

In formal gardens, specimen trees are usually planted in the centre of the lawn. In less formal settings an offset tree adds a dynamic sense of movement to a scheme, and can lead the eye to the view down the garden. Specimens can mark the transition from one area of the garden to another, and providing a foil for a specimen enhances its effect – for example, by planting it in a swathe of gravel, amongst ground cover plants, or by still water where it can be reflected.

Trees contrasted with plants
As well as providing a contrast of texture with other plants, trees can also be planted to enhance the perspective of the garden.

Using specimen trees

Specimens are trees with a particularly attractive or well-shaped outline. They look their best when sited on their own, so that they stand out against the rest of the garden. Magnolia x kewensis 'Wada's Memory' makes a magnificent specimen tree, with its profusion of large, fragrant, white flowers that appear before the leaves from mid- to late spring.

Features of interest

A tree's form provides a framework to display other features of interest at different times of the year. Foliage is the most important, by virtue of its mass and duration. The shape, colour, and texture of leaves provide infinite variation, from the delicate, fern-like foliage of *Gleditsia triacanthos* 'Sunburst' to the large, architectural leaves of *Paulownia tomentosa*. Plants with dark or variegated foliage offer the potential of subtle or dramatic associations with plain, green-leaved species. Surface texture adds another dimension: glossy leaves give glittering reflections and can be contrasted with leaves of a matt texture.

Even the most transient of flowers can create memorable effects, ranging from the delicate profusion of the spring cherries (*Prunus* species) to the tropical opulence of the jacarandas. Trees that bloom in autumn, winter, and early spring are amongst the most valuable, providing interest in the darkest seasons. Choose flower colours to complement the wider scheme, and shelter those with scent so that the still air captures their fragrance.

Fruits, berries, and pods often rival flowers in beauty, and many berrying trees attract wildlife. Do not overlook more subtle fruits, such as the pods of magnolias or the coloured keys of maples.

Trees in containers
Container-grown trees have a striking effect and can be moved to vary the garden design or for their own protection in winter.

The colour and texture of bark can be fully appreciated in winter. Choose from the stark whites of the birches, the mahogany-reds of some *Prunus*, the striations of the snake-bark acers, or the peeling mosaics of *Eucalyptus*.

Trees for screens and shelter belts
Large-scale tree planting can be used to screen unsightly buildings and roads, whilst also deadening noise and filtering dust. They can provide shelter from wind and frost for other plants nearby. Tree selection is very important. Lombardy poplars (*Populus nigra* 'Italica') are often planted as screens, but their height and narrow outline not only highlight what they are intended to conceal, but also offer little protection from wind at ground level. Stands of mixed deciduous and evergreen trees provide a more effective barrier.

Hedges are the most dense and compact form of screening, and a number of trees tolerate close clipping and prove invaluable as formal hedging. Yew (*Taxus baccata*) is the classic backdrop in traditional English gardens; hornbeam (*Carpinus betulus*), holly (*Ilex aquifolium*), and beech (*Fagus sylvatica*), also create visually impenetrable but very effective wind-filtering screens. For informal, flowering hedges try cherry plum (*Prunus cerasifera*) or strawberry tree (*Arbutus unedo*).

Trees in containers
Growing trees in large pots or tubs greatly extends their design potential. On patios, in courtyards – anywhere where soil space is at a premium – containerized trees create a verdant and colourful effect, and give height and structure to the design. Trees in large containers may be used to frame an entrance or to flank wide steps, while tender trees may be grown in containers, displayed outdoors in summer, then moved to a light, frost-free place as the cold weather draws in.

Dwarf conifers
As a group, the dwarf conifers are unique in their diversity of shape and form. They range from globose to spire- and cone-shape, with habits including prostrate, erect, and weeping. Textures vary from soft and feathery to firm and spiky, and their colours encompass almost metallic shades of gold, silver, bronze and steel blues, as well as rich blue-greens and dark greens.

Their compact form is well suited to small, modern gardens, where larger trees are impractical. Adaptable and easy to grow – in raised beds and borders, as well as in rock gardens – dwarf conifers are a garden essential. Even the tiniest of them may be used effectively to create miniature landscapes in troughs or other containers.

Adaptable dwarf conifers
Dwarf conifers are invaluable in the garden and are available in a wide variety of shapes, sizes, colours, and textures.

PLANTER'S GUIDE TO TREES

FOR EXPOSED SITES

Acer pseudoplatanus 'Simon
  Louis Frères',
  A. pseudoplatanus
  f. *erythrocarpum*
Betula pendula 'Tristis'
Crataegus laevigata 'Paul's
  Scarlet', *C.* x *lavallei*
  'Carrierei'
Fagus sylvatica, F. sylvatica
  f. *pendula, F. sylvatica*
  f. *purpurea*
Fraxinus excelsior
Juniperus communis
  'Hibernica'
Laburnum alpinum,
  L. x *watereri* 'Vossii'
Picea abies
Pinus contorta, P. nigra,
  P. ponderosa, P. sylvestris
  'Fastigiata'
Populus x *canadensis* and cvs.
Quercus robur f. *fastigiata*
Salix alba
Sorbus aria 'Lutescens'
  S. aucuparia
Taxus baccata 'Aurea',
  T. baccata 'Dovastonii
  Aurea'
Tilia cordata 'Rancho'

FOR SMALL GARDENS

Acer capillipes, A. griseum,
  A. palmatum 'Koreanum'
Arbutus x *andrachnoides*
Betula albosinensis, B. ermanii
  B. pendula 'Tristis'
  B. utilis var. *jacquemontii*
Catalpa bignonioides 'Aurea'
Cercis siliquastrum
Cornus florida

Crataegus laevigata 'Paul's
  Scarlet', *C.* x *lavallei*
  'Carrierei'
Eucryphia x *nymansensis*
Gleditsia triacanthos
  'Sunburst'
Laburnum x *watereri* 'Vossii'
Malus (many)
Pinus halepensis
Prunus (many)
Pyrus calleryana
  'Chanticleer', *P. salicifolia*
  'Pendula'
Sorbus cashmiriana,
  S. commixta, S. vilmorinii

FOR CONTAINERS

Abies koreana
Acer negundo 'Variegatum'
  A. palmatum 'Coreanum'
Chamaecyparis lawsoniana
  'Gnom', *C. lawsoniana*
  'Minima', *C. obtusa* 'Nana
  Pyramidalis'
Cordyline australis
  'Atropurpurea'
Ficus benjamina 'Variegata'
Ilex compact species and cvs.
Juniperus chinensis 'Stricta'
  J. scopulorum 'Skyrocket'
Pinus mugo 'Gnom'
Prunus 'Kiku-shidare-zakura',
  P. subhirtella 'Pendula
  Rubra'
Taxus baccata 'Dovastonii
  Aurea'
Thuja orientalis 'Aurea
  Nana', *T. occidentalis*
  'Caespitosa'

SPECIMEN TREES

Araucaria araucana
Abies procera 'Glauca'
Acer griseum, A. rubrum
Alnus cordata
Betula albosinensis
Carpinus betulus 'Fastigiata'
Cedrus atlantica f. *glauca,*
  C. libani

Ginkgo biloba
Liquidambar styraciflua
Liriodendron tulipifera
Magnolia campbellii 'Charles
  Raffill'
Metasequoia glyptostroboides
Nyssa sylvatica
Picea breweriana, P. omorika,
  P. bungeana
Prunus maackii
Salix x *sepulcralis* var.
  chrysocoma
Sequoiadendron giganteum
Tsuga heterophylla

POLLUTION TOLERANT

Acer (not Japanese maples)
Aesculus (all)
Ailanthus altissima
Alnus cordata, A. glutinosa
  'Imperialis', *A. incana*
Amelanchier (all)
Betula papyrifera
Carpinus betulus and cvs.
Catalpa bignonioides
Crataegus (most)
Davidia involucrata
Fraxinus (all)
Laburnum (all)
Liriodendron tulipifera
Malus (all)
Morus nigra
Platanus (all)
Populus (most)
Prunus avium, P. padus and
  cvs.
Prunus (all Japanese
  cherries)
Quercus ilex,
  Q. x *hispanica*
  'Lucombeana'

Salix (most)
Sorbus aria
  'Lutescens' and variants,
  S. aucuparia and variants

CATALOGUE OF
GARDEN
TREES

Hippocastanaceae	COMMON HORSE-CHESTNUT

AESCULUS HIPPOCASTANUM

Habit Vigorous, spreading. **Flowers** Tubular, flared at the mouth. They appear in large, conical, upright panicles in mid- to late spring. White, flushed with pink, yellow at the centre.
Fruits Rounded, spiny, green husk, enclosing 1 or 2 glossy brown conkers. **Leaves** Deciduous, divided into 5–7 narrowly oval, pointed leaflets. Dark green, turning yellow and orange-brown in autumn.
• NATIVE HABITAT Mountain woods of N. Greece and Albania.

• CULTIVATION Grow in sun or semi-shade in any fertile, well-drained soil. Very old trees sometimes develop downward-growing branches that turn sharply upwards where they meet the ground, thus forming natural layers. It is a reliably flowering species, often grown as a parkland tree and suitable as a specimen in larger gardens.
• PROPAGATION By seed in autumn.

HEIGHT
To 25m
(80ft)

SPREAD
20m (70ft)

Hippocastanaceae	

AESCULUS × *CARNEA* 'Briotii' ♈

Habit Broadly columnar or round-headed.
Flowers Tubular, flared at mouth, in upright,
conical spires in late spring. Rich bright red.
Fruits Smooth or slightly spiny husks enclosing
glossy brown conkers. *Leaves* Deciduous, divided,
with 5–7 twisted, sharply toothed leaflets. Dark green.
• NATIVE HABITAT Garden origin.
• CULTIVATION Grow in sun or semi-shade in any
fertile, well-drained soil.
• PROPAGATION By budding in late summer or by
grafting in winter.

Hippocastanaceae	CHINESE HORSE-CHESTNUT

AESCULUS CHINENSIS

Habit Slow-growing, spreading. *Flowers* Small,
tubular, in long, slender spires in mid-summer.
White. *Leaves* Deciduous, divided into 7 long,
narrow, oblong-oval leaflets. Glossy bright green.
• NATIVE HABITAT Forests of N. China.
• CULTIVATION Grow in sun or semi-shade in any
fertile, well-drained soil.
• PROPAGATION By seed in autumn.

☼ ◊
❀ ❀ ❀

HEIGHT
To 20m
(70ft)

SPREAD
15m (50ft)

☼ ◊
❀ ❀ ❀

HEIGHT
20m (70ft)
or more

SPREAD
10m (30ft)

Aceraceae	BIG LEAF MAPLE, OREGON MAPLE

ACER MACROPHYLLUM

Habit Broadly columnar. *Flowers* Small, fragrant,
in long, pendent clusters in spring. Yellow.
Fruits 2 seeds, fused together, each with a wing.
Leaves Deciduous, deeply lobed. Dark green,
turning orange and gold in autumn.
Bark Vertically fissured. Grey-brown.
• NATIVE HABITAT Damp woodland and canyons of
W. North America.
• CULTIVATION Grow in full sun or light, dappled
shade in fertile, moisture-retentive soil.
• PROPAGATION By seed in autumn.

Salicaceae	ABELE, SILVER-LEAVED POPLAR, WHITE POPLAR

POPULUS ALBA

Habit Broadly columnar. *Flowers* Drooping
catkins, with male and female on separate plants.
Fruits Small capsules enclosing tiny seeds in
white cotton. *Leaves* Deciduous, wavy-margined,
3–5 lobes. Dark green above, silvery-white beneath,
turning yellow in autumn.
• NATIVE HABITAT Woods of Europe, N. Africa,
C. and W. Asia.
• CULTIVATION Grow in deep, fertile, moisture-
retentive soil. Plant away from buildings and drains.
• PROPAGATION By hardwood cuttings in winter.

☼ ◊
❀ ❀ ❀

HEIGHT
To 20m
(70ft)

SPREAD
15m (50ft)

☼ ◊
❀ ❀ ❀

HEIGHT
To 20m
(70ft)

SPREAD
15m (50ft)
or more

Salicaceae	JAPANESE POPLAR

POPULUS MAXIMOWICZII

Habit Vigorous, upright, conical. **Flowers** Male and female catkins on separate plants.
Fruits Pendent, female catkins bear seeds clothed in silky hair in late summer. **Leaves** Deciduous, oval, heart-shaped at base. Balsam-scented. Bright green, white beneath, turning yellow in autumn.
• NATIVE HABITAT Woodlands of E. Asia.
• CULTIVATION Grow in deep, fertile, moisture-retentive soil. Plant at least 30m (100ft) away from buildings and drains.
• PROPAGATION By hardwood cuttings in winter.

HEIGHT
To 20m
(70ft)

SPREAD
10m (30ft)

Fagaceae	SPANISH CHESTNUT, SWEET CHESTNUT

CASTANEA SATIVA 'Albomarginata'

Habit Broadly columnar. **Flowers** Tiny, in clustered catkins, in summer. Creamy-yellow.
Fruits Prickly husks enclosing edible nuts. Brown.
Leaves Deciduous, lance-shaped. Dark green, margined white, turning yellow in autumn.
• NATIVE HABITAT Species occurs in woodlands of S. Europe, N.W. Africa, S.W. Asia. Garden origin.
• CULTIVATION Grow in sun or semi-shade, in fertile, well-drained soil.
• PROPAGATION By budding in summer or by grafting in late winter.

HEIGHT
25m (80ft)

SPREAD
15m (50ft)

Magnoliaceae	TULIP TREE

LIRIODENDRON TULIPIFERA
'Aureomarginatum'

Habit Vigorous, broadly columnar, spreading with age. **Flowers** Tulip-shaped, carried at branch tips of mature trees in mid-summer. Pale green, with orange markings at the base. **Leaves** Deciduous, lobed. Dark green, with yellow margins above, blue-white beneath, turning butter-yellow in autumn.
• NATIVE HABITAT Garden origin.
• CULTIVATION Tolerates semi-shade. Grow in deep, moist but well-drained, slightly acid soil.
• PROPAGATION By budding in late summer.

HEIGHT
To 20m
(70ft)

SPREAD
To 10m
(30ft)

Rosaceae	BLACK CHERRY, RUM CHERRY

PRUNUS SEROTINA

Habit Broadly columnar, irregularly spreading.
Flowers Small, fragrant, in upright or drooping spikes at branch tips, in early summer. White.
Fruits Small, edible cherries. Black when ripe.
Leaves Deciduous, elliptic to lance-shaped. Glossy dark green, turning yellow in autumn.
• NATIVE HABITAT Pasture and woods of North America.
• CULTIVATION Grow in any but waterlogged soil.
• PROPAGATION By seed in autumn or by softwood cuttings in summer.

HEIGHT
To 20m
(70ft)

SPREAD
10m (40ft)
or more

Sterculiaceae	FLAME BOTTLE TREE, FLAME TREE

BRACHYCHITON ACERIFOLIUS

Habit Spreading, with a rounded crown.
Flowers Small, in dense clusters, on bare branches from spring to late summer. Brilliant scarlet.
Leaves Deciduous, 3–7 lobes, heart-shaped at the base. Lustrous dark green.
• NATIVE HABITAT Tropical forests of Australia.
• CULTIVATION Grown as a house or conservatory plant. Grow in a free-draining, sandy soil or compost. Prune after flowering to restrict size.
• PROPAGATION By seed in spring.
• OTHER NAMES *Sterculia acerifolia.*

☀ ◌

Min.
7–10°C
(45–50°F)

HEIGHT
To 20m
(80ft)

SPREAD
20m (80ft)

Fagaceae	PURPLE BEECH, COPPER BEECH

FAGUS SYLVATICA Purple Group

Habit Round-headed, broadly spreading.
Leaves Deciduous, oval, with wavy margins. Purple and silky when young, turning rich copper in autumn. *Bark* Smooth. Pale grey.
• NATIVE HABITAT Species grows in woodlands of Europe. Garden origin.
• CULTIVATION Tolerates chalky and acid soils, provided they are well drained. Excellent for hedging. Trim in summer.
• PROPAGATION By budding in late summer or by seed in autumn. Seed-raised plants are variable.

☀ ◌
❀❀❀

HEIGHT
30m (100ft)

SPREAD
25m (80ft)

Aceraceae	

ACER PLATANOIDES 'Crimson King' ♈

Habit Vigorous, spreading. *Flowers* Tiny, in dense clusters in mid-spring. Yellow, tinged red.
Fruits Small, round seed, with large papery wings.
Leaves Deciduous, large, palmately lobed, each lobe with long, slender points. Deep red-purple, turning orange in autumn.
• NATIVE HABITAT Garden origin.
• CULTIVATION Tolerates semi-shade and almost any fertile, well-drained soil.
• PROPAGATION By grafting in late winter or early spring or by budding in summer.

☀ ◌
❀❀❀

HEIGHT
18m (60ft)

SPREAD
15m (50ft)
or more

Salicaceae	GREY POPLAR

POPULUS X *CANESCENS*

Habit Vigorous, broadly columnar.
Flowers Catkins, in spring. Male: greyish-red; female: green, on separate plants
Leaves Deciduous, rounded to oval, toothed. Grey when young, later glossy dark green and grey beneath, turning yellow in autumn.
Bark Diamond-shaped markings. Grey.
• NATIVE HABITAT A natural hybrid occurring in river valleys from C. Europe to Russia.
• CULTIVATION Grow in moist, fertile soil.
• PROPAGATION By hardwood cuttings in winter.

☀ ◗
❀❀❀

HEIGHT
To 25m
(80ft)

SPREAD
To 15m
(50ft)

Salicaceae	

POPULUS × *CANADENSIS* 'Robusta'

Habit Fast-growing, conical, with upright branches. *Flowers* Long, male catkins in spring. Red. *Leaves* Deciduous, broadly triangular. Bronze-red on emergence, later glossy dark green. *Bark* Vertically fissured. Pale grey.
• NATIVE HABITAT Garden origin.
• CULTIVATION Grow in deep, fertile, moisture-retentive soil. Excellent for windbreaks and shelter-belt plantings. As with most species of poplar, the deeply penetrating root system may cause extensive damage, so plant at least 30m (100ft)
away from buildings, walls, and drains, especially on clay soils. This, and other *Populus* species, are susceptible to bacterial canker and fungal diseases. A male clone, *P.* × *canadensis* 'Robusta' does not produce the fruits that in female clones such as 'Regenerata' or 'Marylandica' give rise to woolly litter as they ripen.
• PROPAGATION By hardwood cuttings in winter.

HEIGHT
To 30m
(100ft)

SPREAD
12m (40ft)
or more

Salicaceae	

POPULUS × *CANADENSIS*
'Serotina de Selys'
Habit Vigorous, columnar. *Flowers* Catkins in spring. Red. *Leaves* Deciduous, broadly triangular. Pale green when young, later grey-green, turning yellow in autumn.
• NATIVE HABITAT Garden origin.
• CULTIVATION Grow in deep, fertile, moisture-retentive soil. Plant at least 30m (100ft) away from buildings, walls, and drains, especially on clay soils.
• PROPAGATION By hardwood cuttings in winter.
• OTHER NAMES *P.* × *canadensis* 'Serotina Erecta'.

☼ ◐
❀ ❀ ❀

HEIGHT
To 25m
(80ft) or
more

SPREAD
6m (20ft)

Betulaceae	GREY ALDER

ALNUS INCANA
Habit Open, with a conical crown.
Flowers Upright catkins, on bare branches in early spring. Male: drooping, reddish; female: small, red, on same plant. *Fruits* Small, woody, cone-like.
Leaves Deciduous, oval, pointed, toothed. Dull dark green, grey-downy beneath.
• NATIVE HABITAT Mountains of Europe and the Caucasus.
• CULTIVATION Tolerates wet or waterlogged soil.
• PROPAGATION By seed in autumn or by hardwood cuttings in early winter.

☼ ◐
❀ ❀ ❀

HEIGHT
17m (55ft)

SPREAD
7m (22ft)

Fagaceae	

QUERCUS MACRANTHERA
Habit Broadly spreading, with a dense, rounded, crown. *Fruits* Acorns, to 2.5cm (1in) long. Cups clothed in hairy scales. *Leaves* Deciduous, oval, to 15cm (6in) long, with deeply cut, rounded lobes. Dark green above, paler and hairy beneath.
• NATIVE HABITAT Dry, mountain woodlands in the Caucasus.
• CULTIVATION Tolerates semi-shade and lime-rich soils. Grow in deep, fertile, well-drained soil.
• PROPAGATION By seed in autumn.

☼ ◌
❀ ❀ ❀

HEIGHT
To 20m
(70ft)

SPREAD
15m (50ft)

Fagaceae	WEEPING BEECH

FAGUS SYLVATICA 'Pendula'   ♛
Habit Weeping. *Leaves* Deciduous, oval, wavy-margined. Bright green and silky when young, turning rich yellow and old gold in autumn.
Bark Smooth. Pale grey.
• NATIVE HABITAT Woodlands, often on chalk or limestone soils, in Europe.
• CULTIVATION Tolerates chalky and acid soils, provided they are well drained. A beautiful specimen for large gardens.
• PROPAGATION By budding in late summer or by seed in autumn. Seed-raised plants are variable.

☼ ◌
❀ ❀ ❀

HEIGHT
15m (50ft)
or more

SPREAD
20m (70ft)

Fagaceae	

QUERCUS ROBUR f. FASTIGIATA

Habit Upright, columnar, dense. **Fruits** Acorns, to 4cm (1½in) long, one-third enclosed by a cup.
Leaves Deciduous, elliptic to broadly oval, lobed. Dark green above, bluish-green beneath.
Bark Fissured. Pale grey.
• NATIVE HABITAT Woodlands of Europe.
• CULTIVATION Tolerates semi-shade and lime-rich soils. Grow in deep, fertile, well-drained soil.
• PROPAGATION By budding in late summer or by seed in autumn. Seed-raised plants are variable.

HEIGHT
20m (70ft)
or more

SPREAD
6m (20ft) or more

Betulaceae	ITALIAN ALDER

ALNUS CORDATA

Habit Fast-growing, broadly conical.
Flowers Upright catkins, on bare branches, in early spring. Male: drooping, reddish; female: small, red. **Fruits** Small, woody, cone-like.
Leaves Deciduous, broadly oval to rounded, heart-shaped at the base, leathery. Glossy dark green.
• NATIVE HABITAT Deciduous, mountain woodlands of C. and S. Italy and Corsica.
• CULTIVATION Tolerates dry, wet soils.
• PROPAGATION By seed in autumn or by hardwood cuttings in early winter.

HEIGHT
25m (80ft)

SPREAD
11m (35ft)

Fagaceae	ALGERIAN OAK, MIRBECK'S OAK

QUERCUS CANARIENSIS

Habit Dense, columnar when young, becoming broader with age. **Fruits** Acorns, one-third enclosed by a cup. **Leaves** Deciduous or semi-evergreen, broadly oval to elliptic, shallowly lobed. Dark green above, paler beneath. **Bark** Fissured.
• NATIVE HABITAT Woodlands of N. Africa and S.W. Europe.
• CULTIVATION Tolerates semi-shade, clay, and lime-rich soils. Grow in deep, well-drained soil.
• PROPAGATION By seed in autumn.
• OTHER NAMES Q. mirbeckii.

HEIGHT
20m (70ft)

SPREAD
15m (50ft)

Salicaceae	LOMBARDY POPLAR

POPULUS NIGRA 'Italica'　　　🏆

Habit Very fast-growing, narrowly columnar, with strongly upright branches. **Flowers** Male catkins in mid-spring. Red. **Leaves** Deciduous, rounded, diamond-shaped. Bright green.
• NATIVE HABITAT Garden origin.
• CULTIVATION Grow in deep, fertile, moisture-retentive soil. Plant at least 30m (100ft) away from buildings, walls, and drains, especially on clay soils. Good for screens and windbreaks. Susceptible to bacterial canker and fungal diseases.
• PROPAGATION By hardwood cuttings in winter.

☀ 💧
❀ ❀ ❀

HEIGHT
To 30m
(100ft)

SPREAD
5m (15ft)

Aceraceae	LOBEL'S MAPLE

ACER LOBELII

Habit Upright, narrowly columnar.
Flowers Tiny, in erect clusters, in late spring. Yellow-green. **Fruits** 2 seeds, fused together, each with a green wing. **Leaves** Deciduous, with 5 wavy-edged, pointed lobes. Glossy dark green, turning yellow in autumn.
• NATIVE HABITAT Mountain woods of S. Italy.
• CULTIVATION Tolerates semi-shade and almost any fertile, well-drained soil. Excellent for planting in confined spaces.
• PROPAGATION By seed in autumn.

☀ 💧
❀ ❀

HEIGHT
To 20m
(70ft)

SPREAD
5m (15ft)

Juglandaceae	ENGLISH WALNUT, PERSIAN WALNUT

JUGLANS REGIA　　　🏆

Habit Slow-growing, dense, broadly spreading.
Flowers Catkins, with male and female on same plant, in late spring. Yellow-green. **Fruits** Smooth husks, enclosing edible, creamy-white nuts.
Leaves Deciduous, aromatic, with 5–7 elliptic leaflets. Bronzed when young, later dark green.
• NATIVE HABITAT Stream sides and valleys from S.E. Europe to China.
• CULTIVATION Grow in deep, fertile soil. Needs long, hot summers to ripen fruits.
• PROPAGATION By seed in autumn.

☀ 💧
❀ ❀ ❀

HEIGHT
30m (100ft)

SPREAD
20m (70ft)

Tiliaceae	LIME, LINDEN

TILIA OLIVERI

Habit Open, spreading, with broadly rounded crown. **Flowers** Small, fragrant, cup-shaped, in clusters in summer. Greenish-yellow, with pale green bracts. **Fruits** Round, smooth, winged, to 1cm (½in) across. Grey-green. **Leaves** Deciduous, heart-shaped, pointed. Dark green above, silvery-white beneath.

• NATIVE HABITAT Woodlands of C. China.
• CULTIVATION Tolerates semi-shade. It does best when grown in deep, fertile soil that is moisture-retentive but well drained. Unlike many limes, it is usually unaffected by aphids and so does not cause problems with dripping honeydew and the unsightly mould that this subsequently causes. It makes a stately specimen tree and is shown to its best advantage when planted alone as a specimen in large gardens. It is distinguished among all the limes by its very handsome foliage.

• PROPAGATION By seed in autumn.

HEIGHT
15m (50ft)
or more

SPREAD
10m (30ft)

| Fagaceae | CHINKAPIN OAK, YELLOW CHESTNUT OAK |

QUERCUS MUEHLENBERGII

Habit Dense, round-headed. *Fruits* Acorns to 2cm (¾in) long, half enclosed in a cup with downy scales. *Leaves* Deciduous, oblong to lance-shaped, sharply toothed. Bright green, colouring well in autumn. *Bark* Flaky. Grey.
• NATIVE HABITAT Woodlands of North America.
• CULTIVATION Tolerates semi-shade and lime-rich soils. Grow in deep, fertile, well-drained soil.
• PROPAGATION By seed in autumn.

HEIGHT
18m (60ft)

SPREAD
15m (50ft)

| Ulmaceae | MEDITERRANEAN HACKBERRY, SOUTHERN NETTLE TREE |

CELTIS AUSTRALIS

Habit Broadly columnar, spreading with age. *Flowers* Insignificant. *Fruits* Small, round, berry-like. Purple-black. *Leaves* Deciduous, lance-shaped to oval, pointed, sharply toothed. Dark green above, grey-green beneath, and hairy.
• NATIVE HABITAT Dry, rocky slopes of S. Europe and S.W. Asia.
• CULTIVATION Grow in any fertile soil. Performs best in areas with long, hot summers.
• PROPAGATION By seed in autumn.

HEIGHT
To 20m (70ft)

SPREAD
15m (50ft)

| Platanaceae | LONDON PLANE |

PLATANUS X *HISPANICA*

Habit Vigorous, broadly columnar, the crown spreading with age. *Flowers* Insignificant, with male and female on same plant. *Fruits* Spherical, bristly, in clusters of 2–4. *Leaves* Deciduous, with 3–5 large, sharply toothed lobes. Bright green. *Bark* Flaky. Cream, pink-grey, and brown.
• NATIVE HABITAT Garden origin.
• CULTIVATION Grow in deep, fertile soil.
• PROPAGATION By hardwood cuttings in early winter.
• OTHER NAMES *P.* x *acerifolia.*

HEIGHT
28m (95ft)

SPREAD
20m (70ft)

| Fagaceae | RAULI BEECH |

NOTHOFAGUS PROCERA

Habit Broadly conical. *Leaves* Deciduous, oval to lance- or trowel-shaped, regularly toothed and veined. Bronzed when young, later matt dark green, turning orange, red, and gold in autumn.
• NATIVE HABITAT Forests of Argentina and Chile.
• CULTIVATION Grow in deep, fertile, neutral to acid soil. Shelter from strong winds. Makes an elegant specimen in woodland gardens and other sheltered sites.
• PROPAGATION By seed in autumn.
• OTHER NAMES *N. nervosa.*

HEIGHT
25m (80ft)

SPREAD
15m (50ft)

Lauraceae	

SASSAFRAS ALBIDUM

Habit Upright, open, later spreading, suckering.
Flowers Insignificant, in spring. Yellowish.
Fruits Small, egg-shaped berries. Blue.
Leaves Deciduous, aromatic, elliptic to oval, sometimes 3-lobed. Bright green above, blue-green beneath, turning yellow, red, or purple in autumn.
• NATIVE HABITAT Woodlands and thickets of E. North America.
• CULTIVATION Grow in deep, fertile, preferably neutral to acid soil. Young growth is susceptible to late frosts. An elegant and unusual specimen for the large garden. The leaves emit a curious fragrance of orange and vanilla when crushed. Sassafras roots are used commercially in the making of perfumes and root beer.
• PROPAGATION By seed or suckers in autumn or by root cuttings in winter.
• OTHER NAMES *S. officinale.*

HEIGHT
22m (75ft)

SPREAD
15m (50ft)
or more

CONTENTS

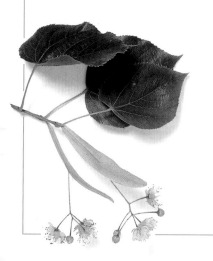

A DORLING KINDERSLEY BOOK

Produced for Dorling Kindersley by
Cooling Brown (*Book Packaging*)
9-11 High Street, Hampton, Middlesex TW12 2SA

MANAGING EDITOR Francis Ritter
MANAGING ART EDITOR Derek Coombes

First published in Great Britain in 1996
by Dorling Kindersley Limited
9 Henrietta Street, London WC2E 8PS

(w)635 976l

A CIP catalogue record for this book
is available from the British Library

ISBN 0-7513-017-52

Colour reproduction by Colourscan, Singapore
Printed and bound by Star Standard Industries, Singapore

THE ROYAL HORTICULTURAL SOCIETY
PLANT ❦ GUIDES
GARDEN TREES

DORLING KINDERSLEY
London • New York • Stuttgart • Moscow

THE ROYAL HORTICULTURAL SOCIETY

PLANT ❦ GUIDES

GARDEN
TREES

Juglandaceae	BLACK WALNUT

JUGLANS NIGRA ♆

Habit Fast-growing, dense, broadly spreading.
Flowers Catkins, male and female on same plant,
in late spring. Yellow-green. **Fruits** Smooth husks
enclosing edible nuts. **Leaves** Deciduous, large,
aromatic, with 11–17 slender, pointed leaflets.
Glossy dark green.
• NATIVE HABITAT Rich woodlands of C. and S.
United States.
• CULTIVATION Grow in deep, fertile soil. Needs
long, hot summers to ripen fruits.
• PROPAGATION By seed in autumn.

☼ ◊
❀❀❀

HEIGHT
To 30m
(100ft)

SPREAD
20m (65ft)

Juglandaceae	HEARTNUT, JAPANESE WALNUT

JUGLANS AILANTIFOLIA var. *CORDIFORMIS*

Habit Spreading, with a broad-domed crown.
Flowers Catkins. Male: to 30cm (12in) long;
female: 10cm (4in), on the same plant in late spring.
Greenish. **Fruits** Slightly hairy, poisonous husks
enclosing edible nuts. **Leaves** Deciduous, large,
with 11–17 elliptic, short-pointed, hairy leaflets.
Dark green above, paler beneath.
• NATIVE HABITAT Damp areas in Japan.
• CULTIVATION Grow in any deep, fertile soil.
• PROPAGATION By seed in autumn.
• OTHER NAMES *J. cordiformis.*

☼ ◊
❀❀❀

HEIGHT
15m (50ft)
or more

SPREAD
15m (50ft)

Fagaceae	WATER OAK

QUERCUS NIGRA

Habit Spreading, with a narrowly dome-shaped
crown. **Fruits** Acorns, to 1.5cm (¾in) long, half
enclosed by scaly cups. **Leaves** Deciduous or
semi-evergreen, variably lobed, especially on young
plants. Glossy rich green.
• NATIVE HABITAT Damp habitats in S.E. United
States.
• CULTIVATION Grow in deep, fertile, moisture-
retentive soil.
• PROPAGATION By seed in autumn.
• OTHER NAMES *Q. aquatica.*

☼ ◊
❀❀❀

HEIGHT
18m (60ft)
or more

SPREAD
12m (40ft)

Fagaceae	ROBLE BEECH

NOTHOFAGUS OBLIQUA

Habit Fast-growing, broadly columnar, with
slender, arching branches. **Leaves** Deciduous,
oval, toothed, smooth. Deep green above, blue-
green beneath, turning orange and red in autumn.
• NATIVE HABITAT Forests of Argentina and Chile.
• CULTIVATION Tolerates semi-shade. Grow in
deep, fertile, preferably neutral to acid soil. Shelter
from strong winds. Grows rapidly to make a
handsome specimen in woodland gardens and in
other sheltered sites.
• PROPAGATION By seed in autumn.

☼ ◊
❀❀❀

HEIGHT
25m (80ft)
or more

SPREAD
15m (50ft)

Sterculiaceae	CHINESE PARASOL TREE

FIRMIANA SIMPLEX

Habit Robust, vigorous, rounded. **Flowers** Small, bell-shaped, in long, showy panicles in summer. Lemon-yellow. **Fruits** Leaf-like, with seeds at the edges. **Leaves** Deciduous, large, 3–5 lobes. Dark green.
• NATIVE HABITAT Forests of Japan to Vietnam.
• CULTIVATION Tolerates partial shade. Grow in a fertile, moisture-retentive soil or compost. Water freely when in growth, otherwise sparingly.
• PROPAGATION By seed when ripe or in spring.
• OTHER NAMES *F. platanifolia, Sterculia platanifolia.*

☼ ◊
Min. 2°C
(36°F)

HEIGHT
18m (60ft)
less in cult.

SPREAD
10m (30ft)

Tiliaceae	PENDENT SILVER LIME, WEEPING LIME

TILIA 'Petiolaris' ♉

Habit Broadly columnar, with pendent branches. **Flowers** Toxic to bees. Small, fragrant, cup-shaped, in drooping clusters in mid-summer. Creamy-yellow. **Fruits** Rounded, woody. Grey-green. **Leaves** Deciduous, heart-shaped, pointed. Dark green above, silver beneath.
• NATIVE HABITAT Origin uncertain.
• CULTIVATION Tolerates semi-shade. Grow in deep, fertile soil. Prone to aphid infestation.
• PROPAGATION By grafting in late summer.
• OTHER NAMES *T. petiolaris, T. tomentosa* 'Petiolaris'.

☼ ◊
✽✽✽

HEIGHT
28m (90ft)

SPREAD
18m (60ft)

Fagaceae	

QUERCUS PETRAEA 'Columnea'

Habit Dense, slender, upright. **Fruits** Acorns, to 3cm (1¼in) long, one-third enclosed by a cup. **Leaves** Deciduous, large, wavy-edged. Bronze when young, later a leathery, dark green. **Bark** Vertically ridged. Grey.
• NATIVE HABITAT Garden origin.
• CULTIVATION Tolerates semi-shade, coastal conditions, and a wide range of soil types.
• PROPAGATION By grafting in late winter.

☼ ◊
✽✽✽

HEIGHT
20m (70ft)
or more

SPREAD
6m (30ft)

Fagaceae	

QUERCUS CASTANEIFOLIA

Habit Broadly spreading. **Fruits** Acorns, to 2.5cm (1in) long, half enclosed in a cup with long scales. **Leaves** Deciduous, oblong to narrowly oval, with sharp, triangular teeth. Very glossy, dark green above, grey beneath. **Bark** Smooth. Grey.
• NATIVE HABITAT Forests of the Caucasus and N. Iran.
• CULTIVATION Tolerates semi-shade and lime-rich soils. Grow in fertile soil.
• PROPAGATION By seed in autumn.

☼ ◊
✽✽✽

HEIGHT
25m (80ft)

SPREAD
18m (60ft)

Fagaceae	COMMON BEECH, EUROPEAN BEECH

FAGUS SYLVATICA ♀

Habit Broadly spreading. **Fruits** Small, bristly husks enclosing 2 edible nuts. **Leaves** Deciduous, oval, with wavy margins. Brilliant green on emergence, later mid- to dark green, turning copper-gold in autumn. **Bark** Smooth. Silver-grey.
• NATIVE HABITAT Woodlands, usually on chalk, in Europe.
• CULTIVATION Tolerates semi-shade and thrives in well-drained, acid and alkaline soils. Excellent for hedging. Trim in summer.
• PROPAGATION By seed in autumn.

☼ ◐
❄ ❄ ❄

HEIGHT
30m (100ft)

SPREAD
15m (50ft)

Fagaceae	HUNGARIAN OAK

QUERCUS FRAINETTO

Habit Fast-growing, spreading, with a large, domed crown. **Fruits** Acorns, to 2cm (¾in) long, half enclosed in a cup. **Leaves** Deciduous, long, oval-oblong, with deeply cut, rounded lobes. Dark green above, grey-green beneath. **Bark** Deeply fissured. Dark grey.
• NATIVE HABITAT Woodlands of S.E. Europe.
• CULTIVATION Tolerant of almost any well-drained soils, including chalky ones.
• PROPAGATION By seed in autumn.
• OTHER NAMES *Q. conferta, Q. pannonica.*

☼ ◐
❄ ❄ ❄

HEIGHT
To 25m
(80ft)

SPREAD
20m (70ft)

Salicaceae	

POPULUS ALBA 'Raket'

Habit Narrow, upright. **Flowers** Catkins; male and female on separate plants. **Fruits** Small capsules enclosing seeds in white cotton. **Leaves** Deciduous, wavy-margined, 3–5 lobes. Dark green above, silvery-white beneath, yellow in autumn.
• NATIVE HABITAT Garden origin.
• CULTIVATION Tolerates coastal conditions. Grow in deep, fertile, moisture-retentive soil. Plant at least 30m (100ft) away from buildings and drains.
• PROPAGATION By hardwood cuttings in winter.
• OTHER NAMES *P. alba* 'Rocket'.

☼ ◐
❄ ❄ ❄

HEIGHT
To 20m
(70ft) or
more

SPREAD
5m (15ft) or
more

Fagaceae	PIN OAK

QUERCUS PALUSTRIS   ♛

Habit Fast-growing, spreading, with slender branches, pendulous at the tips. **Fruits** Acorns, to 1.5cm (⅝in) long, up to one-third enclosed in a broad, shallow cup. **Leaves** Deciduous, deeply lobed. Shining deep green above, turning scarlet in autumn. **Bark** Smooth. Grey-brown.
• NATIVE HABITAT Swampy woodlands of S.E. Canada and N.E. United States.
• CULTIVATION Tolerates semi-shade and very moist soils. Grow in deep, fertile soil.
• PROPAGATION By seed in autumn.

☼ ◊
❀ ❀ ❀

HEIGHT
20m (70ft)

SPREAD
12m (40ft)

Juglandaceae	SHAG-BARK HICKORY

CARYA OVATA   ♛

Habit Broadly columnar. **Flowers** Catkins, in late spring. Male: clusters of 3, to 13cm (5in) long, green-yellow; female: inconspicuous, on same plant. **Fruits** Green husk enclosing edible, white nut. **Leaves** Deciduous, with 5 taper-pointed, toothed leaflets. Dark yellow-green, golden yellow in autumn. **Bark** Peeling in strips. Grey-brown.
• NATIVE HABITAT Woodland and valleys of E. North America.
• CULTIVATION Grow in deep, fertile soil.
• PROPAGATION By seed in autumn.

☼ ◊
❀ ❀ ❀

HEIGHT
22m (76ft)

SPREAD
18m (60ft)

Fagaceae	HOLM OAK

QUERCUS ILEX   ♛

Habit Broadly spreading, with a rounded crown. **Fruits** Acorns, to 2cm (¾in) long, one-third enclosed in a cup. **Leaves** Evergreen, elliptic to narrowly oval. Glossy dark green above, silvery-grey and hairy beneath. **Bark** Rugged. Black.
• NATIVE HABITAT Woodland and dry scrub on hillsides around the Mediterranean.
• CULTIVATION Tolerates both dry and chalky soils, and coastal exposure, but grows best in deep, fertile soils in mild areas.
• PROPAGATION By seed in autumn.

☼ ◊
❀ ❀ ❀

HEIGHT
25m (80ft)

SPREAD
To 20m
(70ft)

Fagaceae	RED OAK

QUERCUS RUBRA   ♛

Habit Fast-growing, broadly spreading. **Fruits** Acorns, to 3cm (1¼in) long, one-quarter enclosed in a shallow cup. **Leaves** Deciduous, long, elliptic-oval, sharply lobed, with slender teeth. Dark green, paler beneath, turning red in autumn.
• NATIVE HABITAT Woodlands of E. North America.
• CULTIVATION Tolerant of urban pollution and almost any well-drained soil, including chalky soils.
• PROPAGATION By seed in autumn.
• OTHER NAMES *Q. borealis* var. *maxima*.

☼ ◊
❀ ❀ ❀

HEIGHT
25m (80ft)

SPREAD
18m (60ft)

Fagaceae	LAUREL OAK

QUERCUS LAURIFOLIA

Habit Broadly conical, becoming increasingly round-headed with age. *Fruits* Acorns, almost round, flattish at the base, to 1.5cm (⅝in) long, one-third enclosed in a cup. *Leaves* Deciduous or semi-evergreen, narrowly oblong to lance-shaped, shallowly lobed or unlobed, smooth. Glossy green, bronze-tinted when young. *Bark* Scaly. Grey.
• NATIVE HABITAT Woodland on sandy soils, and at the edges of coastal swamps in E. United States.
• CULTIVATION Tolerates semi-shade and moist but not waterlogged soils. Grow in deep, fertile soil.

A handsome tree that retains its leaves well into winter, giving a semi-evergreen appearance. This, and other semi-evergreen oaks, thrives best if given shelter from cold, dry, winter winds. The leaves resemble those of *Laurus nobilis*, the bay laurel, hence the common name.
• PROPAGATION By seed in autumn.

HEIGHT
18m (60ft)

SPREAD
12m (40ft)

Magnoliaceae	TULIP TREE

LIRIODENDRON TULIPIFERA

Habit Broadly columnar, spreading with age.
Flowers Tulip-shaped, at branch tips, in mid-summer. Pale green, tepals banded orange at the base. **Leaves** Deciduous, lobed, with middle lobe cut off or notched at the tip. Dark green above, paler beneath, turning butter-yellow in autumn.
• NATIVE HABITAT Deciduous woods of E. North America.
• CULTIVATION Tolerates semi-shade. Grow in fertile, moisture-retentive, slightly acid soil.
• PROPAGATION By seed in autumn.

HEIGHT
28m (95ft)

SPREAD
20m (70ft)

Juglandaceae	

PTEROCARYA X *REHDERIANA*

Habit Very fast-growing, broadly spreading, suckering. **Flowers** Tiny catkins, with male and female on same plant. Greenish. **Fruits** Winged, in long pendulous catkins, to 45cm (18in) long. **Leaves** Deciduous, divided into 11–21 oblong leaflets, with winged leaf stalks. Dark green. **Bark** Purple-brown; pale orange within fissures.
• NATIVE HABITAT Garden origin.
• CULTIVATION Grow in any deep, fertile soil.
• PROPAGATION By softwood cuttings in summer or by suckers in autumn.

HEIGHT
25m (80ft)

SPREAD
20m (65ft)

Simaroubaceae	TREE OF HEAVEN

AILANTHUS ALTISSIMA

Habit Fast-growing, broadly columnar.
Flowers Small, in large panicles, from mid- to late summer. Male and female usually on separate plants. Yellowish-green. **Fruits** Winged, pink-tinted. **Leaves** Deciduous, with 15–30 paired, lance-shaped to oval, pointed leaflets. Dark green.
• NATIVE HABITAT Mountain woodlands of China.
• CULTIVATION Grow in deep, fertile soil.
• PROPAGATION By seed in autumn or by suckers or root cuttings in winter.
• OTHER NAMES *A. glandulosa.*

HEIGHT
To 25m
(80ft) or
more

SPREAD
15m (52ft)

Fagaceae	

FAGUS SYLVATICA 'Dawyck Gold'

Habit Dense, columnar. **Leaves** Deciduous, oval, with wavy margins. Bright yellow on emergence, later yellow-green, turning copper-gold in autumn. **Bark** Silver-grey. Smooth.
• NATIVE HABITAT Garden origin.
• CULTIVATION Thrives in light shade and in well-drained soils, both acid and alkaline.
• PROPAGATION By budding in late summer.

HEIGHT
18m (60ft)

SPREAD
5m (15ft)

Tiliaceae	CAUCASIAN LIME

TILIA 'Euchlora' ♀

Habit Broadly columnar. *Flowers* Small, fragrant, cup-shaped, in drooping clusters in mid-summer. Creamy-yellow. *Leaves* Deciduous, broadly oval, pointed, unequally heart-shaped at the base. Dark green above, paler beneath.
• NATIVE HABITAT Origin uncertain.
• CULTIVATION Tolerates semi-shade. Grow in deep, fertile soil. Usually resistant to aphids and free of honeydew.
• PROPAGATION By grafting in late summer.
• OTHER NAMES *Tilia x euchlora.*

☼ ◊
❀❀❀

HEIGHT
20m (70ft)

SPREAD
10m (30ft)

Tiliaceae	COMMON LIME

TILIA X EUROPAEA

Habit Vigorous, broadly columnar. *Flowers* Small, fragrant, cup-shaped, in drooping clusters in mid-summer. Pale yellow. *Leaves* Deciduous, broadly oval with heart-shaped base, with a short-pointed tip. Dark green above, paler below.
• NATIVE HABITAT Woodlands of Europe.
• CULTIVATION Tolerates semi-shade. Grow in deep, fertile soil. Often infested with aphids, which drip honeydew on the ground beneath.
• PROPAGATION By grafting in late summer.
• OTHER NAMES *Tilia x vulgaris.*

☼ ◊
❀❀❀

HEIGHT
35m (120ft)

SPREAD
15m (50ft)

Bombacaceae	SILK-FLOSS TREE

CHORISIA SPECIOSA

Habit Fast-growing. Trunk covered with stout spines and swollen at the base. *Flowers* Large, cup-shaped. Pink to burgundy, petals creamy and spotted at the base in autumn. *Fruits* Capsules enclosing seeds in silky floss. *Leaves* Deciduous, lance-shaped, toothed. Pale green. *Bark* Thorny.
• NATIVE HABITAT Tropical Brazil and Argentina.
• CULTIVATION Grow as a house or conservatory plant. Water moderately when in growth, sparingly when leafless. Prune in spring to restrict growth.
• PROPAGATION By seed in spring.

☼ ◊

Min. 10°C
(50°F)

HEIGHT
15m (50ft)

SPREAD
10m (30ft)

Aceraceae	

ACER RUBRUM 'Scanlon' ♀

Habit Broadly columnar. *Flowers* Small, in dense clusters on bare branches, in spring. Red. *Fruits* Small, round seed, with papery wings. Red. *Leaves* Deciduous, 3–5 lobes. Dark green, turning brilliant red in autumn.
• NATIVE HABITAT Garden origin.
• CULTIVATION Tolerates some lime, but grow in fertile, moisture-retentive, neutral to acid soil for best autumn colour.
• PROPAGATION By grafting in late winter or early spring or by budding in summer.

☼ ◊
❀❀❀

HEIGHT
15m (50ft)

SPREAD
5m (15ft)

Hamamelidaceae	SWEET GUM

LIQUIDAMBAR STYRACIFLUA

Habit Broadly conical, spreading with age.
Leaves Deciduous, alternate, palmate, with 5–7 pointed, finely toothed lobes. Glossy green, turning brilliant orange, red, and purple in autumn.
• NATIVE HABITAT Damp woodlands of E. United States.
• CULTIVATION Tolerates semi-shade. Does not thrive on shallow chalk. Grow in fertile, moist but well-drained soil.
• PROPAGATION By softwood cuttings in summer or by seed in autumn.

☼ ◊
❀ ❀ ❀

HEIGHT
25m (80ft)

SPREAD
18m (60ft)

Fagaceae	SCARLET OAK

QUERCUS COCCINEA

Habit Broadly spreading. **Fruits** Acorns, to 2.5cm (1in) long, up to one half enclosed in a shiny cup.
Leaves Deciduous, elliptic, deeply lobed, with bristly teeth, persisting for several weeks. Glossy dark green above, paler beneath, turning brilliant scarlet in autumn,
• NATIVE HABITAT Sandy woods of E. North America.
• CULTIVATION Tolerates semi-shade, but colours best in sun. Grow in deep, fertile soil.
• PROPAGATION By seed in autumn.

☼ ◊
❀ ❀ ❀

HEIGHT
To 20m (70ft)

SPREAD
15m (50ft)

Fagaceae	NORTHERN PIN OAK

QUERCUS ELLIPSOIDALIS

Habit Broadly spreading. **Fruits** Acorns, to 2cm (¾in) long, one-third to one-half enclosed in a cup.
Leaves Deciduous, elliptic, deeply lobed, each lobe with slender, pointed teeth. Glossy dark green above, paler beneath, turning deep purplish-red, then crimson in autumn.
• NATIVE HABITAT Dry woodlands of E. and C. North America.
• CULTIVATION Tolerates semi-shade, but colours best in sun. Grow in deep, fertile soil.
• PROPAGATION By seed in autumn.

☼ ◊
❀ ❀ ❀

HEIGHT
20m (70ft)

SPREAD
18m (60ft)

Aceraceae	

ACER PSEUDOPLATANUS 'Erythrocarpum'

Habit Vigorous, broadly columnar, spreading with age. **Flowers** Tiny, in pendulous clusters in spring.
Fruits Small, round seed, with papery, bright red wings. **Leaves** Deciduous, with 5 coarsely toothed lobes. Dark green.
• NATIVE HABITAT Mountain woods from Europe to S.W. Asia.
• CULTIVATION Grow in any but waterlogged soil.
• PROPAGATION By grafting in late winter or early spring, by budding in summer, or by seed in autumn. Seed-raised plants are variable.

☼ ◊
❀ ❀ ❀

HEIGHT
20m (70ft)

SPREAD
15m (50ft)

Aceraceae	

ACER RUBRUM 'Schlesingeri'

Habit Round-headed, broadly columnar.
Flowers Small, in dense clusters, on bare branches in spring. Red. **Fruits** 2 seeds, fused together, each with a red wing. **Leaves** Deciduous, 3–5 lobes. Dark green, turning brilliant scarlet in early autumn.
• NATIVE HABITAT Garden origin.
• CULTIVATION Tolerates some lime, but grow in fertile, moisture-retentive, neutral to acid soil for best autumn colour.
• PROPAGATION By grafting in late winter or early spring or by budding in summer.

HEIGHT 20m (70ft)
SPREAD 11m (35ft)

Aceraceae	SCARLET MAPLE, RED MAPLE, SWAMP MAPLE

ACER RUBRUM

Habit Round-headed, broadly columnar.
Flowers Small, in dense clusters on bare branches in spring. Red. **Fruits** 2 seeds, fused together, each with a red wing. **Leaves** Deciduous, 3–5 lobes. Dark green, turning brilliant red and scarlet in autumn.
• NATIVE HABITAT Damp soils in E. North America.
• CULTIVATION Tolerates some lime, but grow in fertile, moisture-retentive, neutral to acid soil for best autumn colour.
• PROPAGATION By seed in autumn.

HEIGHT 20m (70ft)
SPREAD 10m (30ft)

Cercidiphyllaceae	KATSURA TREE

CERCIDIPHYLLUM JAPONICUM ♔

Habit Fast-growing, open, spreading.
Leaves Deciduous, rounded, heart-shaped at the base. Fallen leaves smell like burnt toffee. Bronze when young, turning smooth, bluish-green, then yellow, bronze-purple, and red in autumn.
• NATIVE HABITAT Mountain woods of Himalayas and Japan.
• CULTIVATION Tolerates dappled shade. Grow in any deep, fertile soil. Autumn colour is best on acid soils. Young leaves may be damaged by late frosts.
• PROPAGATION By seed in autumn.

HEIGHT 20m (70ft)
SPREAD 15m (50ft)

Nyssaceae	BLACK GUM, SOUR GUM

NYSSA SYLVATICA ♔

Habit Slow-growing, broadly conical-columnar.
Leaves Deciduous, oval to elliptic, blunt-pointed. Glossy dark green above, blue-green beneath, turning yellow, orange, and scarlet in autumn.
• NATIVE HABITAT Swamps and damp woods of E. North America.
• CULTIVATION Tolerates semi-shade. Grow in fertile, neutral to acid soil. Resents transplanting. Performs best in areas with long, hot summers.
• PROPAGATION By softwood cuttings in summer or by seed in autumn.

HEIGHT 20m (70ft)
SPREAD 11m (35ft)

Fagaceae	WHITE OAK

QUERCUS ALBA

Habit Broadly spreading. **Fruits** Acorns, to 2.5cm (1in) long, one-quarter enclosed in a cup.
Leaves Deciduous, broadly oval, tapered at the base, deeply and irregularly lobed. Pink-tinted when young, turning glossy bright green, then rich purple-red in autumn.
• NATIVE HABITAT Dry woodlands of S.E. Canada and E. United States.
• CULTIVATION Unsuitable for chalky soils. Grow in deep, fertile soil.
• PROPAGATION By seed in autumn.

☼ ◊
✿ ✿ ✿

HEIGHT
15m (50ft)

SPREAD
11m (35ft)

Bignoniaceae	AFRICAN TULIP TREE, FLAME-OF-THE-FOREST

SPATHODEA CAMPANULATA

Habit Dense, with a rounded crown.
Flowers Tulip- shaped, in dense clusters, throughout the year. Scarlet. **Fruits** Woody capsules with poisonous seeds. **Leaves** Evergreen, with 4–9 pairs of oblong-oval leaflets. Dark green.
• NATIVE HABITAT Forests of tropical Africa.
• CULTIVATION Container-grown plants seldom bloom. Grow in fertile soil or compost. Water freely when in growth, otherwise moderately.
• PROPAGATION By seed in spring or by semi-ripe cuttings in summer.

☼ ◊

Min. 13°C
(55°F)

HEIGHT
20m (70ft)

SPREAD
10m (30ft)

Ulmaceae	JAPANESE ZELKOVA, KEAKI

ZELKOVA SERRATA ♔

Habit Broadly spreading, with a rounded crown, branches ascending. **Leaves** Deciduous, oval, sharply pointed, and toothed. Dark green, turning yellow, orange, or red in autumn.
• NATIVE HABITAT Stream sides in woodlands of China, Japan, and Korea.
• CULTIVATION Grow in fertile, moist, but well-drained soil. Best with shelter from strong, cold winds.
• PROPAGATION By seed in autumn.
• OTHER NAMES Z. acuminata, Planera acuminata.

☼ ◊
✿ ✿ ✿

HEIGHT
20m (70ft)

SPREAD
12m (40ft)

Fagaceae	FERN-LEAF BEECH

FAGUS SYLVATICA var. HETEROPHYLLA ♔ 'Aspleniifolia'

Habit Dense, broadly columnar.
Leaves Deciduous, narrowly lance-shaped, deeply cut into long, slender lobes. Dark green, turning copper-gold in autumn. **Bark** Smooth. Silver-grey.
• NATIVE HABITAT Garden origin.
• CULTIVATION Thrives in light shade and in well-drained soils, both acid and alkaline.
• PROPAGATION By budding in late summer.

☼ ◊
✿ ✿ ✿

HEIGHT
25m (80ft)

SPREAD
15m (40ft)

Rosaceae	GEAN, MAZZARD, WILD CHERRY

PRUNUS AVIUM ♈

Habit Broadly columnar. *Flowers* Cup-shaped, in clusters in spring with, or just before, the leaves. White, pinkish when in bud. *Fruits* Small, edible, sweet or bitter cherries. Red. *Leaves* Deciduous, elliptic to oblong, pointed, sharply toothed. Bronze when young, turning matt dark green, then yellow and red-crimson in autumn.
• NATIVE HABITAT Woods throughout Europe.
• CULTIVATION Grow in any but waterlogged soil. A beautiful specimen for the wild garden.
• PROPAGATION By seed in autumn.

☼ ◊
❀ ❀ ❀

HEIGHT
20m (70ft)

SPREAD
100m (30ft)

Aceraceae	

ACER PLATANOIDES 'Lorbergii'

Habit Vigorous, spreading. *Flowers* Tiny, in dense clusters in mid-spring. Yellow. *Fruits* Small, round seed, with large, papery wings. *Leaves* Deciduous, deeply divided, with 5 slender, long-pointed lobes. Pale green, turning yellow and orange in autumn.
• NATIVE HABITAT Species grows in mountain woods of Europe and S.W. Asia. Garden origin.
• CULTIVATION Tolerates semi-shade and almost any fertile, well-drained soil.
• PROPAGATION By grafting in late winter or early spring or by budding in summer.

☼ ◊
❀ ❀ ❀

HEIGHT
20m (70ft)

SPREAD
11m (35ft)

Ulmaceae	WILLOW OAK

QUERCUS PHELLOS

Habit Broadly spreading. *Fruits* Acorns, to 1.5cm (⅝in) long, one-quarter enclosed in a shallow cup. *Leaves* Deciduous, long, narrow, willow-like, smooth. Bright green, turning yellow, orange, and brown in autumn.
• NATIVE HABITAT Moist soils and swamps of E. United States.
• CULTIVATION Unsuitable for chalky soils. Grow in deep, fertile soil.
• PROPAGATION By seed in autumn. Acorns mature in their second year.

☼ ◊
❀ ❀ ❀

HEIGHT
20m (70ft)

SPREAD
11m (35ft)

Oleaceae	COMMON ASH

FRAXINUS EXCELSIOR ♈

Habit Vigorous, broadly columnar.
Flowers Small, purple, apetalous. Male and female appear before the leaves on the same or separate plants in spring. *Fruits* Winged keys, in large, dense clusters. *Leaves* Deciduous, divided into 9–13 lance-shaped, sharply toothed leaflets. Dark green.
• NATIVE HABITAT Damp woodland and hedgerows of Europe.
• CULTIVATION Grow in any fertile, well-drained but not too dry soil.
• PROPAGATION By seed in autumn.

☼ ◊
❀ ❀ ❀

HEIGHT
30m (100ft)

SPREAD
20m (65ft)

| Leguminosae | |

SOPHORA JAPONICA 'Violacea'

Habit Broadly spreading, with a rounded crown.
Flowers Small, fragrant, pea-like, in large sprays in
late summer and early autumn. White, flushed lilac-
pink. *Fruits* A pod, approximately 8cm (3in) in
length. *Leaves* Deciduous, with 7–17 oval,
pointed leaflets. Dark green, turning yellow in
autumn.
• NATIVE HABITAT Woodlands in dry mountain
valleys of China.
• CULTIVATION Tolerant of poor, dry soils and
urban pollution. Grow in any fertile, well-drained

soil. Plants do not flower until reaching maturity,
which may be at about 30 years of age. Although
the tree grows vigorously, it needs long, hot
summers to flower profusely and prefers a warm
climate. The pod is rarely set in cool temperate
climates.
• PROPAGATION By grafting in late winter to
early spring.

HEIGHT
20m (70ft)

SPREAD
20m (70ft)

Myrtaceae	MOUNTAIN GUM

EUCALYPTUS DALRYMPLEANA ☙

Habit Vigorous, fast-growing, open, columnar.
Flowers Small, in clusters of 3, in late summer-autumn. *Leaves* Evergreen; juvenile: rounded, without stalks; adult: lance-shaped. Bronze on emergence, then blue-green.
Bark Peeling. Pinkish-grey, creamy-white beneath.
• NATIVE HABITAT Mountains of S.E. Australia and Tasmania.
• CULTIVATION Grow in fertile, well-drained soil and provide shelter from cold winds.
• PROPAGATION By seed in spring or autumn.

☀ ◇
❋ ❋

HEIGHT
20m (70ft)

SPREAD
8m (25ft)

Betulaceae	CANOE BIRCH, PAPER BIRCH

BETULA PAPYRIFERA

Habit Vigorous, open, broadly conical.
Flowers Catkins. Males to 10cm (4in) long; females shorter, on same plant. Greenish.
Leaves Deciduous, oval, with tapering points, toothed. Dark green, turning golden yellow in autumn. *Bark* Peeling. White.
• NATIVE HABITAT Woods and mountains of North America.
• CULTIVATION Grow in moist, well-drained soil.
• PROPAGATION By softwood cuttings in summer or by seed in autumn. Seed-raised plants variable.

☀ ◇
❋ ❋ ❋

HEIGHT
20m (70ft)

SPREAD
8m (25ft)

Betulaceae	GOLD BIRCH, ERMAN'S BIRCH, RUSSIAN ROCK BIRCH

BETULA ERMANII

Habit Elegant, open, broadly conical.
Flowers Upright catkins. Male: to 10cm (4in) long; female: shorter, on same plant. Greenish.
Leaves Deciduous, oval, heart-shaped at the base, pointed, toothed. Glossy green, turning yellow in autumn. *Bark* Peeling in strips. Creamy-white.
• NATIVE HABITAT Forests of N.E. Asia and Japan.
• CULTIVATION Grow in moist, well-drained soil.
• PROPAGATION By softwood cuttings in early summer or by seed in autumn. Seed-raised plants are variable.

☀ ◇
❋ ❋ ❋

HEIGHT
20m (70ft)

SPREAD
8m (25ft)

Myrtaceae	CIDER GUM

EUCALYPTUS GUNNII   ♈

Habit Vigorous, fast-growing, conical.
Flowers Small, in clusters of 3, in late spring-
summer. White. **Leaves** Evergreen. Juvenile:
rounded, stalkless. Grey-blue. Adult: oval to lance-
shaped. Silvery, turning smooth, grey-green.
Bark Peeling. Grey, greenish, and orange, creamy-
white beneath.
• NATIVE HABITAT Mountain forests of Tasmania.
• CULTIVATION Grow in fertile, well-drained soil.
Shelter from cold winds.
• PROPAGATION By seed in spring or autumn.

☼ ◊
❀❀

HEIGHT
20m (70ft)

SPREAD
8m (25ft)

Moraceae	

FICUS ELASTICA 'Doescheri'   ♈

Habit Vigorous, upright, then spreading.
Leaves Evergreen, large, oblong to oval, leathery.
Lustrous dark green, splashed with grey-green and
yellow.
• NATIVE HABITAT Garden origin.
• CULTIVATION Grow as a house or conservatory
plant. Tolerates partial shade. Grow in a fertile,
free-draining soil or compost. Water freely when in
growth and sparingly in low temperatures.
• PROPAGATION By leaf-bud, stem-tip cuttings, or
air-layering in summer.

☼ ◊

Min. 10°C
(50°F)

HEIGHT
17m (55ft)

SPREAD
10m (30ft)
or more

Moraceae	BANYAN TREE

FICUS BENGHALENSIS

Habit Spreading, with stilt-like prop roots.
Flowers Insignificant. **Fruits** Small, fig-like.
Brown. **Leaves** Evergreen, oval, to 20cm (8in)
long, leathery. Rich green, with paler veins.
• NATIVE HABITAT Humid tropical forests of S. Asia.
• CULTIVATION Grow as a house or conservatory
plant in cooler climates. Tolerates partial shade.
Grow in a fertile, free-draining soil or compost.
Water freely when in growth.
• PROPAGATION By leaf-bud cuttings, stem-tip
cuttings, or air-layering in summer.

☼ ◊

Min. 10°C
(50°F)

HEIGHT
18m (60ft)

SPREAD
22m (76ft)

Myrtaceae	MOUNT WELLINGTON PEPPER-MINT, TASMANIAN SNOW GUM

EUCALYPTUS COCCIFERA   ♈

Habit Vigorous, fast-growing, broadly spreading.
Flowers Small, in clusters of 3–7 in early summer.
White. **Leaves** Evergreen. Juvenile: rounded,
without stalks. Adult: aromatic, lance-shaped,
hooked at the tip, smooth. Green to grey-green.
Bark Peeling. Blue-grey, creamy-white beneath.
• NATIVE HABITAT Mountains of Tasmania.
• CULTIVATION Grow in fertile, well-drained soil
and provide shelter from freezing winds.
• PROPAGATION By seed in spring or autumn.

☼ ◊
❀❀

HEIGHT
18m (60ft)

SPREAD
8m (25ft)

| Palmae | ALEXANDRA PALM, NORTHERN BANGALOW PALM |

ARCHONTOPHOENIX ALEXANDRAE

Habit Erect, unbranched. **Flowers** In sprays on mature trees. Cream to yellow. **Leaves** Evergreen, feather-shaped, arching, to 3.5m (11ft) long.
• NATIVE HABITAT Rainforests of E. Australia.
• CULTIVATION Grown as a conservatory plant in cooler climates. Tolerant of some shade. Grow in a humus-rich, free-draining soil or compost. Provide good light, but shade from hot summer sun to avoid foliage scorch. Water moderately when in growth but sparingly when temperatures are low. The tree will not reach its full height potential when grown in cultivation. In cooler climates the young plants make handsome specimens for display in the home or conservatory, although these palms will seldom reach a sufficient size to enable flowering.
• PROPAGATION By seed in spring at not less than 24°C (75°F).

☼ ◊

Min. 15°C
(59°F)

HEIGHT
To 25m
(80ft)

SPREAD
7m (22ft)

Fagaceae	TURNER'S OAK

QUERCUS × TURNERI

Habit Dense, rounded, broadly spreading.
Fruits Acorns, to 2cm (¾in) long, one-half
enclosed in a cup. **Leaves** Semi-evergreen, oblong
to broadly oval, tapering at the base, with 3–5
triangular teeth on each side. Glossy dark green.
• NATIVE HABITAT Garden origin.
• CULTIVATION Tolerates lime-rich soils and semi-
shade. Grow in deep, fertile soil.
• PROPAGATION By grafting in late winter.

HEIGHT
20m (70ft)

SPREAD
18m (60ft)

Fagaceae	

NOTHOFAGUS DOMBEYI

Habit Open-branched, broadly columnar.
Leaves Evergreen, small, narrowly oval, finely and
sharply toothed. Sometimes loses its leaves in very
cold winters. Glossy dark green.
• NATIVE HABITAT Mountain forests of Argentina
and Chile.
• CULTIVATION Grow in deep, fertile, neutral to
acid soil, ensuring shelter from cold and strong
winds. Makes an exceptionally elegant specimen in
woodland gardens and other sheltered sites.
• PROPAGATION By seed in autumn.

HEIGHT
20m (70ft)

SPREAD
10m (30ft)

Betulaceae	WEEPING BIRCH

BETULA PENDULA 'Tristis'

Habit Slender, elegant, open, with pendulous
branchlets. **Flowers** Catkins, drooping or upright.
Male: to 6cm (2½in) long; female: shorter, on the
same plant. Greenish. **Leaves** Deciduous,
triangular to diamond-shaped. Bright green, turning
yellow in autumn. **Bark** White. Black fissures with
age.
• NATIVE HABITAT Garden origin.
• CULTIVATION Grow in moist, well-drained soil.
• PROPAGATION By softwood cuttings in summer.

HEIGHT
20m (70ft)

SPREAD
7m (22ft)

Fagaceae	CORK OAK

QUERCUS SUBER

Habit Broadly spreading, with a rounded crown.
Fruits Acorns, to 3cm (1¼in) long, one-half
enclosed in a cup. *Leaves* Evergreen, oval to
oblong, stiff, usually toothed. Glossy dark green
above, grey-felted beneath. *Bark* Thick, rugged,
corky. Pale grey. Cork is used commercially.
• NATIVE HABITAT Woodlands on hillsides around
W. Mediterranean.
• CULTIVATION Tolerates dry soils but grows best
on deep, fertile soils and in mild areas.
• PROPAGATION By seed in autumn.

☼ ◌
❄❄

HEIGHT
20m (70ft)

SPREAD
20m (70ft)

Palmae	SOUTHERN WASHINGTONIA

WASHINGTONIA ROBUSTA

Habit Fast-growing, upright, unbranched.
Flowers Tiny, in large, long-stalked sprays in
summer. Creamy-white. *Fruits* Small, spherical
berries. Black. *Leaves* Evergreen, fan-shaped, leaf-
blade and petioles both to 1m (3ft) long. Mid-green.
• NATIVE HABITAT Baja California to Mexico.
• CULTIVATION Grow as a conservatory plant in
cooler climates. Grow in a fertile soil or compost
with sharp sand added. Water moderately in
summer, otherwise sparingly.
• PROPAGATION By seed in spring.

☼ ◌
Min. 8°C
(46°F)

HEIGHT
15m (50ft)

SPREAD
3m (10ft)

Palmae	QUEEN PALM

SYAGRUS ROMANZOFFIANA

Habit Upright, unbranched. *Flowers* Small, in
huge clusters on mature plants. Yellow.
Fruits Egg-shaped, berry-like. Orange.
Leaves Arching, feather-shaped, with leaflets to
3–5m (10–15ft) long. Lustrous dark green.
• NATIVE HABITAT Dry, open forests of Brazil.
• CULTIVATION Grow as a house or conservatory
plant in cooler climates. Tolerates partial shade.
Grow in a humus-rich soil or compost.
• PROPAGATION By seed in spring.
• OTHER NAMES *Arecastrum romanzoffianum.*

☼ ◌
Min. 13°C
(55°F)

HEIGHT
16m (52ft)

SPREAD
10m (30ft)

Fagaceae	LUCOMBE OAK

QUERCUS × *HISPANICA* 'Lucombeana' ♔

Habit Broadly conical or with a dense, rounded,
billowing crown. *Fruits* Acorns, to 2.5cm (1in)
long, one-third enclosed in a cup. *Leaves* Semi-
evergreen, oval-elliptic or oblong, coarsely toothed.
Glossy dark green above, downy-grey beneath.
Bark Slightly corky. Grey.
• NATIVE HABITAT Garden origin.
• CULTIVATION Tolerates lime-rich soils and semi-
shade. Grow in deep, fertile soil. A very beautiful
specimen for large gardens.
• PROPAGATION By grafting in late winter.

☼ ◌
❄❄❄

HEIGHT
30m (80ft)

SPREAD
20m (70ft)

Proteaceae	MACADAMIA NUT

MACADAMIA INTEGRIFOLIA

Habit Spreading. **Flowers** Small, in panicles in spring. Creamy-yellow. **Fruits** Edible nuts. Brown. **Leaves** Evergreen, oblong to broadly oval, leathery, in whorls of 3. Dark green.
• NATIVE HABITAT Tropical highland forests of E. Australia.
• CULTIVATION Tolerates semi-shade. Grow in humus-rich, moisture-retentive soil or compost. Water freely when in growth, otherwise moderately. Prune if necessary in autumn. The tree rarely bears fruit when cultivated in cool temperate zones. It makes an interesting foliage specimen when grown in a warm conservatory. In tropical and sub-tropical regions it is grown as an ornamental shade tree and also on a commercial basis for its crisp, oil-rich, sweet nuts. Large trees are susceptible to damage in strong winds.
• PROPAGATION By seed in autumn or spring.

Min.
10–13°C
(50–55°F)

HEIGHT
20m (70ft)

SPREAD
15m (50ft)

Platanaceae	ORIENTAL PLANE

PLATANUS ORIENTALIS

Habit Vigorous, broadly columnar, the crown spreading with age. **Flowers** Tiny, insignificant. Male and female on same plant. **Fruits** Spherical, bristly, in pendent clusters of up to 6. Brown. **Leaves** Deciduous, palmately lobed, with sharply cut, slender, toothed lobes. Glossy bright green. **Bark** Flaky. Cream, pinkish-brown, and grey.
• NATIVE HABITAT Mountain woodlands and riversides in S.E. Europe.
• CULTIVATION Grow in deep, fertile soil.
• PROPAGATION By seed in autumn.

HEIGHT
25m (80ft)

SPREAD
25m (80ft)

Betulaceae	CHINESE RED BIRCH

BETULA ALBOSINENSIS

Habit Elegant, open-branched, with a broadly conical crown. **Flowers** Catkins. Male: to 6cm (2½in) long, yellow; female: upright, green, on same plant. **Leaves** Deciduous, oval, sharply toothed with tapering point. Glossy green, turning yellow in autumn. **Bark** Peeling in strips. Coppery-red to orange-red, shining, cream colour beneath.
• NATIVE HABITAT Mountain woods of W. China.
• CULTIVATION Grow in moist, well-drained soil.
• PROPAGATION By softwood cuttings in summer. Birches hybridize freely; seed-raised plants variable.

HEIGHT
18m (60ft)

SPREAD
9m (28ft)

Fagaceae	

NOTHOFAGUS BETULOIDES

Habit Narrowly columnar, broadening with age, sometimes shrubby. **Leaves** Evergreen, oval to elliptic, to 2.5cm (1in) long, blunt-toothed at margins. Glossy, very dark green, paler and conspicuously veined beneath.
• NATIVE HABITAT Evergreen forests in Chile and Argentina.
• CULTIVATION Tolerates dappled shade. Grow in deep, fertile, well-drained soil. Shelter from cold, dry winds. Unsuitable for chalky soils.
• PROPAGATION By seed in autumn.

HEIGHT
20m (70ft)

SPREAD
6m (20ft)

Lauraceae	CALIFORNIA LAUREL, HEAD-ACHE TREE, OREGON MYRTLE

UMBELLULARIA CALIFORNICA

Habit Broadly spreading. **Flowers** Small, apetalous, in clusters in late winter-early spring. Yellow-green sepals. **Fruits** Egg-shaped berries. Deep purple. **Leaves** Evergreen, aromatic, elliptic to oblong. Glossy bright green or yellow-green.
• NATIVE HABITAT Scrub and evergreen forest in canyons of S.W. Oregon and California, US.
• CULTIVATION Grow in fertile, moist but well-drained soil. Provide shelter from cold, dry winds. Leaves emit poisonous vapour when crushed.
• PROPAGATION By seed in autumn.

HEIGHT
20m (70ft)

SPREAD
12m (40ft)

Salicaceae	GOLDEN WILLOW

SALIX ALBA var. *VITELLINA* ♀

Habit Fast-growing, broadly spreading.
Leaves Deciduous, lance-shaped. Green, paler beneath. ***Bark*** Young twigs egg-yolk yellow.
• NATIVE HABITAT Riversides and damp meadows from Europe to W. Asia.
• CULTIVATION Grow in any but very dry soil. Often grown for bright winter twigs. Pollard annually in early spring or every other year. Do not plant within 30m (100ft) of buildings.
• PROPAGATION By semi-ripe cuttings in summer or by hardwood cuttings in winter.

☼ ◊
❀ ❀ ❀

HEIGHT
20m (70ft)

SPREAD
10m (30ft)

Rosaceae	

MALUS HUPEHENSIS ♀

Habit Vigorous, broadly spreading, with ascending branches. ***Flowers*** Large, fragrant, shallowly cup-shaped, in profusion in mid-spring. White, pink in bud. ***Fruits*** Round, red crab apples, to 1cm (⅜in) across, in red-stalked clusters.
Leaves Deciduous, elliptic to oval, taper-pointed, finely toothed. Dark green.
• NATIVE HABITAT Mountain woodlands of China.
• CULTIVATION Tolerates some shade, but blooms best in sun. Grow in any but waterlogged soil.
• PROPAGATION By seed in autumn.

☼ ◊
❀ ❀ ❀

HEIGHT
12m (40ft)

SPREAD
12m (40ft)

Salicaceae	GOLDEN WEEPING WILLOW

SALIX × *SEPULCRALIS* var. *CHRYSOCOMA* ♀

Habit Weeping, broadly spreading.
Leaves Deciduous, narrowly lance-shaped. Bright green, later dark green; blue-green beneath.
• NATIVE HABITAT Garden origin.
• CULTIVATION Grows in any but very dry soil, but seen to best effect near water. Do not plant within 30m (100ft) of buildings. Prone to fungal cankers.
• PROPAGATION By semi-ripe cuttings in summer or by hardwood cuttings in winter.
• OTHER NAMES *S. alba* 'Tristis', *S.* 'Chrysocoma'.

☼ ◊
❀ ❀ ❀

HEIGHT
20m (70ft)

SPREAD
15m (50ft)

Salicaceae	VIOLET WILLOW

SALIX DAPHNOIDES

Habit Fast-growing, broadly conical. ***Flowers*** Male catkins in spring. Silvery, with yellow anthers.
Leaves Deciduous, narrowly elliptic. Glossy dark green above, blue-green beneath. ***Bark*** Young shoots dark purple, bloomed white.
• NATIVE HABITAT Damp woodlands in Europe.
• CULTIVATION Grow in any but very dry soil. Often grown for winter twigs. Pollard annually in early spring or every other year.
• PROPAGATION By semi-ripe cuttings in summer or by hardwood cuttings in winter.

☼ ◊
❀ ❀ ❀

HEIGHT
10m (30ft)

SPREAD
7m (22ft)

Rosaceae	MANCHURIAN CRAB

MALUS BACCATA var. *MANDSCHURICA*

Habit Vigorous, broadly spreading, with a rounded crown. *Flowers* Fragrant, shallowly cup-shaped, in profusion in mid-spring. White. *Fruits* Small, egg-shaped, long-persistent. Red or yellow.
Leaves Deciduous, elliptic to oval, taper-pointed, finely toothed. Dark green above, paler beneath.
• NATIVE HABITAT Scrub and woodlands of N.E. Asia.
• CULTIVATION Tolerates some shade, but blooms best in sun. Grow in any but waterlogged soil.
• PROPAGATION By budding in summer or by grafting in late winter.

HEIGHT 15m (50ft)

SPREAD 11m (35ft)

Rosaceae	CALLERY PEAR

PYRUS CALLERYANA 'Chanticleer'

Habit Narrowly conical, symmetrical.
Flowers Small, 5-petalled, in sprays in spring. White. *Leaves* Deciduous, oval to elliptic. Glossy dark green, turning purplish or scarlet in autumn.
• NATIVE HABITAT Garden origin.
• CULTIVATION Tolerant of urban conditions. Grow in any fertile, well-drained soil. Resistant to fireblight. A beautiful tree for confined spaces.
• PROPAGATION By budding in summer or by grafting in winter.
• OTHER NAMES *P. calleryana* 'Cleveland Select'.

HEIGHT 13m (43ft)

SPREAD 6m (20ft)

Rosaceae	ST LUCIE CHERRY

PRUNUS MAHALEB

Habit Bushy, round-headed. *Flowers* Small, fragrant, cup-shaped, in clusters from mid- to late spring. White. *Fruits* Small, bitter cherries. Black.
Leaves Deciduous, broadly oval to rounded, toothed. Dark green, turning yellow in autumn.
• NATIVE HABITAT In woods and thickets on dry hillsides of C. and S. Europe.
• CULTIVATION Grow in any but waterlogged soil. Flowers may not be freely carried on young plants, but become more profuse with age.
• PROPAGATION By seed in autumn.

HEIGHT 10m (30ft)

SPREAD 8m (25ft)

Styraceae	MOUNTAIN SILVER BELL, SNOWDROP TREE

HALESIA MONTICOLA

Habit Fast-growing, conical or spreading.
Flowers Small, bell-shaped, in a profusion of pendent clusters in late spring. White. *Fruits* Four papery wings. *Leaves* Deciduous, elliptic to broadly oval-oblong, pointed. Bright green, later mid-green.
• NATIVE HABITAT North Carolina, Arkansas, US.
• CULTIVATION Grow in moist but well-drained, neutral to acid soil. Shelter from cold winds.
• PROPAGATION By softwood cuttings in summer or by seed in autumn.
• OTHER NAMES *H. carolina* var. *monticola*.

HEIGHT 12m (40ft)

SPREAD 8m (28ft)

| Cornaceae | MOUNTAIN DOGWOOD, PACIFIC DOGWOOD |

CORNUS NUTTALLII

Habit Broadly conical. **Flowers** Tiny, in
hemispherical clusters, in late spring and
sometimes again in autumn. Green, surrounded by
4–7 large, conspicuous, creamy-white bracts,
flushed pink with age. **Leaves** Deciduous, oval, to
15cm (6in) long, pointed. Dark green, turning
yellow or red in autumn.
• NATIVE HABITAT Lowland forests and mountain
forests of W. North America.
• CULTIVATION Tolerates light, dappled shade.
Grow in fertile, freely draining soil. Dislikes
shallow, chalky soils. An elegant and beautiful
specimen tree, it is also well suited to open areas in
woodland gardens. It is notable for its beautiful
habit, having an open crown of ascending branches
arising from a straight, fluted bole. The flower
buds are clearly visible at the branch tips in winter.
• PROPAGATION By seed in autumn.

HEIGHT
12m (40ft)

SPREAD
8m (25ft)

Rosaceae	

PRUNUS AVIUM 'Plena' ♛

Habit Round-headed, spreading.
Flowers Double, cup-shaped, in large clusters in spring with or just before leaves. Pure white.
Fruits Small, edible, sweet or bitter cherries. Red.
Leaves Deciduous, elliptic to oblong, pointed, sharply toothed. Bronze when young, turning matt dark green, then yellow and red-crimson in autumn.
• NATIVE HABITAT Garden origin.
• CULTIVATION Grow in any but waterlogged soil. One of the most beautiful of the flowering cherries.
• PROPAGATION By softwood cuttings in summer.

☼ ◊
❀ ❀ ❀

HEIGHT 12m (40ft)

SPREAD 12m (40ft)

Oleaceae	FLOWERING ASH, MANNA ASH

FRAXINUS ORNUS ♛

Habit Broadly spreading, round-headed.
Flowers Tiny, fragrant, in large, conical clusters from late spring to early summer. Creamy-white.
Fruits Seeds, with papery wings, in clusters.
Leaves Deciduous, divided into 5–9, oblong to oval, pointed leaflets. Matt dark green.
• NATIVE HABITAT Woodland on dry slopes from S. Europe to S.W. Asia.
• CULTIVATION Grow in any fertile soil, provided it is not too dry.
• PROPAGATION By seed in autumn.

☼ ◊
❀ ❀ ❀

HEIGHT 15m (50ft)

SPREAD 13m (43ft)

Rosaceae	BIRD CHERRY

PRUNUS PADUS

Habit Conical when young, spreading with age.
Flowers Small, fragrant, in upright or drooping spikes in mid- to late spring. White. **Fruits** Small, rounded to egg-shaped cherries. Glossy black.
Leaves Deciduous, elliptic, pointed, finely toothed. Dark green, turning yellow or red in autumn.
• NATIVE HABITAT Stream sides in open areas and in woods throughout Europe.
• CULTIVATION Grow in any but waterlogged soil. A beautiful specimen for the wild garden.
• PROPAGATION By seed in autumn.

☼ ◊
❀ ❀ ❀

HEIGHT 15m (50ft)

SPREAD 10m (30ft)

Ericaceae	MADRONA

ARBUTUS MENZIESII ♛

Habit Broadly columnar, spreading with age.
Flowers Small, urn-shaped, in upright panicles in late spring. White. **Fruits** Small, strawberry-like berries. Orange-red. **Leaves** Evergreen, elliptic. Glossy dark green above, bluish beneath.
Bark Peeling. Red-brown, golden-olive beneath.
• NATIVE HABITAT Forests of W. North America.
• CULTIVATION Tolerates dappled shade. Grow in fertile, humus-rich soil. Shelter from winds.
• PROPAGATION By seed in autumn or by semi-ripe cuttings in summer.

☼ ◊ pH
❀ ❀ ❀

HEIGHT 15m (50ft)

SPREAD 15m (50ft)

Meliaceae	BEAD TREE, CHINABERRY

MELIA AZEDARACH

Habit Round-headed, spreading. *Flowers* Small, fragrant, star-shaped, in spring. Pinkish-lilac. *Fruits* Small, round, berry-like. Orange-yellow. *Leaves* Deciduous, divided into many oval to elliptic leaflets. Dark green
• NATIVE HABITAT N. India and China.
• CULTIVATION Tolerant of very dry soil and coastal conditions. Grow in any well-drained soil. Flowers best in areas with long, hot summers.
• PROPAGATION By seed in autumn.

☼ ◌
❀ ❀

HEIGHT
10m (30ft)

SPREAD
10m (30ft)

Rosaceae	HILL CHERRY

PRUNUS SERRULATA var. *SPONTANEA*

Habit Broadly spreading. *Flowers* Cup-shaped, in profusion from mid- to late spring. White to pale pink. *Fruits* Cherries, to 2.5cm (1in) long. Dark purplish-red. *Leaves* Deciduous, oblong to oval-elliptic, pointed, toothed. Bronze when young, then dark green, turning yellow through red in autumn.
• NATIVE HABITAT Woods, in the hills and mountains of China, Japan, and Korea.
• CULTIVATION Grow in any but waterlogged soil.
• PROPAGATION By seed in autumn.
• OTHER NAMES *P. jamasakura.*

☼ ◌
❀ ❀ ❀

HEIGHT
12m (40ft)

SPREAD
12m (40ft)

Rosaceae	

PRUNUS 'Kanzan'   ♛

Habit Vigorous, vase-shaped, with ascending branches, spreading with age. *Flowers* Large, double, in dense clusters, carried with the emerging leaves from mid- to late spring. Bright purplish-pink. *Leaves* Deciduous, oval, long-pointed. Coppery-bronze on emergence, then dark green.
• NATIVE HABITAT Garden origin.
• CULTIVATION Grow in any but waterlogged soil.
• PROPAGATION By softwood cuttings in summer, by budding in summer, or by grafting in winter.
• OTHER NAMES *P.* 'Sekiyama'.

☼ ◌
❀ ❀ ❀

HEIGHT
To 10m
(30ft)

SPREAD
9m (28ft)

Rosaceae	

MALUS 'Profusion'

Habit Vigorous, spreading. **Flowers** Cup-shaped, in profuse clusters from mid- to late spring. Deep purplish-red. **Fruits** Tiny, rounded crab apples. Red-purple. **Leaves** Deciduous. Bronze-purple on emergence, later dark green, veined crimson.
• NATIVE HABITAT Garden origin.
• CULTIVATION Tolerates semi-shade. Grow in any but waterlogged soil. Susceptible to fireblight.
• PROPAGATION By budding in late summer or by grafting in mid-winter.
• OTHER NAMES *M.* x *moerlandsii* 'Profusion'.

☼ ◌
❀ ❀ ❀

HEIGHT
To 10m
(30ft)

SPREAD
9m (28ft)

Scrophulariaceae	

PAULOWNIA TOMENTOSA

Habit Broadly columnar. **Flowers** Fragrant, foxglove-like, in large, upright panicles in spring. Pinkish-lilac. **Leaves** Deciduous, broadly oval, heart-shaped at the base, sometimes lobed, hairy. Dark green above, densely hairy beneath.
• NATIVE HABITAT Mountains of China.
• CULTIVATION Grow in any fertile soil. Flowers best in regions with long, hot summers.
• PROPAGATION By seed in autumn or spring or by root cuttings in winter.
• OTHER NAMES *P. imperialis*.

☼ ◌
❀ ❀ ❀

HEIGHT
14m (46ft)

SPREAD
10m (30ft)

Leguminosae	

GLEDITSIA TRIACANTHOS 'Sunburst'

Habit Spreading. **Leaves** Deciduous, finely divided into many slender leaflets. Bright golden-yellow on emergence, becoming dark green. Young and mature leaves make effective contrasts.
• NATIVE HABITAT Garden origin.
• CULTIVATION Tolerates urban pollution. Grow in any well-drained soil.
• PROPAGATION By budding in late summer.
• OTHER NAMES *G. triacanthos* 'Inermis Aurea'.

☼ ◌
❀ ❀ ❀

HEIGHT
To 10m
(30ft)

SPREAD
10m (30ft)

MAGNOLIAS

Magnolias are a genus of deciduous, evergreen or semi-evergreen shrubs and trees. They are usually found in woodland and forests, often in mountainous areas, and mainly in the northern hemisphere. Some have been known in cultivation in China for over 1400 years.

Magnolias are usually exceptionally long-lived, and are much valued for their elegant habit and beautiful, often intensely fragrant flowers. These range from the tough but delicate-looking, star-shaped blooms of *M. stellata* to the exotic, goblet-shaped blooms of *M.* x *soulangeana*.

Magnolias are among the most handsome of plants when grown as free-standing specimens; they are not only gloriously beautiful in flower, they often offer an architectural branch framework in winter. Some also produce interesting fruits. The buds and flowers of early-flowering species may be damaged by

frosts, so avoid planting in frost pockets. Most also need shelter from strong winds, as their branches can be brittle. All grow best on deep, fertile, moisture-retentive but well-drained soils that are humus-rich, and preferably neutral or acid. Some, such as *M. kobus*, *M. wilsonii*, and *M. grandiflora*, tolerate lime, provided that the soil is deep and humus-rich. Grow in sun or light, dappled shade.

Magnolias generally require little pruning, other than to remove dead wood and badly placed branches, although overgrown specimens can be cut back hard. This should be done after flowering for early-flowering deciduous species, and in early spring for late-flowering evergreens.

Propagate species by seed in autumn or by semi-ripe cuttings in summer. Cultivars, hybrids, and variants are propagated by semi-ripe cuttings in summer or by grafting in winter.

M. KOBUS 'Norman Gould'
Habit Slow-growing, spreading, sometimes shrubby.
Flowers Fragrant, star-shaped, opening from silky buds in mid-spring. White.
Leaves Deciduous, narrowly oblong-oval. Dark green.
• HEIGHT 5m (15ft).
• SPREAD 5m (15ft).

M. kobus 'Norman Gould'

☼ ◊ ❀❀❀

M. x KEWENSIS 'Wada's Memory'
Habit Dense, broadly conical.
Flowers Fragrant, large, on bare branches from mid- to late spring. Creamy-white to pure white. *Leaves* Aromatic. Deciduous, oval. Red-purple, then dark green.
• OTHER NAMES *M.* 'Wada's Memory'.
• HEIGHT 9m (30ft).
• SPREAD 6m (20ft).

M. x *kewensis* 'Wada's Memory'

☼ ◊ ❀❀❀   ♛

M. KOBUS
Habit Broadly conical.
Flowers Fragrant, up to 10cm (4in) across, in profusion in spring. Creamy-white tepals, flushed pink at the base.
Leaves Slightly aromatic. Deciduous, elliptic to oval, tapering at the base. smooth. Dark green.
• CULTIVATION
Blooms at about 10–15 years of age.
• HEIGHT To 20m (70ft), often less.
• SPREAD 10m (30ft).

M. kobus

☼ ◊ ❀❀❀

M. CYLINDRICA
Habit Spreading,
sometimes shrubby.
Flowers Fragrant,
upright, opening on bare
branches in spring.
Narrow, creamy-white
tepals and sepals.
Leaves Deciduous,
broadly to elliptic. Dark
green above, paler and
downy beneath.
• HEIGHT 9m (28ft).
• SPREAD 6m (20ft).

M. cylindrica

☼ ◊ ❀❀❀   ♈

M. SALICIFOLIA
Habit Broadly conical.
Flowers Fragrant, large,
opening on bare branches
in early spring. Narrow,
white tepals and sepals.
Leaves Aromatic.
Deciduous, oval to lance-
shaped or elliptic.
Reddish when young,
then dark green above,
blue-green beneath.
• HEIGHT 10m (30ft).
• SPREAD 5m (15ft).

M. salicifolia
Anise magnolia

☼ ◊ ❀❀❀   ♈

M. × WIESNERI
Habit Open, bushy,
spreading.
Flowers Fragrant, large,
saucer-shaped, opening
from tight, round buds in
late spring. White, with
crimson stamens.
Leaves Deciduous,
broadly oval, leathery.
Dark green.
• OTHER NAMES
M. × watsonii.
• HEIGHT 7m (22ft).
• SPREAD 7m (22ft).

M. × wiesneri

☼ ◊ ❀❀❀

M. WILSONII
Habit Open, spreading.
Flowers Fragrant, large,
pendent, cup- then
saucer-shaped, in late
spring–early summer.
White; crimson stamens.
Leaves Deciduous,
elliptic-oblong to lance-
shaped. Matt green, silky
beneath.
• CULTIVATION
Tolerates semi-shade.
• HEIGHT 8m (25ft).
• SPREAD 6m (20ft).

M. wilsonii

☼ ◊ ❀❀❀   ♈

M. DENUDATA
Habit Rounded,
spreading, sometimes
shrubby.
Flowers Fragrant, very
large, goblet-shaped, on
bare branches from mid-
to late spring. White.
Leaves Deciduous, oval.
Mid-green, softly hairy
beneath.
• OTHER NAMES
M. heptapeta.
• HEIGHT 10m (30ft) or
more.
• SPREAD 10m (30ft).

M. denudata
Lily tree, Yulan

☼ ◊ ❀❀   ♈

M. 'Charles Coates'
Habit Rounded, open,
spreading. *Flowers* Very
fragrant, carried with the
emerging leaves in late
spring and early summer.
Creamy-white with an
inner ring of red stamens.
Leaves Deciduous, oval,
wedge-shaped at base, to
25cm (10in) long. Light
green.
• HEIGHT To 6m (20ft).
• SPREAD 5m (15ft).

M. 'Charles Coates'

☼ ◊ ❀❀❀

M. 'Manchu Fan'
Habit Vigorous, upright.
Flowers Fragrant, large,
goblet-shaped, in late
spring. Creamy-white;
innermost tepals flushed
purple-pink at base.
Leaves Deciduous,
elliptic. Pale green when
young, turning darker.
• HEIGHT 10m (30ft) or
more.
• SPREAD 10m (30ft).

M. 'Manchu Fan'
Gresham hybrid

☼ ◊ ❀❀❀

M. FRASERI
Habit Broadly
spreading, open-
branching.
Flowers Fragrant,
saucer-shaped, opening
from vase-shaped buds at
the branch tips in late
spring–early summer.
Rich creamy-white.
Leaves Deciduous,
large, heart-shaped at
base, soft. Bronzed at
first, then pale green.
• HEIGHT To 14m (56ft).
• SPREAD To 12m (40ft).

M. fraseri

☼ ◊ ❁❁❁

M. GRANDIFLORA
'Exmouth'
Habit Dense, broadly
conical **Flowers** Very
fragrant, large, cup-
shaped. Appear
intermittently from mid-
summer to early autumn.
Creamy-white.
Leaves Evergreen,
narrow, elliptic, glossy.
Soft green above, with
red-brown felt beneath.
• HEIGHT To 25m (80ft).
• SPREAD 12m (40ft).

M. grandiflora
'Exmouth'

☼ ◊ ❁❁❁   ♛

M. TRIPETALA
Habit Conical, open,
broadly spreading with
age. **Flowers** Large, from
slender buds at branch
tips in late spring to early
summer. Creamy-white,
with narrow tepals.
Leaves Deciduous, oval
to elliptic, pointed. Dark
green above, hairy; grey-
green beneath.
• HEIGHT 12m (40ft).
• SPREAD 10m (30ft).

M. tripetala
Umbrella tree

☼ ◊ ❁❁❁

M. HYPOLEUCA
Habit Vigorous,
pyramidal.
Flowers Very fragrant,
large, cup-shaped, in
early summer. Creamy-
white, pink-flushed, with
crimson stamens.
Leaves Deciduous, very
large, broadly oval. Deep
green.
• OTHER NAMES
M. obovata.
• HEIGHT 16m (52ft).
• SPREAD 8m (25ft).

M. hypoleuca

☼ ◊ ❁❁❁   ♛

M. SPRENGERI
Habit Open, spreading.
Flowers Fragrant. Large,
bowl-shaped, on bare
branches in mid-spring.
White, sometimes tinted
red or pink.
Leaves Deciduous,
broadly oval, wedge-
shaped at base. Dark
green.
• HEIGHT 12m (40ft).
• SPREAD 10m (30ft).

M. sprengeri

☼ ◊ ❁❁

M. x VEITCHII
'Peter Veitch'
Habit Very vigorous,
spreading.
Flowers Fragrant, large,
goblet-shaped, on bare
branches in spring.
Waxy-white, flushed
pink-purple.
Leaves Deciduous,
broadly oval-oblong,
pointed. Bronzed when
young, then dark green.
• HEIGHT To 25m (80ft).
• SPREAD 8m (25ft).

M. x veitchii
'Peter Veitch'
Gresham hybrid

☼ ◊ ❁❁❁

M. *CAMPBELLII*
Habit Upright, broadly
conical. *Flowers* Slightly
fragrant, very large, cup-
shaped, on bare branches
from late winter to early
spring. Pale pink to deep
pink.
Leaves Deciduous,
oblong-oval, pointed.
Dark green, paler below,
flushed purple when
young.
• HEIGHT 16m (52ft).
• SPREAD 11m (35ft).

M. campbellii
Pink tulip tree

☼ ◊ ❀❀

M. *CAMPBELLII*
subsp. *MOLLICOMATA*
Habit Upright, broadly
conical. *Flowers* Slightly
fragrant, large, cup-
shaped, in late winter to
early spring. Pale lilac-
pink. *Leaves* Deciduous,
oblong-oval, pointed.
Dark green, often hairy
beneath, flushed purple
when young.
• HEIGHT 16m (52ft) or
more.
• SPREAD 11m (35ft).

M. campbellii subsp.
mollicomata

☼ ◊ ❀❀❀

M. **'Heaven Scent'**
Habit Vigorous,
spreading. *Flowers* Very
fragrant, narrowly cup-
shaped, in late spring.
Pale pink, flushed deep
pink at base; tepal
reverse-striped magenta.
Leaves Deciduous,
oblong-oval. Dark green.
• HEIGHT 10m (30ft) or
more.
• SPREAD 10m (30ft).

M. **'Heaven Scent'**
Gresham hybrid

☼ ◊ ❀❀❀   ♥

M. *CAMPBELLII*
'Wakehurst'
Habit Open, spreading.
Flowers Fragrant, large,
narrowly bowl-shaped, on
bare branches in mid-
spring. Purplish-pink,
rich pink within.
Leaves Deciduous, oval
to lance-shaped or
elliptic. Dark green.
• HEIGHT 15m (50ft).
• SPREAD 10m (30ft).

M. campbellii
'Wakehurst'

☼ ◊ ❀❀

M. *CAMPBELLII*
'Charles Raffill'
Habit Vigorous, upright,
later spreading.
Flowers Fragrant, large,
cup-shaped, in mid-
spring. Rose-purple,
white within. Margins
flushed pink-purple.
Leaves Deciduous,
oblong-oval, pointed.
Mid-green.
• HEIGHT 16m (52ft) or
more.
• SPREAD 11m (35ft).

M. campbellii
'Charles Raffill'

☼ ◊ ❀❀❀

M. *CAMPBELLII*
'Darjeeling'
Habit Upright, broadly
conical. *Flowers* Slightly
fragrant, large, cup-
shaped, on bare branches
in late winter to early
spring. Rose-pink.
Leaves Deciduous,
oblong-oval, pointed.
Dark green, paler below.
Purplish when young.
• HEIGHT 16m (52ft).
• SPREAD 11m (35ft).

M. campbellii
'Darjeeling'

☼ ◊ ❀❀

Styraceae	JAPANESE SNOWBELL

STYRAX JAPONICA ♀

Habit Open, broadly spreading. *Flowers* Slightly fragrant, small, pendent, bell-shaped, carried beneath the branches in early to mid-summer. White. *Leaves* Deciduous, elliptic to oval. Rich glossy green, turning yellow or red in autumn.
• NATIVE HABITAT Open areas, usually on damp ground, in China, Japan, and Korea.
• CULTIVATION Tolerates dappled shade. Grow in neutral to acid soil and shelter from cold winds.
• PROPAGATION By softwood cuttings in summer or by seed in autumn.

☀ ◐ pH
❄ ❄ ❄

HEIGHT
10m (30ft)

SPREAD
8m (25ft)

Betulaceae	EASTERN HOP HORNBEAM, IRONWOOD

OSTRYA VIRGINIANA

Habit Broadly conical-rounded. *Flowers* Catkins. Male: to 5cm (2in) long, yellow; female: small, green, on same plant in spring. *Fruits* Nuts, enclosed in pale, bladder-like husks, carried in short, pendent clusters. *Leaves* Deciduous, ovate, toothed. Dark green, turning rich yellow in autumn.
• NATIVE HABITAT Woodlands of E. North America.
• CULTIVATION Tolerates dappled shade. Grow in any fertile, well-drained soil.
• PROPAGATION By seed in autumn.

☀ ◐
❄ ❄ ❄

HEIGHT
15m (50ft)

SPREAD
12m (40ft)

Rosaceae	HIMALAYAN WHITEBEAM

SORBUS VESTITA

Habit Broadly conical. *Flowers* Small, flattened clusters in late spring-early summer. White. *Fruits* Small, rounded to pear-shaped, berry-like. Green, flecked brown. *Leaves* Deciduous, elliptic, veined. Dark grey-green above, silvery-white and downy beneath.
• NATIVE HABITAT Forests in the Himalayas.
• CULTIVATION Fertile, moisture-retentive soil.
• PROPAGATION By softwood cuttings in summer or by seed in autumn.
• OTHER NAMES *S. cuspidata.*

☀ ◐
❄ ❄ ❄

HEIGHT
15m (50ft)

SPREAD
10m (30ft)

Nyssaceae	DOVE TREE, GHOST TREE, POCKET-HANDKERCHIEF TREE

DAVIDIA INVOLUCRATA

Habit Broadly conical. *Flowers* Tiny, in rounded heads, with conspicuous purple anthers, surrounded by large, white, papery bracts of unequal size, in late spring. *Fruits* Rounded berry, 2.5cm (1in) across. Green, ripening to purple.
Leaves Deciduous, heart-shaped, with slender, pointed tip. Bright green, felted beneath.
Bark Peeling vertically in small flakes. Orange-brown.
• NATIVE HABITAT Moist, mountain woods in China.

• CULTIVATION Tolerates semi-shade. Grow in any moisture-retentive soil. Provide shelter from strong winds. Flowers only when mature. The numerous papery bracts give the appearance of handkerchiefs hanging from the tree.
• PROPAGATION By semi-ripe cuttings in early summer or by seed in autumn.

HEIGHT
14m (46ft)

SPREAD
10m (30ft)

Bignoniaceae	INDIAN BEAN TREE, EASTERN CATALPA

CATALPA BIGNONIOIDES 🏆

Habit Broadly spreading. **Flowers** Trumpet-shaped, 2-lipped, in upright panicles in mid- to late summer. White, yellow- and purple-spotted. **Fruits** Long, pendent pods. **Leaves** Deciduous, heart-shaped, pointed at the tip. Light green.
• NATIVE HABITAT Woods and stream sides of S.E. United States.
• CULTIVATION Grow in fertile, well-drained soil. Shelter from strong winds. Flowers only when mature. Thrives in areas with long, hot summers.
• PROPAGATION By seed in autumn.

☀ ◉
❀ ❀ ❀

HEIGHT
15m (50ft)

SPREAD
15m (50ft)

Bignoniaceae	WESTERN CATALPA, NORTHERN CATALPA

CATALPA SPECIOSA

Habit Broadly columnar. **Flowers** Trumpet-shaped, 2-lipped, in upright panicles in mid-summer. White, purple-spotted. **Fruits** Long, narrow, pendent pods. **Leaves** Deciduous, broadly oval, taper-pointed at the tip. Dark green.
• NATIVE HABITAT Damp woods, swamps, and riverbanks of C. United States.
• CULTIVATION Grow in deep, fertile, well-drained soil. Provide shelter from strong winds. Thrives in areas with long, hot summers.
• PROPAGATION By seed in autumn.

☀ ◉
❀ ❀ ❀

HEIGHT
15m (50ft)

SPREAD
15m (50ft)

Theaceae	JAPANESE STEWARTIA

STEWARTIA PSEUDOCAMELLIA 🏆

Habit Broadly columnar. **Flowers** Shallowly cup-shaped, opening from silky buds in mid-summer. Glistening white, with golden stamens.
Leaves Deciduous, oval to elliptic, finely toothed. Dark green, turning yellow and red in autumn.
Bark Peeling. Red-brown, grey-pink beneath.
• NATIVE HABITAT Mountain woods of Japan.
• CULTIVATION Grow in rich, neutral to acid soil. Shelter from cold winds. Prefers shade at the roots.
• PROPAGATION By softwood cuttings in summer or by seed in autumn.

☀ ◉ pH
❀ ❀ ❀

HEIGHT
15m (50ft)

SPREAD
10m (30ft)

Fagaceae	VARIEGATED TURKEY OAK

QUERCUS CERRIS 'Argenteovariegata'

Habit Broadly spreading, with a rounded crown.
Fruits Acorns to 2.5cm (1in) long, half enclosed in a cup clothed with long, slender scales.
Leaves Deciduous, elliptic to oblong, deeply lobed. Glossy dark green, margined yellow, fading to cream.
• NATIVE HABITAT Garden origin.
• CULTIVATION Tolerates semi-shade, chalky soils, and coastal conditions. Grow in deep, fertile, well-drained soil.
• PROPAGATION By grafting in late winter.
• OTHER NAMES Q. cerris 'Variegata'.

☀ ◉
❀ ❀ ❀

HEIGHT
15m (50ft)

SPREAD
10m (30ft)

Rosaceae	

SORBUS ARIA 'Lutescens' ♆

Habit Dense crown, conical when young, later spreading. *Flowers* Small, in flattened clusters in late spring. White. *Fruits* Small, rounded berries, in clusters. Orange-red. *Leaves* Deciduous, elliptic to oval, toothed, densely clothed in creamy down when young. Grey-green, turning russet and gold in autumn.
• NATIVE HABITAT Garden origin.
• CULTIVATION Tolerant of heavy clay soils, semi-shade, urban pollution, and exposed, coastal conditions. Thrives in both acid and alkaline soils.

Grow in fertile, moisture-retentive but well-drained soil. It makes a beautiful and adaptable specimen tree, well suited to town gardens and having a long season of interest.
• PROPAGATION By softwood cuttings or budding in summer or by grafting in winter.

HEIGHT
13m (43ft)

SPREAD
8m (25ft)

| Hippocastanaceae | INDIAN HORSE-CHESTNUT |

AESCULUS INDICA 'Sydney Pearce'

Habit Vigorous, upright, broadly columnar, later spreading. *Flowers* Tubular to bell-shaped, flared at the mouth, carried freely in narrow, upright panicles in mid-summer. White, flushed pink, marked red and yellow. *Fruits* Scaly, spineless husk enclosing a single, small, shiny 'conker'. *Leaves* Deciduous, with 5–7 lance-shaped, stalked leaflets. Bronze when young, turning dark olive green.
• NATIVE HABITAT Garden origin.
• CULTIVATION Tolerates dappled shade. Grow in fertile, moisture-retentive but well-drained soil. This elegant, low-branching tree flowers much later than the common horse-chestnut and bears its blooms near ground level where they can be seen more clearly.
• PROPAGATION By budding in late summer or by grafting in late winter.

HEIGHT
13m (43ft)

SPREAD
13m (43ft)

Aceraceae	

ACER PSEUDOPLATANUS 'Simon Louis Frères'

Habit Broadly spreading, with a domed crown.
Leaves Deciduous, with 5 coarsely toothed lobes.
Pink on emergence, later streaked yellowish and
pale green above, green beneath.
• NATIVE HABITAT Garden origin.
• CULTIVATION Tolerates exposure and almost
any soil. Smaller and slower-growing than the
species. An attractive specimen for open sites.
• PROPAGATION By grafting in late winter or early
spring or by budding in summer.

☼ ◊
❀ ❀ ❀

HEIGHT
12m (40ft)
or more

SPREAD
19m (30ft)

Aceraceae	VARIEGATED BOX ELDER

ACER NEGUNDO 'Variegatum'

Habit Fast-growing, broadly columnar.
Leaves Deciduous, with 3–5 lance-shaped to
oblong, toothed, pointed, sometimes lobed leaflets.
Bright green, irregularly margined creamy-white.
• NATIVE HABITAT Garden origin.
• CULTIVATION Grow in any fertile, moisture-
retentive but well-drained soil. Prune out any
branches with all-green leaves.
• PROPAGATION By grafting in late winter or early
spring or by budding in summer.
• OTHER NAMES *A. negundo* 'Argenteovariegatum'.

☼ ◊
❀ ❀ ❀

HEIGHT
14m (46ft)

SPREAD
7m (22ft)

Bignoniaceae	

JACARANDA MIMOSIFOLIA

Habit Vigorous, rounded. *Flowers* Narrowly bell-
shaped, in large panicles in spring and early
summer. Vivid blue-purple, white at throat. Seldom
flowers at less than 3m (10ft) tall. *Leaves*
Deciduous, fern-like, elliptic. Green.
• NATIVE HABITAT Dry forests, Argentina, Bolivia.
• CULTIVATION Grow under glass as a foliage pot
plant. Water freely in growth, otherwise sparingly.
• PROPAGATION By seed in spring or by semi-ripe
cuttings in summer.
• OTHER NAMES *J. acutifolia, J. ovalifolia*.

☼ ◊

Min. 7°C
(45°F)

HEIGHT
13m (43ft)

SPREAD
8m (25ft)

Rosaceae	

SORBUS THIBETICA 'John Mitchell'   ♔

Habit Vigorous, broadly conical, rounded with
age. *Flowers* Tiny, in small clusters in late spring.
Creamy-white. *Fruits* Small, round berries.
Orange-brown. *Leaves* Deciduous, large, rounded-
elliptic. Green above, densely silver-downy beneath.
• NATIVE HABITAT Garden origin.
• CULTIVATION Grow in fertile, moisture-
retentive soil.
• PROPAGATION By softwood cuttings or budding
in summer or by grafting in winter.
• OTHER NAMES *S.* 'Mitchellii'.

☼ ◊
❀ ❀ ❀

HEIGHT
13m (43ft)

SPREAD
7m (22ft)

Meliaceae	

TOONA SINENSIS

Habit Broadly columnar. **Flowers** Small, fragrant, in large, drooping panicles in mid-summer. White.
Leaves Deciduous, with 10–24 oblong to lance-shaped leaflets. Pinkish-bronze on emergence, later dark green, turning yellow in autumn.
Bark Shaggy, peeling in strips.
• NATIVE HABITAT Woodlands in China.
• CULTIVATION Grow in any fertile soil.
• PROPAGATION By seed in autumn or by root cuttings in winter.
• OTHER NAMES *Cedrela sinensis*.

HEIGHT
15m (50ft)

SPREAD
7m (22ft)

Rhamnaceae	JAPANESE RAISIN TREE

HOVENIA DULCIS

Habit Broadly conical, later spreading.
Flowers Small, in clusters. Greenish-yellow with red, fleshy, edible leaf-stalks in summer.
Leaves Deciduous, broadly oval, pointed at tip, heart-shaped at the base, coarsely toothed. Very glossy dark green.
• NATIVE HABITAT E. Asia; native range uncertain.
• CULTIVATION Grow in fertile soil, in a sheltered site. Young growth susceptible to frost damage.
• PROPAGATION By softwood cuttings in summer or by seed in autumn.

HEIGHT
13m (43ft)

SPREAD
10m (30ft)

Salicaceae	WEEPING ASPEN

POPULUS TREMULA 'Pendula'

Habit Vigorous, weeping. **Flowers** Catkins.
Male: long, pendent, purplish; female: greenish, on separate plants, in late winter to early spring.
Leaves Deciduous, rounded to broadly oval, with rounded teeth. Bronze on emergence, later dark grey-green; yellow in autumn. The long, flat, leaf-stalks cause 'trembling' in a breeze.
• NATIVE HABITAT Garden origin.
• CULTIVATION Grow in deep, fertile soil. Plant at least 30m (100ft) away from drains and buildings.
• PROPAGATION By hardwood cuttings in winter.

HEIGHT
15m (50ft)

SPREAD
7m (22ft)

Betulaceae	AMERICAN HORNBEAM, BLUE BEECH, WATER BEECH

CARPINUS CAROLINIANA

Habit Broadly spreading. **Flowers** Catkins. Male: pendent, yellowish; female: small, upright, on same plant in spring. **Fruits** Nuts, with 2–3 toothed bracts. Green. **Leaves** Deciduous, oval, taper-pointed, toothed. Blue-green, turning orange-red in autumn.
• NATIVE HABITAT Swamps and damp woods of E. North America and Mexico.
• CULTIVATION Tolerates semi-shade. Grow in any deep, fertile, moisture-retentive soil.
• PROPAGATION By seed in autumn.

HEIGHT
10m (30ft)
or more

SPREAD
8m (25ft)

Fagaceae	BLACK JACK OAK

QUERCUS MARILANDICA

Habit Broadly spreading. *Fruits* Acorns, to 2cm (¾in) long, half enclosed in hairy-scaly cup.
Leaves Deciduous, triangular, with 3 pointed lobes at the broad tip. Glossy dark green above, tawny beneath, turning yellow, red, and brown in autumn.
• NATIVE HABITAT Woods, often in poor, sandy soils, of E. United States.
• CULTIVATION Grow in deep, fertile soil. Unsuitable for chalky soils. Tolerates semi-shade.
• PROPAGATION By seed in autumn.

HEIGHT
12m (40ft)

SPREAD
10m (30ft)

Sabiaceae	

MELIOSMA VEITCHIORUM

Habit Rounded, with stout, upright branches.
Flowers Small, fragrant, in large panicles in late spring. White. *Fruits* Rounded, berry-like. Rich violet. *Leaves* Deciduous, with 7–9 oval to oblong leaflets. Dark green, with red leaf-stalks.
• NATIVE HABITAT W. and C. China.
• CULTIVATION Grow in deep, fertile, freely draining soil, in a warm, sheltered site. Flowers reliably only in areas with long, hot summers. Makes an attractive architectural specimen.
• PROPAGATION By seed in autumn.

HEIGHT
12m (40ft)

SPREAD
7m (22ft)

Araliaceae	CASTOR ARALIA

KALOPANAX PICTUS

Habit Broadly columnar. *Flowers* Tiny, in large, rounded clusters in late summer. White.
Fruits Small, round, berry-like. Blue-black.
Leaves Deciduous, with 5–7 toothed lobes. Glossy dark green. *Bark* Spiny, deeply fissured.
• NATIVE HABITAT Riversides and damp forests from China and E. Russia to Japan and Korea.
• CULTIVATION Grow in moist, well-drained soil.
• PROPAGATION By softwood cuttings in summer.
• OTHER NAMES *K. septemlobus.*

HEIGHT
12m (40ft)

SPREAD
8m (25ft)

Oleaceae	ARIZONA ASH

FRAXINUS VELUTINA

Habit Open, rounded, spreading.
Leaves Deciduous, with 3–5 paired, lance-shaped to elliptic leaflets. Dull green, usually clothed in velvety-grey down, turning yellow in autumn.
• NATIVE HABITAT In moist soils by riverbanks, in canyons, desert grasslands, and oak and pine forest of S.W. United States.
• CULTIVATION Tolerates dry and alkaline soils, but grows best in moisture-retentive but well-drained soil.
• PROPAGATION By seed in autumn.

HEIGHT
12m (40ft)

SPREAD
8m (25ft)

Leguminosae	

GLEDITSIA JAPONICA

Habit Pyramidal, very spiny. **Leaves** Deciduous, finely divided, fern-like, with tiny, oblong to lance-shaped leaflets. Bright green. **Bark** Shoots are purplish when young.
• NATIVE HABITAT Woodlands of Japan.
• CULTIVATION Grow in any fertile, well-drained soil in a warm, sunny site. A delicate and graceful tree, suitable for specimen plantings.
• PROPAGATION By seed in autumn.

☼ ◊
❀ ❀ ❀

HEIGHT
15m (50ft)

SPREAD
15m (50ft)

Fagaceae	OREGON WHITE OAK

QUERCUS GARRYANA

Habit Slow-growing, dense, rounded, spreading. **Fruits** Edible acorns, to 3cm (1¼in) long, up to one-third enclosed in a thin, shallow cup. **Leaves** Deciduous, elliptic, rounded at both ends, with deep, rounded lobes. Glossy bright green.
• NATIVE HABITAT Deciduous woodlands, in valleys and on mountains of W. North America.
• CULTIVATION Tolerates semi-shade. Grow in any deep, fertile, well-drained soil.
• PROPAGATION By seed in autumn.

☼ ◊
❀ ❀ ❀

HEIGHT
15m (50ft)

SPREAD
10m (30ft)

Fagaceae	BURR OAK, MOSSY-CUP OAK

QUERCUS MACROCARPA

Habit Slow-growing, broadly spreading. **Fruits** Acorns, to 5cm (2in) long, half or more enclosed in a cup fringed with long scales. **Leaves** Deciduous, oblong-oval, lobed. Glossy dark green, but paler, sometimes white-downy, beneath. Turns pale yellow and brown in autumn.
• NATIVE HABITAT Rich woodlands of E. North America.
• CULTIVATION Unsuitable for chalky soils. Tolerates semi-shade. Grow in deep, fertile soil.
• PROPAGATION By seed in autumn.

☼ ◊
❀ ❀ ❀

HEIGHT
15m (50ft)

SPREAD
10m (30ft)

Rubiaceae	

EMMENOPTERYS HENRYI

Habit Open, spreading. **Flowers** Small, with conspicuous white bracts, in large, pyramidal clusters in summer. White. **Leaves** Deciduous, elliptic-oval, pointed. Bronze-purple when young, lustrous dark green above, paler beneath.
• NATIVE HABITAT C. and W. China, Burma, and Thailand.
• CULTIVATION Tolerates chalk. Grow in a warm, sunny, sheltered site, in deep, fertile, moisture-retentive soil. Flowers best in long, hot summers.
• PROPAGATION By softwood cuttings in summer.

☼ ◊
❀ ❀

HEIGHT
15m (50ft)

SPREAD
12m (40ft)

Fagaceae	

QUERCUS MACROLEPIS

Habit Spreading, with a rounded crown.
Fruits Acorns, to 4.5cm (1¾in) long, two-thirds enclosed in a cup with woody scales. Ripens in second year. *Leaves* Deciduous or semi-evergreen, oblong, with sharp, bristly lobes. Olive grey-green.
• NATIVE HABITAT Dry foothills and mountain woods in the Balkans.
• CULTIVATION Tolerates semi-shade. Grow in any deep, fertile, well-drained soil.
• PROPAGATION By seed in autumn.
• OTHER NAMES *Q. ithaburensis* subsp. *macrolepis.*

HEIGHT
13m (43ft)

SPREAD
13m (43ft)
or more

Tiliaceae	

TILIA CORDATA 'Rancho'

Habit Dense, conical, spreading when young.
Flowers Fragrant, small, cup-shaped, in clusters in mid-summer. *Leaves* Deciduous, small, oval, taper-pointed, heart-shaped at the base. Glossy dark green.
• NATIVE HABITAT Garden origin.
• CULTIVATION Tolerates semi-shade. Grow in deep, fertile soil. May be infested by aphids which drip sticky honeydew onto the ground beneath.
• PROPAGATION By grafting in late summer.

HEIGHT
13m (43ft)

SPREAD
6m (20ft)

Flacourtiaceae	

IDESIA POLYCARPA

Habit Broadly spreading. *Flowers* Fragrant, small, in drooping clusters in mid-summer. Yellow-green. *Fruits* Small berries, in pendent clusters. Red. *Leaves* Deciduous, heart-shaped. Bronze-purple when young, turning glossy dark green, with red veins and leaf-stalks.
• NATIVE HABITAT Mountains of China and Japan.
• CULTIVATION Prefers a fertile, neutral to acid soil or deep soil over chalk. Grow in a sunny site.
• PROPAGATION By softwood cuttings in summer or by seed in autumn.

HEIGHT
13m (43ft)

SPREAD
11m (33ft)

Fagaceae	

QUERCUS RUBRA 'Aurea'

Habit Slow-growing, broadly columnar to spreading. *Fruits* Acorns, to 3cm (1¼in) long, one-quarter enclosed in a shallow cup.
Leaves Deciduous, long, elliptic-oval, sharply lobed, with slender teeth. Clear yellow when young, later mid-green, turning red in autumn.
• NATIVE HABITAT Garden origin.
• CULTIVATION Tolerant of urban pollution and almost any well-drained soils, including chalky ones. Tolerates semi-shade, but colours best in sun.
• PROPAGATION By grafting in late winter.

HEIGHT
15m (50ft)

SPREAD
10m (30ft)

Betulaceae	

ALNUS GLUTINOSA 'Imperialis'

Habit Open, with a conical crown.
Flowers Catkins. Male: drooping, reddish; female: small, upright, on same plant, red, on bare branches in early spring. *Fruits* Small, woody, cone-like. Dark brown. *Leaves* Deciduous, delicately cut into pointed lobes. Smooth above, with tufts of hairs in the vein axils beneath. Dark green. *Bark* Fissured. Dark grey.
• NATIVE HABITAT Species occurs by rivers in N. Africa, W. Asia, and N. Europe.
• CULTIVATION Tolerates wet or even waterlogged soil. *Alnus glutinosa* 'Imperialis' makes an elegant and graceful specimen for waterside plantings. It is especially attractive in winter, when the woody 'cones' are clearly visible. It is one of the most lime-tolerant of alders.
• PROPAGATION By budding in late summer or by hardwood cuttings in early winter.

HEIGHT
12m (40ft)

SPREAD
5m (15ft)

Rutaceae	

PHELLODENDRON CHINENSE

Habit Spreading, with a rounded crown.
Flowers Small, in pendent racemes in early summer. Greenish. **Fruits** Berry-like, in dense clusters, on female trees. Black. **Leaves** Aromatic, deciduous, divided into 7–13 oblong leaflets. Dark green, turning yellow in autumn.
• **NATIVE HABITAT** Mountains of C. China.
• **CULTIVATION** Grow in a sunny, sheltered site in any fertile, well-drained soil.
• **PROPAGATION** By softwood cuttings in summer, by seed in autumn, or by root cuttings in winter.

HEIGHT
10m (30ft)

SPREAD
10m (30ft)

Leguminosae	

ROBINIA PSEUDOACACIA 'Frisia'

Habit Broadly columnar. **Flowers** Fragrant, small, pea-like, in pendent clusters from early to mid-summer. White. **Fruits** Smooth pod. Brown.
Leaves Deciduous, with 11–23 oval leaflets. Golden-yellow on emergence, later yellow-green, turning clear orange-yellow in autumn.
• **NATIVE HABITAT** Garden origin.
• **CULTIVATION** Grow in any but waterlogged soil. Branches may suffer damage in strong winds.
• **PROPAGATION** By suckers in autumn or by root cuttings in winter.

HEIGHT
15m (50ft)

SPREAD
8m (25ft)

Ulmaceae	DICKSON'S GOLDEN ELM

ULMUS CARPINIFOLIA 'Dicksonii'

Habit Slow-growing, dense, conical.
Leaves Deciduous, small, broadly oval. Bright golden-yellow.
• **NATIVE HABITAT** Garden origin.
• **CULTIVATION** Grow in fertile, well-drained soil. Susceptible to (usually fatal) Dutch elm disease, but affected trees may re-sprout from the base.
• **PROPAGATION** By softwood cuttings in summer or by suckers in autumn.
• **OTHER NAMES** *U. carpinifolia* 'Sarniensis Aurea', *U.* 'Dicksonii', *U.* 'Wheatleyi Aurea'.

HEIGHT
12m (40ft)

SPREAD
7m (22ft)

Bignoniaceae	

CATALPA BIGNONIOIDES 'Aurea'

Habit Broadly spreading. **Flowers** Trumpet-shaped, 2-lipped, in large, upright panicles in mid- to late summer. White, yellow- and purple-spotted.
Fruits Long, narrow, pendent pods.
Leaves Deciduous, heart-shaped, pointed at the tip. Bright yellow, bronzed when young.
• **NATIVE HABITAT** Garden origin.
• **CULTIVATION** Grow in deep, fertile, well-drained soil. Provide shelter from strong winds.
• **PROPAGATION** By softwood cuttings in summer or by budding in late summer.

HEIGHT
15m (50ft)

SPREAD
12m (40ft)

Eucryphiaceae	

EUCRYPHIA × *NYMANSENSIS*
Habit Upright, columnar. ***Flowers*** Large,
fragrant, in clusters in late summer-early autumn.
Glistening white, with yellow, pink-tipped stamens.
Leaves Evergreen, elliptic, toothed, sometimes
with 3 leaflets. Glossy dark green.
• NATIVE HABITAT Garden origin.
• CULTIVATION Tolerates semi-shade and some
lime. Grow in fertile, moist, well-drained soil, with
shade at the roots. Shelter from cold, dry winds.
Does best in mild, damp climates.
• PROPAGATION By semi-ripe cuttings in summer.

HEIGHT
15m (50ft)

SPREAD
7m (22ft)

Aceraceae	

ACER DAVIDII 'Madeline Spitta'
Habit Upright, columnar. ***Fruits*** 2 seeds, fused
together, each with a wing, in long, pendent
clusters. Orange-brown in autumn.
Leaves Deciduous, oval, pointed, toothed. Glossy
dark green, turning orange in autumn. ***Bark***
Striped vertically. Grey-green and white.
• NATIVE HABITAT Garden origin.
• CULTIVATION Grow in moisture-retentive soil,
preferably with shelter from cold winds.
• PROPAGATION By grafting in late winter or early
spring or by budding in summer.

HEIGHT
14m (46ft)

SPREAD
7m (22ft)

Myrtaceae	BRUSH CHERRY

SYZYGIUM PANICULATUM
Habit Broadly conical, shrubby. ***Flowers*** Creamy-
white, with reddish sepals, and a brush of long
white anthers. ***Fruits*** Globose, fleshy. Shades of
purple, red, pink, and white. ***Leaves*** Evergreen,
lance-shaped. Coppery, turning glossy dark green.
• NATIVE HABITAT Australia.
• CULTIVATION Grow in fertile soil or compost.
Water freely when in growth, otherwise moderately.
• PROPAGATION By seed in spring or by semi-ripe
cuttings in summer.
• OTHER NAMES *Eugenia australis, E. paniculata.*

Min. 7°C
(45°F)

HEIGHT
13m (43ft)

SPREAD
8m (25ft)

Rosaceae	

SORBUS HUPEHENSIS var. *OBTUSA* ♀

Habit Open, spreading. *Flowers* Small, in open, rounded clusters in late spring. White.
Fruits Small, round, persistent berries. Pink.
Leaves Deciduous, up to 17 paired, sharply toothed, pointed leaflets. Blue-green; scarlet in autumn.
• NATIVE HABITAT Garden origin.
• CULTIVATION Tolerates dappled shade. Grow in any fertile, moisture-retentive soil.
• PROPAGATION By softwood cuttings or budding in summer or by grafting in winter.
• OTHER NAMES *S. hupehensis* 'Rosea'.

☼ ◊
✳ ✳ ✳

HEIGHT
12m (40ft)

SPREAD
8m (25ft)

Rosaceae	

SORBUS COMMIXTA

Habit Delicate, open, broadly conical.
Flowers Small, in broad clusters in late spring. White. *Fruits* Small, round, in long-persistent clusters. Bright orange-red. *Leaves* Deciduous, up to 15 paired, elliptic- to lance-shaped, taper-pointed leaflets. Deep green; orange and red in autumn.
• NATIVE HABITAT Mountain forest, Japan, Korea.
• CULTIVATION Tolerates dappled shade. Grow in any fertile, moisture-retentive soil.
• PROPAGATION By seed in autumn.
• OTHER NAMES *S. discolor* of gardens.

☼ ◊
✳ ✳ ✳

HEIGHT
10m (30ft)

SPREAD
7m (22ft)

Aceraceae	

ACER RUBRUM 'Columnare'

Habit Erect, columnar, slender. *Flowers* Small, in dense clusters, on bare branches in spring. Red. *Fruits* 2 seeds, fused together, each with a wing. Red. *Leaves* Deciduous, 3–5 lobes. Dark green, turning brilliant red and yellow in autumn.
• NATIVE HABITAT Garden origin.
• CULTIVATION Tolerates some lime, but grow in fertile, moisture retentive, neutral to acid soil for best autumn colour. Suitable for confined spaces.
• PROPAGATION By grafting in late winter or early spring or by budding in summer.

☼ ◊
✳ ✳ ✳

HEIGHT
15m (50ft)

SPREAD
6m (20ft)

Rosaceae	MOUNTAIN ASH, ROWAN

SORBUS AUCUPARIA

Habit Broadly conical. **Flowers** Small, creamy-white, in large clusters in late spring.
Fruits Round berries in dense clusters. Orange-red. **Leaves** Deciduous, with up to 15 paired, toothed, lance-shaped leaflets. Dark green above, blue-green beneath, turning red in autumn.
• NATIVE HABITAT Woods, heaths, and moorland throughout Europe and Asia.
• CULTIVATION Tolerates dappled shade. Grow in any fertile, moisture-retentive soil.
• PROPAGATION By seed in autumn.

HEIGHT
To 15m
(50ft)

SPREAD
7m (22ft)

Rosaceae	

MALUS TSCHONOSKII   ♀

Habit Broadly conical, dense, with upswept branches. **Flowers** 5-petalled, in small clusters in late spring. White flushed pink, with yellow anthers. **Fruits** Small, rounded crab apples. Yellow-green, flushed red. **Leaves** Deciduous, broadly oval, sharply and irregularly toothed, pointed. Glossy mid-green, turning golden-bronze to red and purple in autumn.
• NATIVE HABITAT Woodlands of Japan.
• CULTIVATION Grow in any but waterlogged soil.
• PROPAGATION By seed in autumn.

HEIGHT
12m (40ft)
or more

SPREAD
7m (22ft)

Aceraceae	

ACER RUFINERVE   ♀

Habit Broadly columnar. **Flowers** Small, in upright clusters in spring. Yellow-green.
Fruits 2 seeds, fused together, each with a red wing. **Leaves** Deciduous, with 3 coarsely toothed lobes. Dark green; red in autumn. **Bark** Striped white and pale green, with diamond-shaped markings.
• NATIVE HABITAT Mountain woods of Japan.
• CULTIVATION Tolerates lime, but grow in moisture-retentive, neutral to acid soil for best autumn colour. Excellent for confined spaces.
• PROPAGATION By seed in autumn.

HEIGHT
10m (30ft)

SPREAD
7m (22ft)

Theaceae	

STEWARTIA MONADELPHA

Habit Broadly columnar. **Flowers** Shallowly cup-shaped, opening from silky buds in summer. Glistening white, with golden stamens.
Leaves Deciduous, elliptic, toothed. Dark green, turning deep red-purple in autumn. **Bark** Peeling. Red-brown, grey-fawn beneath.
• NATIVE HABITAT Woods in Japan and Korea.
• CULTIVATION Grow in humus-rich soil. Shelter from cold winds. Prefers shade at the roots.
• PROPAGATION By softwood cuttings in summer or by seed in autumn.

HEIGHT
12m (40ft)

SPREAD
8m (25ft)

Aceraceae	

ACER SACCHARUM 'Temple's Upright'

Habit Upright, narrowly conical.
Leaves Deciduous, 5 lobes, heart-shaped at the base. Dark green; brilliant orange and red in autumn.
• NATIVE HABITAT Garden origin.
• CULTIVATION Tolerates lime, but grow in fertile, moisture-retentive, neutral to acid soil for best autumn colour. Excellent for planting in confined spaces.
• PROPAGATION By grafting in late winter or early spring or by budding in summer.
• OTHER NAMES *A saccharum* 'Monumentale'.

☼ ◊
❀ ❀ ❀

HEIGHT
15m (50ft)

SPREAD
3m (10ft)

Aceraceae	

ACER CISSIFOLIUM subsp. HENRYI

Habit Broadly spreading. **Flowers** Tiny, in long, slender racemes. Yellow. **Fruits** 2 seeds, fused together, each with a red wing. **Leaves** Deciduous, divided into 3 elliptic, taper-pointed leaflets. Dark green, turning bright orange and red in autumn.
• NATIVE HABITAT Mountain woods of C. China.
• CULTIVATION Tolerates lime, but grow in moisture-retentive, neutral to acid soil for best autumn colour.
• PROPAGATION By seed in autumn.
• OTHER NAMES *A. henryi.*

☼ ◊
❀ ❀ ❀

HEIGHT
8m (25ft)

SPREAD
10m (30ft)

Hippocastanaceae	SWEET BUCKEYE, YELLOW BUCKEYE

AESCULUS FLAVA ♈

Habit Broadly conical. **Flowers** Appear in conical, upright panicles in late spring to early summer. Yellow, blotched pink. **Fruits** Smooth, rounded husks enclosing usually 2 small, shiny chestnuts. **Leaves** Deciduous, with 5 oval, sharply toothed, short-stalked leaflets. Dark green; red in autumn.
• NATIVE HABITAT Damp woods, E. United States.
• CULTIVATION Tolerates dappled shade. Grow in fertile, moisture-retentive but well-drained soil.
• PROPAGATION By seed in autumn.
• OTHER NAMES *A. octandra.*

☼ ◊
❀ ❀ ❀

HEIGHT
15m (50ft)

SPREAD
10m (30ft)

Hamamelidaceae	PERSIAN IRONWOOD

PARROTIA PERSICA ♈

Habit Short-trunked, broadly spreading.
Flowers Tiny, apetalous, on bare branches in spring. Crimson anthers. **Leaves** Deciduous, elliptic to oval, wavy-margined. Green, turning yellow, orange, and crimson in autumn.
Bark Flaking. Grey-fawn.
• NATIVE HABITAT Forests of Caucasus, Iran.
• CULTIVATION Grow in deep, fertile soil. Autumn colour is best on neutral to acid soils.
• PROPAGATION By softwood cuttings in summer or by seed in autumn.

☼ ◊
❀ ❀ ❀

HEIGHT
8m (25ft)

SPREAD
12m (40ft)

Nyssaceae	CHINESE TUPELO

NYSSA SINENSIS ♈

Habit Broadly conical. **Leaves** Deciduous, oblong-lance-shaped to elliptic. Dark green, flushed red when young, turning yellow, orange, and rich scarlet in autumn.
• NATIVE HABITAT Stream sides and mountain woodland in C. China.
• CULTIVATION Tolerates semi-shade. Grow in fertile, neutral to acid soil. Resents transplanting and performs best in areas with long, hot summers.
• PROPAGATION By softwood cuttings in summer or by seed in autumn.

☼ ◑
❋ ❋ ❋

HEIGHT
10 (30ft)

SPREAD
10m (30ft)

Aceraceae	SNAKE-BARK MAPLE

ACER CAPILLIPES ♈

Habit Broadly conical, with ascending branches. **Leaves** Deciduous, with 3 slender-pointed, toothed lobes. Bright green, turning yellow, orange, and crimson in autumn. **Bark** Green and grey, with vertical white stripes.
• NATIVE HABITAT Mountain stream banks and woods in Japan.
• CULTIVATION Tolerates dappled shade but colours best in sun. Grow in fertile, humus-rich, well-drained soil.
• PROPAGATION By seed in autumn.

☼ ◑
❋ ❋ ❋

HEIGHT
11m (33ft)

SPREAD
8m (25ft)

Rosaceae	

CRATAEGUS × LAVALLEI 'Carrierei' ♈

Habit Vigorous, broadly spreading. **Flowers** 5-petalled, to 2.5cm (1in) across, in flattened clusters in late spring-early summer. White. **Fruits** Rounded haws, to 2cm (¾in) across. Red. **Leaves** Deciduous, elliptic, tapered at base, leathery. Glossy dark green; red in late autumn.
• NATIVE HABITAT Garden origin.
• CULTIVATION Tolerant of urban pollution, coastal exposure, and any but waterlogged soil.
• PROPAGATION By budding in late summer.
• OTHER NAMES *C. carrierei.*

☼ ◊
❋ ❋ ❋

HEIGHT
10m (30ft)

SPREAD
10m (30ft)

Fagaceae	BARTRAM'S OAK

QUERCUS X HETEROPHYLLA

Habit Spreading, with a broadly domed crown.
Fruits Acorns to 3cm (1¼in) long, one-quarter
enclosed in a shallow cup. **Leaves** Deciduous,
variable, oblong to lance-shaped or broadly oval and
deeply lobed. Glossy bright green, turning scarlet
and yellow in autumn.
• NATIVE HABITAT Damp woodlands in
E. United States.
• CULTIVATION Unsuitable for chalk soils. Grow
in deep, fertile, moisture-retentive soil.
• PROPAGATION By grafting in late winter.

☼ ◊
❀❀❀

HEIGHT
15m (50ft)

SPREAD
12m (40ft)

Leguminosae	YELLOWWOOD

CLADRASTIS LUTEA 🏆

Habit Broadly spreading, round-headed.
Flowers Fragrant, small, pea-like, in hanging
clusters in early summer. White, marked yellow.
Leaves Deciduous, with 7–9 rounded-oval leaflets.
Dark green, turning clear yellow in autumn.
• NATIVE HABITAT Woods and rocky bluffs in
S.E. United States.
• CULTIVATION Grow in any fertile soil. Older
specimens are prone to damage by strong winds.
• PROPAGATION By seed in autumn or by root
cuttings in late winter.

☼ ◊
❀❀❀

HEIGHT
12m (40ft)

SPREAD
10m (30ft)

Rosaceae	

SORBUS 'Joseph Rock' 🏆

Habit Upright, broadly columnar. **Flowers** Small,
in flattened heads in late spring and early summer.
White. **Fruits** Small, round. Creamy-yellow,
becoming orange-yellow. **Leaves** Deciduous, with
15–19 narrowly oblong, toothed leaflets. Bright
green, turning orange, red, and purple in autumn.
• NATIVE HABITAT Uncertain, probably China.
• CULTIVATION Grow in fertile, moisture-
retentive soil. Is very susceptible to fireblight.
• PROPAGATION By softwood cuttings or budding
in summer or by grafting in winter.

☼ ◊
❀❀❀

HEIGHT
10m (30ft)

SPREAD
7m (22ft)

Moraceae	BLACK MULBERRY

MORUS NIGRA 🏆

Habit Broadly spreading, with a rounded crown.
Flowers Tiny. Male and female on separate
plants. **Fruits** Small, oval, fleshy, edible clusters.
Dark red to black. **Leaves** Deciduous, heart-
shaped, toothed. Glossy dark green, turning yellow
in autumn.
• NATIVE HABITAT Long cultivated, hence origin
obscure.
• CULTIVATION Grow in any fertile soil, in a
warm, sunny, sheltered site, for good cropping.
• PROPAGATION By seed in autumn.

☼ ◊
❀❀❀

HEIGHT
12m (40ft)

SPREAD
15m (50ft)

Betulaceae	WEST HIMALAYAN BIRCH

BETULA UTILIS var. *JACQUEMONTII*

Habit Open, broadly conical. *Flowers* Catkins. Male: to 15cm (6in) long; female: shorter, upright, inconspicuous, on same plant. *Leaves* Deciduous, oval, with tapering point, toothed. Dark green, turning rich golden-yellow in autumn.
Bark Smooth, peeling. Shining white, with pale brown markings.
• NATIVE HABITAT High mountain forests of the Himalaya.
• CULTIVATION Grow in any moist but well-drained soil, in an open, sunny position. It makes a beautiful tree for specimen plantings and is especially effective in group plantings against a dark backdrop, where the brilliant white bark may be seen to best advantage.
• PROPAGATION By softwood cuttings in early summer or by seed in autumn. Birches hybridize readily. Seed may not come true.

HEIGHT
15m (50ft)

SPREAD
7.5m (23ft)

Magnoliaceae	

MICHELIA DOLTSOPA

Habit Broadly spreading. **Flowers** Fragrant, magnolia-like, in late winter-early spring. Many white to pale yellow petals. **Leaves** Evergreen or semi-evergreen, oval. Glossy dark green.
• NATIVE HABITAT Forests of E. Himalaya.
• CULTIVATION Tolerates partial shade. Grow in humus-rich soil. Suitable for mild, sheltered sites or cool conservatories. Water freely when in full growth, less in winter.
• PROPAGATION By semi-ripe cuttings in summer or by seed in autumn or spring.

☼ ◊ pH
❄

HEIGHT
12m (40ft)

SPREAD
12m (40ft)

Leguminosae	MIMOSA, SILVER WATTLE

ACACIA DEALBATA ♀

Habit Fast-growing, broadly conical.
Flowers Fragrant, tiny, in globular clusters, carried in dense panicles in late winter to early spring. Yellow. **Leaves** Evergreen, feathery, with many tiny leaflets. Blue-green.
• NATIVE HABITAT Mountain gullies and stream sides in S.E. Australia and Tasmania.
• CULTIVATION Grow in any well-drained soil in a warm, sunny, sheltered site.
• PROPAGATION By seed in spring.

☼ ◊
❄ ❄

HEIGHT
13m (43ft)

SPREAD
8m (25ft)

Myrtaceae	CHRISTMAS TREE, POHUTUKAWA

METROSIDEROS EXCELSA

Habit Robust, rounded, wide-spreading, often multi-stemmed. **Flowers** Carried in broad clusters in winter. Small petals with many long, showy, crimson stamens. **Leaves** Evergreen, elliptic to oblong, leathery. Grey-green above, densely white-downy beneath.
• NATIVE HABITAT Warm to temperate coastal forests in New Zealand.
• CULTIVATION Grow in fertile, free-draining soil or compost. Water freely when in growth, less in low temperatures. The tree may be pruned after flowering, if necessary. It makes a handsome specimen when grown in large containers in the conservatory and may bear flowers, even on quite young plants.
• PROPAGATION By semi-ripe cuttings in summer or by seed in spring.
• OTHER NAMES *M. tomentosa.*

☼ ◊

Min. 3°C
(37°F)

HEIGHT
13m (43ft)

SPREAD
13m (43ft)

Ericaceae	

ARBUTUS × *ANDRACHNOIDES*

Habit Dense, bushy when young, later broadly spreading. **Flowers** Small, urn-shaped, in pendent clusters at the branch tips, from autumn to spring. White. **Fruits** Small, strawberry-like, ripening with the previous year's flowers. Red.
Leaves Evergreen, oval to elliptic, toothed. Glossy dark green, paler beneath. **Bark** Peeling in strips. Red-brown.
• NATIVE HABITAT Thickets and woodland of Greece.
• CULTIVATION Tolerates chalky soil, but prefers a deep, fertile, humus-rich soil. Provide shelter from cold, dry winds, especially when young. A fine specimen for open areas in the woodland garden, *A.* × *andrachnoides* is a naturally occurring hybrid between *A. andrachne* and *A. unedo*.
• PROPAGATION By semi-ripe cuttings in late summer.

☼ ◌
❆ ❆

HEIGHT
9m (28ft)

SPREAD
8m (25ft)

Moraceae	

FICUS BENJAMINA 'Variegata'

Habit Dense, round-headed, weeping, often with aerial roots. *Leaves* Evergreen, slender, oval, pointed. Lustrous, rich green, with white variegation.
• NATIVE HABITAT Garden origin.
• CULTIVATION Grow in fertile, free-draining soil or compost. Water freely when in full growth, sparingly when temperatures are low. An elegant specimen for the home or the conservatory.
• PROPAGATION By leaf bud or stem-tip cuttings or by air-layering in summer.

☀ ◊
Min.
15–18°C
(59–64°F)
HEIGHT
13m (43ft)
SPREAD
10m (30ft)

Myrtaceae	GHOST GUM, WHITE SALLY

EUCALYPTUS PAUCIFLORA

Habit Open, broadly spreading. *Flowers* Small, in small clusters in the leaf axils in summer. White. *Leaves* Evergreen. Juvenile: oval to rounded. Grey. Adult: lance-shaped. Glossy grey to deep green. *Bark* Peeling. White and grey; young shoots red to cream.
• NATIVE HABITAT From sea level to mountains of S.E. Australia and Tasmania.
• CULTIVATION Grow in fertile, well-drained soil.
• PROPAGATION By seed in spring or autumn in a cold frame or greenhouse.

☀ ◊
❄❄
HEIGHT
12m (40ft)
SPREAD
7m (22ft)

Myrtaceae	SNOW GUM

EUCALYPTUS PAUCIFLORA subsp. ♀
NIPHOPHILA

Habit Open, spreading. *Flowers* Small, in clusters in leaf axils in summer. White. *Leaves* Evergreen. Juvenile: oval to rounded, dull blue-green. Adult: broadly lance-shaped, glossy green to deep blue-green. *Bark* Peeling. White and grey.
• NATIVE HABITAT Mountains of S.E. Australia and Tasmania.
• CULTIVATION Grow in well-drained soil.
• PROPAGATION By seed in spring or autumn.
• OTHER NAMES *E. niphophila*.

☀ ◊
❄❄
HEIGHT
12m (40ft)
SPREAD
6m (20ft)

Palmae	CHUSAN PALM, CHINESE WINDMILL PALM

TRACHYCARPUS FORTUNEI ♀

Habit Upright, with unbranched trunk. *Flowers* Tiny, fragrant, in large, drooping clusters in early summer; male and female in separate clusters. Yellow. *Fruits* Small, kidney-shaped, 3-lobed berries. Blue-black. *Leaves* Evergreen, fan-shaped, to 120cm (4ft) across. Dark green above, blue-green beneath.
• NATIVE HABITAT Mountains of C. and S. China.
• CULTIVATION Grow in any fertile, well-drained soil. Provide shelter from cold, dry winds.
• PROPAGATION By seed in spring.

☀ ◊
❄❄
HEIGHT
10m (30ft)
SPREAD
2.5m (8ft)

| Rosaceae | AMUR CHERRY, MANCHURIAN CHERRY |

PRUNUS MAACKII

Habit Vigorous, broadly conical.
Flowers Small, fragrant, with prominent stamens, in dense clusters at the tips of old shoots, as the leaves emerge in mid-spring. White. **Fruits** Tiny, rounded, berry-like. Black when ripe.
Leaves Deciduous, oval, long-pointed at the tip, finely toothed. Dark green, turning yellow in autumn. **Bark** Peeling. Shining, golden orange-brown.
• NATIVE HABITAT Woodlands of N.E. Asia.
• CULTIVATION Grow in any but waterlogged soil.

A beautiful species for specimen plantings, especially in small gardens. It has a long season of interest and its attractive bark is seen to best advantage in winter. The shining bark is sometimes obscured by algal growth; remove with clean water and a soft brush in summer.
• PROPAGATION By seed in autumn.

HEIGHT
10m (30ft)

SPREAD
8m (25ft)

Fagaceae	

QUERCUS MYRSINIFOLIA

Habit Open-branched, broadly spreading. **Fruits** Acorns, to 2cm (¾in) long, rounded, pointed at the tip, one-third enclosed in a ridged cup. **Leaves** Evergreen, lance-shaped, short-pointed. Glossy dark green above, blue-green beneath; bronze-red when young,
• NATIVE HABITAT Forests of China and Japan.
• CULTIVATION Unsuitable for chalky soils. Grow in deep, fertile soils, with shelter from winds.
• PROPAGATION By seed in autumn.
• OTHER NAMES *Q. vibrayeana.*

☀ ◊
❀ ❀

HEIGHT
13m (43ft)

SPREAD
7.5m (23ft)

Araliaceae	AUSTRALIAN IVY-PALM, AUSTRALIAN UMBRELLA TREE

SCHEFFLERA ACTINOPHYLLA ♚

Habit Upright, with a broadly spreading crown. **Flowers** Small, in large sprays in summer or autumn. Dull red. **Leaves** Evergreen, oblong, in rosettes at branch tips. Glossy bright green.
• NATIVE HABITAT N. Australia and New Guinea.
• CULTIVATION Grow in fertile, moisture-retentive soil or compost. Water freely in growth. An elegant specimen for the home or conservatory.
• PROPAGATION By seed or air-layering in spring or by semi-ripe cuttings in summer.
• OTHER NAMES *Brassaia actinophylla.*

☀ ◊

Min.
10–13°C
(50–55°F)

HEIGHT
12m (40ft)

SPREAD
9m (28ft)

Aceraceae	MOOSEWOOD

ACER PENSYLVANICUM ♚

Habit Broadly columnar. **Leaves** Deciduous, with 3 triangular, taper-pointed, toothed lobes. Dark olive green, turning clear yellow in autumn. **Bark** Boldly striped in rich jade green and white.
• NATIVE HABITAT Damp woodlands of E. North America.
• CULTIVATION Does not thrive on chalky soils. Tolerates dappled shade, but colours best in sun. Grow in deep, fertile, humus-rich soil.
• PROPAGATION By seed in autumn.
• OTHER NAMES *A. striatum.*

☀ ◊
❀ ❀ ❀

HEIGHT
To 12m
(40ft)

SPREAD
8m (25ft)

Palmae	CHILEAN WINE PALM, COQUITO PALM

JUBAEA CHILENSIS

Habit Slow-growing, with an unbranched trunk. **Flowers** Small, in large clusters between the leaves in spring. Maroon and yellow. **Fruits** Egg-shaped, in woody, yellow capsules. **Leaves** Evergreen, large, feather-shaped. Silvery-green.
• NATIVE HABITAT Coastal valleys of Chile.
• CULTIVATION Grow in fertile soil or compost. Water moderately in growth, otherwise sparingly. An elegant specimen for the home or conservatory.
• PROPAGATION By seed in spring.
• OTHER NAMES *J. spectabilis.*

☀ ◊

Min. 7°C
(45°F)

HEIGHT
12m (40ft)

SPREAD
5m (15ft)

Palmae	CHINESE FAN PALM

LIVISTONA CHINENSIS ♈

Habit Slow-growing, with a stout, unbranched trunk. *Leaves* Evergreen, fan-shaped, 1–3m (3–10ft) across. Dull yellow-green.
• NATIVE HABITAT Damp soils of S. Japan and S. Taiwan.
• CULTIVATION Tolerates partial shade. Grow in fertile, neutral to acid soil or compost. Water moderately when in growth, less in winter. Suitable for pots or tubs in the home or the conservatory.
• PROPAGATION By seed in spring.
• OTHER NAMES *L. oliviformis.*

☼ ◊

Min. 7°C
(45°F)

HEIGHT
12m (40ft)

SPREAD
5m (15ft)

Corynocarpaceae	

CORYNOCARPUS LAEVIGATA

Habit Upright, conical. *Flowers* Small, in panicles in spring to summer. Greenish-white. *Fruits* Plum-like. Orange. *Leaves* Evergreen, elliptic-oblong, leathery. Glossy dark green.
• NATIVE HABITAT New Zealand.
• CULTIVATION Tolerates partial shade. Grow in fertile, moisture-retentive but free-draining soil or compost. Water moderately when in full growth, less in winter. Prune after flowering if necessary.
• PROPAGATION By seed when ripe or by semi-ripe cuttings in summer.

☼ ◊

Min.
7–10°C
(45–50°F)

HEIGHT
14m (46ft)

SPREAD
8m (25ft)

Salicaceae	DRAGON'S CLAW WILLOW

SALIX BABYLONICA var. *PEKINENSIS* ♈ 'Tortuosa'

Habit Fast-growing, spreading, with ascending, twisted shoots. *Leaves* Deciduous, lance-shaped, very contorted. Bright green.
• NATIVE HABITAT Origin uncertain.
• CULTIVATION Grows in any but very dry soil, but does best in fertile, moisture-retentive soil. Plant well away from drains, as roots may invade.
• PROPAGATION By semi-ripe cuttings in summer or by hardwood cuttings in winter.
• OTHER NAMES *S. matsudana* 'Tortuosa'.

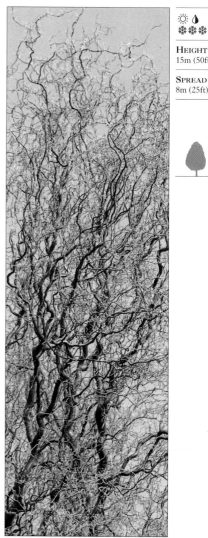

☼ ◊
❀ ❀ ❀

HEIGHT
15m (50ft)

SPREAD
8m (25ft)

Rosaceae	MEDLAR

MESPILUS GERMANICA

Habit Broadly spreading, sometimes shrubby.
Flowers Large, 5-petalled, on short stalks, in late spring to early summer. White. **Fruits** Flattened pear-shape, fleshy, edible when over-ripe. Brown-green. **Leaves** Deciduous, elliptic to oblong. Dark green, turning russet-brown in autumn.
• NATIVE HABITAT Forests, mountain thickets, and woodland edge, in S.W. Asia and S. Europe.
• CULTIVATION Tolerates semi-shade and almost any fertile, free-draining soil.
• PROPAGATION By seed in autumn.

☀ ◊
❀ ❀ ❀

HEIGHT
7.5m (23ft)

SPREAD
8m (25ft)

Rosaceae	

CRATAEGUS LACINIATA

Habit Broadly spreading. **Flowers** Cup-shaped, in dense clusters in early summer. White.
Fruits Rounded-oblong. Red, flushed yellow in autumn. **Leaves** Deciduous, diamond-shaped, deeply lobed. Glossy dark green above, grey-downy beneath. **Bark** Flaking. Grey.
• NATIVE HABITAT Thickets and woodland edge in S.E. Europe and S.W. Asia.
• CULTIVATION Grow in any but waterlogged soil.
• PROPAGATION By seed in autumn.
• OTHER NAMES *C. orientalis*.

☀ ◊
❀ ❀ ❀

HEIGHT
8m (25ft)

SPREAD
8m (25ft)

Hippocastanaceae	CALIFORNIA BUCKEYE

AESCULUS CALIFORNICA

Habit Broadly spreading, often multi-stemmed.
Flowers Small, fragrant, in dense, slender, upright panicles, to 20cm (8in) long, in summer. Creamy or pale pink. **Fruits** Rough-textured, pear-shaped husks enclosing a single, conker-like seed.
Leaves Deciduous, with 5–7 narrowly oblong, taper-pointed leaflets. Dark blue-green.
• NATIVE HABITAT Dry hillsides and canyons of California.
• CULTIVATION *A. californica* is an easily cultivated species, tolerant of a range of soil types, but preferring deep, fertile, well-drained soil. Provide it with a warm, sunny site, with shelter from cold winds. Avoid planting in frost pocket areas where young growth will be damaged by late frosts.
• PROPAGATION By seed in autumn.

☀ ◊
❀ ❀

HEIGHT
8m (25ft)

SPREAD
10m (30ft)

Cornaceae	

CORNUS FLORIDA 'White Cloud'

Habit Broadly spreading. *Flowers* Tiny, in dense clusters, surrounded by 4 broad, white bracts, in late spring. Green. *Leaves* Deciduous, oval to elliptic, pointed. Dark green, often bronzed, turning red and purple in autumn.
• NATIVE HABITAT Garden origin.
• CULTIVATION Unsuitable for shallow, chalky soils. Tolerates dappled shade. Grow in deep, fertile, moisture-retentive soil.
• PROPAGATION By softwood cuttings in summer.

☼ ◊
❋ ❋ ❋

HEIGHT
8m (25ft)

SPREAD
9.5m (29ft)

Rosaceae	FUJI CHERRY

PRUNUS INCISA

Habit Vigorous, broadly spreading, often shrubby. *Flowers* Delicate, single, saucer-shaped, in clusters in mid-spring. White or pale pink. *Leaves* Deciduous, oval, sharply toothed, taper-pointed. Red-bronze when young, later dark green, hairy above and beneath; orange-red in autumn.
• NATIVE HABITAT Mountain woodlands in Japan.
• CULTIVATION Tolerates chalky soils. Useful as hedging. Trim after flowering.
• PROPAGATION By seed in autumn.

☼ ◊
❋ ❋ ❋

HEIGHT
8m (25ft)

SPREAD
8m (25ft)

Rosaceae	

PRUNUS 'Shogetsu' ♟

Habit Wide-spreading, with a broad, flattened crown. *Flowers* Large, double, with sharply toothed petal margins, opening from pink buds, carried in pendent clusters in late spring. White. *Leaves* Deciduous, oval. Bright green, later dark green, turning rich orange-red in autumn.
• NATIVE HABITAT Garden origin.
• CULTIVATION Grow in any well-drained soils, including chalky ones.
• PROPAGATION By softwood cuttings in summer.
• OTHER NAMES *P.* 'Shimidsu'.

☼ ◊
❋ ❋ ❋

HEIGHT
7m (22ft)

SPREAD
10m (30ft)

Rosaceae	GREAT WHITE CHERRY

PRUNUS 'Taihaku' ♟

Habit Vigorous, broadly spreading. *Flowers* Fragrant, very large, single, saucer-shaped, with notched petal-tips, in clusters in mid-spring. Pure white, pink in bud. *Leaves* Deciduous, oval, finely toothed. Coppery-bronze when young, later dark green, turning red-gold in autumn.
• NATIVE HABITAT Garden origin.
• CULTIVATION Grow in any well-drained soils, including chalky ones.
• PROPAGATION By softwood cuttings in summer.
• OTHER NAMES *P.* 'Tai Haku'.

☼ ◊
❋ ❋ ❋

HEIGHT
8m (25ft)

SPREAD
10m (30ft)

Rosaceae	

PRUNUS 'Ukon' ♀

Habit Vigorous, funnel-shaped, horizontally spreading. *Flowers* Large, fragrant, double or semi-double, in clusters in mid-spring. Pale yellowish, tinted green. *Leaves* Deciduous, oval. Pale bronze on emergence, later dark green, turning rich rusty-red or purple in autumn.
• NATIVE HABITAT Garden origin.
• CULTIVATION Grow in any well-drained soils, including chalky ones.
• PROPAGATION By softwood cuttings in summer.

HEIGHT
8m (25ft)

SPREAD
10m (30ft)

Rosaceae	

PRUNUS 'Amanogawa' ♀

Habit Vigorous, narrowly upright, with strongly ascending branches. *Flowers* Large, double, opening with or before the leaves, in mid-spring. Pale pink, with yellow anthers. *Leaves* Deciduous, oval, finely toothed. Coppery-bronze when young, later dark green, turning red-gold in autumn.
• NATIVE HABITAT Garden origin.
• CULTIVATION Grow in any well-drained soils, including chalky ones. An attractive specimen for small gardens, but branches tend to splay with age.
• PROPAGATION By softwood cuttings in summer.

HEIGHT
8m (25ft)

SPREAD
3m (10ft)

Rosaceae	MOUNT FUJI CHERRY

PRUNUS 'Shirotae' ♀

Habit Broadly spreading, with slightly arching branches. *Flowers* Large, fragrant, single or semi-double, bowl-shaped, in clusters in mid-spring. Pure white. *Leaves* Deciduous, oval, fringed. Bright green on emergence, later dark green, turning red-gold in autumn.
• NATIVE HABITAT Garden origin.
• CULTIVATION Grow in any well-drained soils, including chalky ones.
• PROPAGATION By softwood cuttings in summer.
• OTHER NAMES *P.* 'Mount Fuji'.

HEIGHT
8m (25ft)

SPREAD
10m (30ft)

Rosaceae	YOSHINO CHERRY

PRUNUS X *YEDOENSIS* ♀

Habit Wide-spreading, with a broad, rounded crown. *Flowers* Almond-scented, petals notched at the tip, in delicate clusters in early to mid-spring. Pale pink, fading to white. *Leaves* Deciduous, elliptic, taper-pointed, sharply toothed. Pale green on emergence, later dark green, turning rich red-purple in autumn.
• NATIVE HABITAT Hilly woodlands of Japan.
• CULTIVATION Grow in any well-drained soils, including chalky ones.
• PROPAGATION By softwood cuttings in summer.

HEIGHT
8.5m (26ft)

SPREAD
10m (30ft)

Rosaceae	

PRUNUS 'Pandora' ♈

Habit Broadly upright, with nodding branch tips, sometimes shrubby. *Flowers* Large, single, in profuse clusters in early spring, before the leaves. Pale shell-pink, darker at petal margins, opening from pink buds. *Leaves* Deciduous, oval-elliptic. Bronze-red on emergence, later dark green, and colouring well in autumn in shades of orange and red.

• NATIVE HABITAT Garden origin.
• CULTIVATION Grow in any well-drained soils, including chalky ones. A vigorous hybrid between

P. subhirtella 'Ascendens Rosea' and *P.* x *yedoensis*. This, and the other flowering cherries described in this volume, make exceptionally beautiful specimen trees. Many ornamental cherries are ideal for small gardens, as they are small in stature and most are of interest in spring and again when the foliage colours in autumn.

• PROPAGATION By softwood cuttings in summer.

☀ ◊
❀ ❀ ❀

HEIGHT
10m (30ft)

SPREAD
8m (25ft)

Rosaceae	

PRUNUS 'Spire'   ♈

Habit Vase-shaped, conical when young.
Flowers Large, single, in profusion in early to
mid-spring, with the emerging leaves. Soft almond-
pink. *Leaves* Deciduous, broadly oval, coarsely
toothed, short-pointed at tip. Bronze on emergence,
later matt dark green, turning orange-red in autumn.
• NATIVE HABITAT Garden origin.
• CULTIVATION Grow in any well-drained soils,
including chalky ones.
• PROPAGATION By softwood cuttings in summer.
• OTHER NAMES *P.* x *hillieri* 'Spire'.

☼ ◊
❀ ❀ ❀

HEIGHT
10m (30ft)

SPREAD
7m (22ft)

Rosaceae	SARGENT CHERRY

PRUNUS SARGENTII   ♈

Habit Broadly spreading, round-headed.
Flowers Single, with notched petal-tips, in clusters
in mid-spring with, or just before, the leaves. Pink.
Fruits Shiny, rounded to egg-shaped berries. Purple-
black. *Leaves* Deciduous, elliptic to broadly oval,
long-pointed. Bronze-red when young, later dark
green. Brilliant yellow, red, and maroon in autumn.
• NATIVE HABITAT Mountain woods of Japan.
• CULTIVATION Grow in any well-drained soil.
• PROPAGATION By seed in autumn.
• OTHER NAMES *P. serrulata* var. *sachalinensis.*

☼ ◊
❀ ❀ ❀

HEIGHT
10m (30ft)

SPREAD
15m (50ft)

Rosaceae	

PRUNUS 'Hokusai'

Habit Vigorous, wide-spreading. *Flowers* Large,
semi-double, opening from pink buds, carried in
pendent, long-stalked clusters in mid-spring. Soft
pale pink, darkening at the centre with age.
Leaves Deciduous, oval. Bronze on emergence,
later dark green, turning rich orange-red in autumn.
• NATIVE HABITAT Garden origin.
• CULTIVATION Grow in any well-drained soils
including chalky ones.
• PROPAGATION By softwood cuttings in summer.
• OTHER NAMES *P.* 'Uzu-zakura'.

☼ ◊
❀ ❀ ❀

HEIGHT
8m (25ft)

SPREAD
12m (40ft)

Rosaceae	SPRING CHERRY

PRUNUS x *SUBHIRTELLA* 'Stellata'

Habit Upright, slightly spreading, forming a
rounded crown. *Flowers* Single, with long, narrow,
pointed petals, in large clusters at the branch tips in
early to mid-spring. Clear shell-pink.
Leaves Deciduous, narrowly elliptic, toothed.
Dark green, turning yellow in autumn.
• NATIVE HABITAT Garden origin.
• CULTIVATION Grow in any well-drained soils,
including chalky ones.
• PROPAGATION By softwood cuttings in summer.
• OTHER NAMES *P.* x *subhirtella* 'Pink Star'.

☼ ◊
❀ ❀ ❀

HEIGHT
8m (25ft)

SPREAD
8m (25ft)

Rosaceae	

PRUNUS 'Shirofugen' ♈

Habit Vigorous, wide-spreading, with a flattened crown. **Flowers** Large, fragrant, double, carried in long-stalked clusters in late spring. White, becoming pale pink with age, opening from pink buds. **Leaves** Deciduous, oval. Bronze-crimson when young, then dark green, orange-red in autumn.
• NATIVE HABITAT Garden origin.
• CULTIVATION Grow in any well-drained soils, including chalky ones. One of the latest, and longest, in bloom.
• PROPAGATION By softwood cuttings in summer.

☀ ◊
❀ ❀ ❀

HEIGHT
8m (25ft)

SPREAD
10m (30ft)

Rosaceae	

PRUNUS 'Pink Perfection' ♈

Habit Vase-shaped. **Flowers** Large, double, carried in long-stalked, pendulous clusters in mid- to late spring. Pale rose-pink, opening from deep pink buds. **Leaves** Deciduous, oval. Bronze when young, then dark green, turning orange-red in autumn.
• NATIVE HABITAT Garden origin.
• CULTIVATION Grow in any well-drained soil, including chalky soil.
• PROPAGATION By softwood cuttings in summer.

☀ ◊
❀ ❀ ❀

HEIGHT
8m (25ft)

SPREAD
8m (25ft)

Rosaceae	ALMOND

PRUNUS DULCIS 'Roseoplena'

Habit Broadly spreading. **Flowers** Large, double, opening from deep pink buds, with the leaves in early spring. Pink, fading to pale pink or white. **Leaves** Deciduous, lance-shaped to narrowly elliptic, taper-pointed, finely toothed. Dark green.
• NATIVE HABITAT Species occurs in scrub, woodlands, and on dry hillsides in N. Africa and S.W. Asia. Garden origin.
• CULTIVATION Grow in any but waterlogged soil
• PROPAGATION By softwood cuttings in summer.

☀ ◊
❀ ❀ ❀

HEIGHT
8m (25ft)

SPREAD
8m (25ft)

Rosaceae	

PRUNUS 'Accolade' ♀

Habit Broadly spreading, round-headed.
Flowers Semi-double, in a profusion of pendulous clusters in early spring, with or just before the leaves. Rich pink, deep pink in bud.
Leaves Deciduous, elliptic-oblong, sharply toothed, pointed. Dark green, turning orange-red in autumn.
• NATIVE HABITAT Garden origin.
• CULTIVATION Grow in any well-drained soils, including chalky ones.
• PROPAGATION By softwood cuttings in summer.

☀ ◊
❀ ❀ ❀

HEIGHT
8m (25ft) or more

SPREAD
8m (25ft)

Leguminosae	JUDAS TREE

CERCIS SILIQUASTRUM ♀

Habit Broadly spreading, with a rounded crown.
Flowers Small, pea-like, in clusters in mid-spring, with or before the leaves. Bright pink. *Fruits* Long, purplish-red pods. *Leaves* Deciduous, heart-shaped. Bronze when young, then dark blue-green.
• NATIVE HABITAT Dry, rocky hills of S.E. Europe and W. Asia.
• CULTIVATION Grow in deep, fertile soil, which must be well drained. Flowers best in areas with long, hot summers. An attractive foliage specimen.
• PROPAGATION By seed in autumn.

☀ ◊
❀ ❀ ❀

HEIGHT
10m (30ft)

SPREAD
10m (30ft)

Rosaceae	

PRUNUS 'Kiku-shidare-zakura' ♀

Habit Weeping, with strongly pendulous branches. *Flowers* Large, very double, with pointed petals, densely clustered along pendent branches from mid- to late spring. Deep, clear pink.
Leaves Deciduous, lance-shaped. Pale green and slightly bronzed on emergence, later dark green.
• NATIVE HABITAT Garden origin.
• CULTIVATION Grow in any well-drained soils, including chalky ones.
• PROPAGATION By softwood cuttings in summer.
• OTHER NAMES *P.* 'Cheal's Weeping'.

☀ ◊
❀ ❀ ❀

HEIGHT
To 8m (25ft) usually less

SPREAD
7m (22ft)

Rosaceae	

PRUNUS x *SUBHIRTELLA* 'Pendula Rubra' ♀

Habit Weeping, dome-shaped, with slender branches. *Flowers* Single, in spring, before the leaves. Deep pink, ruby-red in bud.
Leaves Deciduous, lance-shaped, finely toothed. Pale green on emergence, later dark green.
• NATIVE HABITAT Garden origin.
• CULTIVATION Grow in any well-drained soils, including chalky ones.
• PROPAGATION By softwood cuttings in summer.
• OTHER NAMES *P.* x *subhirtella* 'Ibara Ito Sakura'.

☀ ◊
❀ ❀ ❀

HEIGHT
8m (25ft)

SPREAD
8m (25ft)

Rosaceae	

MALUS × *MAGDEBURGENSIS*

Habit Rounded when young, later spreading; sometimes shrubby. **Flowers** Large, semi-double, in dense clusters in late spring. Deep pink, deep red in bud. **Fruits** Small crab apples. Yellow. **Leaves** Deciduous, elliptic, pointed. Dark green, downy beneath.

• NATIVE HABITAT Garden origin.
• CULTIVATION Tolerates dappled shade, but flowers and fruits best in sun. Grow in any but waterlogged soil. This, and other crab apples (*Malus*), makes a beautiful specimen tree for smaller gardens. They have a long season of interest, with flowers in spring and fruits in autumn that are also useful for making jellies and preserves. Many also colour well in autumn.

• PROPAGATION By budding in summer or by grafting in winter.
• OTHER NAMES *M*. 'Magdeburgensis'.

HEIGHT
7m (22ft)

SPREAD
8m (25ft)

Rosaceae	

PRUNUS PERSICA 'Prince Charming'

Habit Upright, bushy-headed. ***Flowers*** Double, carried singly or in pairs, along bare branches in mid-spring. Deep rose-pink. ***Leaves*** Deciduous, narrowly elliptic to lance-shaped. Bright green.
• NATIVE HABITAT Garden origin.
• CULTIVATION Grow in any well-drained soils, including chalky ones. Susceptible to peach leaf curl.
• PROPAGATION By softwood cuttings in summer.

☼ ◊
❄ ❄ ❄

HEIGHT
7m (22ft)

SPREAD
5m (15ft)

Sterculiaceae	

DOMBEYA × CAYEUXII

Habit Bushy, rounded. ***Flowers*** Small, in dense, round, pendent clusters in winter or spring. Pink. ***Leaves*** Evergreen, rounded, toothed, heart-shaped at base, hairy. Dark green.
• NATIVE HABITAT Garden origin.
• CULTIVATION Tolerates partial shade. Grow in fertile, free-draining soil or compost. Water freely when in full growth, less in low temperatures. Prune, if necessary, after flowering.
• PROPAGATION By semi-ripe cuttings in summer.

☼ ◊

Min.
10–13°C
(50–55°F)

HEIGHT
6m (20ft)

SPREAD
7m (22ft)

Rosaceae	

PRUNUS 'Yae-murasaki'

Habit Slow-growing, wide-spreading. ***Flowers*** Semi-double, in profusion in mid-spring. Pink-purple, opening from red buds. ***Leaves*** Deciduous, oval, toothed. Coppery-red when young, later dark green, turning brilliant orange-red in autumn.
• NATIVE HABITAT Garden origin.
• CULTIVATION Grow in any well-drained soils, including chalky ones.
• PROPAGATION By softwood cuttings in summer.
• OTHER NAMES *P.* 'Yae-marasakizakura'.

☼ ◊
❄ ❄ ❄

HEIGHT
5m (15ft)

SPREAD
8m (25ft)

Rosaceae	

MALUS 'Royalty'

Habit Broadly pyramidal, spreading. ***Flowers*** Large, in clusters from mid- to late spring. Crimson-purple, opening from dark red buds. ***Fruits*** Small crab apples. Glossy dark red, black when ripe. ***Leaves*** Deciduous, oval, taper-pointed. Glossy red-purple, turning red in late autumn.
• NATIVE HABITAT Garden origin.
• CULTIVATION Tolerates dappled shade but flowers and fruits best in sun.
• PROPAGATION By budding in summer or by grafting in winter.

☼ ◊
❄ ❄ ❄

HEIGHT
8m (25ft)

SPREAD
8m (25ft)

Rosaceae	

MALUS 'Lemoinei'

Habit Round-headed, spreading. *Flowers* Large, single, in profusion in late spring. Wine-red, dark red in bud. *Fruits* Small, glossy, cherry-like crab apples. Red-purple. *Leaves* Deciduous, oval. Deep red-purple when young, later bronze-red, turning red in late autumn.
• NATIVE HABITAT Garden origin.
• CULTIVATION Tolerates dappled shade. Flowers and fruits best in sun. Avoid waterlogged soil.
• PROPAGATION By budding in summer or by grafting in winter.

☼ ◊
❀ ❀ ❀

HEIGHT
8m (25ft)

SPREAD
8m (25ft)

Aceraceae	

ACER PSEUDOPLATANUS ♈
'Brilliantissimum'

Habit Slow-growing, spreading, with a domed crown. *Leaves* Deciduous, with 5 coarsely toothed lobes. Brilliant shrimp-pink on emergence, later pale with green veins, becoming yellow-green.
• NATIVE HABITAT Garden origin.
• CULTIVATION Tolerates exposure and almost any soil. Smaller and slower-growing than the species. An attractive specimen for smaller gardens.
• PROPAGATION By grafting in late winter or early spring or by budding in summer.

☼ ◊
❀ ❀

HEIGHT
6m (20ft) or more

SPREAD
8m (25ft)

Hippocastanaceae	

AESCULUS × NEGLECTA 'Erythroblastos' ♈

Habit Slow-growing, broadly columnar.
Flowers Small, narrow, in open, upright panicles in summer. Creamy-white, flushed peach-pink.
Leaves Deciduous, with 5 elliptic, taper-pointed, finely toothed leaflets. Bright pink, later yellow, then dark green, turning orange and red in autumn.
• NATIVE HABITAT Garden origin. Species occurs on the coastal plains of S.E. United States.
• CULTIVATION Grow in any deep, fertile soil.
• PROPAGATION By budding in late summer or by grafting in winter.

☼ ◊
❀ ❀ ❀

HEIGHT
10m (30ft)

SPREAD
8m (25ft)

Leguminosae	KOWHAI

SOPHORA TETRAPTERA ♈

Habit Open, spreading, with slender branches.
Flowers Small, tubular, in pendulous racemes in late spring. Golden-yellow. *Leaves* Semi-evergreen or deciduous, with up to 20 pairs of tiny, elliptic leaflets. Dark green.
• NATIVE HABITAT Forest margins and open woods in New Zealand and Chile.
• CULTIVATION Grow in any well-drained soil, in a warm, sunny, sheltered site.
• PROPAGATION By seed in autumn or by semi-ripe cuttings in summer.

☼ ◊
❀ ❀ ❀

HEIGHT
10m (30ft)

SPREAD
5m (15ft)

| Cornaceae | WEDDING CAKE TREE |

CORNUS CONTROVERSA 'Variegata'

Habit Slow-growing, tiered, horizontally branching. **Flowers** Tiny, in large, flattened heads in summer. White. **Leaves** Deciduous, alternate, broadly oval to elliptic, taper-pointed. Bright green, broadly margined with creamy-white.
• NATIVE HABITAT Species occurs in thickets and woodland in E. Asia. Garden origin.
• CULTIVATION Tolerates dappled shade. Grow in deep, fertile, moisture-retentive soil. The tree requires no regular pruning, which would spoil the gracefully tiered habit; the branches and foliage are held in distinctive, well-separated horizontal layers. It is an excellent specimen for open areas in the woodland garden, and as it is very slow-growing, it is also suitable for medium-sized gardens as a lawn specimen. *C. alternifolia* 'Argentea' is similar, but smaller.
• PROPAGATION By grafting in winter.

HEIGHT
8m (25ft) or more

SPREAD
8m (25ft)

Cornaceae	

CORNUS ALTERNIFOLIA 'Argentea' ♀

Habit Dense, with tiered, horizontally spreading branches. **Flowers** Tiny, in small heads in spring. Creamy. **Leaves** Deciduous, alternate, narrowly oval. Bright green, margins variegated creamy-white.
• NATIVE HABITAT Species occurs in damp woods of E. North America. Garden origin.
• CULTIVATION Tolerates dappled shade. Grow in deep, fertile, moisture-retentive soil.
• PROPAGATION By grafting in winter.
• OTHER NAMES *C. alternifolia* 'Variegata'.

☼ ◊
❁ ❁ ❁

HEIGHT
8m (25ft)

SPREAD
8m (25ft)

Aceraceae	HAWTHORN MAPLE

ACER CRATAEGIFOLIUM 'Veitchii'

Habit Bushy, round-headed to conical. **Flowers** Small, in slender racemes in spring. Yellow-green. **Fruits** 2 seeds, fused together, each with a red-tinged wing. **Leaves** Deciduous, with 3 toothed lobes, the middle lobe long and taper-pointed. Dark green, blotched white and pale green, turning pink and red-purple in autumn.
• NATIVE HABITAT Garden origin.
• CULTIVATION Grow in any fertile soil.
• PROPAGATION By grafting in late winter or early spring or by budding in summer.

☼ ◊
❁ ❁ ❁

HEIGHT
9m (28ft)

SPREAD
8m (25ft)

Rosaceae	YELLOW HAW

CRATAEGUS FLAVA

Habit Spreading, with a broadly rounded crown. **Flowers** Small, in neat, rounded clusters in late spring and early summer. Creamy-white, with pink anthers. **Fruits** Rounded to pear-shaped, edible. Yellow. **Leaves** Deciduous, small, broadly oval to oblong, leathery. Bright green.
• NATIVE HABITAT E. North America.
• CULTIVATION Tolerates coastal conditions and exposed sites. Grow in any but waterlogged soil.
• PROPAGATION By seed in autumn.

☼ ◊
❁ ❁ ❁

HEIGHT
8m (25ft) or more

SPREAD
10m (30ft)

Myrtaceae	WILLOW MYRTLE, WILLOW PEPPERMINT

AGONIS FLEXUOSA

Habit Graceful, weeping. **Flowers** Small, in profuse clusters on mature trees, in spring and summer. White. **Leaves** Aromatic, evergreen, narrowly lance-shaped, leathery. Bronze-red and silky when young, later dark green.
• NATIVE HABITAT Coastal areas of W. Australia.
• CULTIVATION Best grown as a conservatory plant in cooler climates. Grow in moisture-retentive, well-drained soil or compost.
• PROPAGATION By seed in spring or by semi-ripe cuttings in summer.

☼ ◊

Min. 10°C (50°F)

HEIGHT
7m (22ft)

SPREAD
3m (10ft)

Malvaceae	

HOHERIA ANGUSTIFOLIA

Habit Narrowly columnar. *Flowers* Shallowly cup-shaped, with narrow petals, from mid- to late summer. White. *Leaves* Evergreen, narrowly oblong to lance-shaped, toothed or serrated. Dark green.
• NATIVE HABITAT Damp forests of New Zealand.
• CULTIVATION Tolerates semi-shade. Grow in fertile, humus-rich soil. Shelter from cold, dry winds. In cold areas, provide the shelter of a south- or southwest-facing wall. It makes a very attractive small tree and is suitable for growing in the shrub border or as a free-standing specimen. The honey-scented flowers of this and other species of *Hoheria* are attractive to honey bees and butterflies.
• PROPAGATION By seed in autumn or by semi-ripe cuttings in summer.
• OTHER NAMES *H. populnea* var. *angustifolia.*

☼ ◊
✿ ✿

HEIGHT
To 10m
(30ft)

SPREAD
4m (12ft)

Cornaceae	

CORNUS 'Porlock'

Habit Graceful, open, broadly spreading.
Flowers Tiny, in rounded clusters in summer.
Green, surrounded by large, creamy-white bracts,
flushed pink with age. *Fruits* Pendent, strawberry-
like, in profusion in autumn. Red.
Leaves Deciduous, oval, taper-pointed. Dark
green, turning red in autumn. *Bark* Smooth,
flaking at the base. Grey, with shallow orange
fissures.
• NATIVE HABITAT Garden origin.
• CULTIVATION Tolerates dappled shade.

Grow in deep, fertile, moisture-retentive soil. This,
and the very similar *C.* 'Norman Hadden', makes
an elegant and graceful specimen for the smaller
garden, of interest in summer and again in autumn,
with fruit and foliage colour. It is also suitable for
woodland gardens.
• PROPAGATION By softwood cuttings in summer.

HEIGHT
8m (25ft)

SPREAD
8m (25ft)

Eucryphiaceae	NIRRHE

EUCRYPHIA GLUTINOSA ♀

Habit Narrowly columnar. **Flowers** Fragrant, large, 4-petalled, in late summer. Glistening white, with a prominent boss of stamens, **Fruits** Woody capsules. **Leaves** Semi-evergreen or deciduous, with 3–5 elliptic-oblong, toothed leaflets. Glossy dark green, often turning orange-red in autumn.
• NATIVE HABITAT Forests and riversides, Chile.
• CULTIVATION Grow in humus-rich, moisture-retentive, neutral to acid soil.
• PROPAGATION By semi-ripe cuttings in late summer or by seed in autumn (may not come true).

☀: ◐ pH
❀❀

HEIGHT
10m (30ft)

SPREAD
6m (20ft)

Eucryphiaceae	LEATHERWOOD, PINKWOOD

EUCRYPHIA LUCIDA

Habit Dense, narrowly columnar. **Flowers** Fragrant, large, with 4 rounded petals, cup-shaped at first, opening flat in late summer. Glistening white with pink anthers. **Leaves** Evergreen, narrowly oblong, leathery. Dark green, blue-white beneath.
• NATIVE HABITAT Mountain woods, Tasmania.
• CULTIVATION Grow in humus-rich, moisture-retentive, neutral to acid soil. Provide shelter from cold, dry winds.
• PROPAGATION By semi-ripe cuttings in late summer.

☀: ◐ pH
❀❀

HEIGHT
8m (25ft)

SPREAD
4m (12ft)

Malvaceae	LACEBARK

HOHERIA LYALLII ♀

Habit Broadly conical. **Flowers** Shallowly cup-shaped, in a profusion of rounded clusters in mid-summer. White. **Leaves** Deciduous, oval, pointed, heart-shaped at the base, with neat, rounded teeth. Grey-green, downy-white above and beneath.
• NATIVE HABITAT Forest margins and damp mountain woodlands of New Zealand.
• CULTIVATION Grow in fertile, humus-rich soil with shelter from cold, dry winds.
• PROPAGATION By seed in autumn or by semi-ripe cuttings in summer.

☀: ◐
❀❀

HEIGHT
6m (20ft)

SPREAD
4m (12ft)

Leguminosae	

MAACKIA AMURENSIS

Habit Spreading, with an irregularly rounded crown. **Flowers** Small, pea-like, in dense, upright spikes from mid- to late summer. Creamy-white. **Leaves** Deciduous, with 7–11 broadly oval to elliptic leaflets. Dark green.
• NATIVE HABITAT Mountain scrub and woodlands in E. Asia.
• CULTIVATION Grow in any fertile soil. Blooms best in a warm, sunny, sheltered site.
• PROPAGATION By seed in autumn.

☀: ◐
❀❀❀

HEIGHT
7m (22ft)

SPREAD
9m (28ft)

Leguminosae	SILK TREE

ALBIZIA JULIBRISSIN

Habit Broadly spreading, with a domed or flat-topped crown. *Flowers* Dense, round clusters of fine, clear pink stamens, carried in racemes from late summer to early autumn. *Fruits* Pods, to 15cm (6in) long. *Leaves* Deciduous, feathery, finely divided, with many small leaflets. Dark green.
• NATIVE HABITAT Woodlands and riverbanks of S.W. Asia.
• CULTIVATION Grow in a warm, sheltered site, such as a south- or west-facing wall.
• PROPAGATION By seed in autumn.

☼ ◊ ❄

HEIGHT
10m (30ft)

SPREAD
10m (30ft)

Rosaceae	MIDLAND HAWTHORN, PAUL'S SCARLET HAWTHORN

CRATAEGUS LAEVIGATA 'Paul's Scarlet' ♉

Habit Spreading, with a rounded crown. *Flowers* Double, in dense clusters from late spring to summer. Pinkish-scarlet. *Fruits* Small haws. Red. *Leaves* Deciduous, lobed, toothed. Dark green.
• NATIVE HABITAT Garden origin.
• CULTIVATION Tolerant of urban pollution, coastal conditions, and exposed sites, and almost any but waterlogged soil.
• PROPAGATION By budding in late summer.
• OTHER NAMES *C. laevigata* 'Coccinea Plena', *C. oxyacantha* 'Paul's Scarlet'.

☼ ◊ ❄ ❄ ❄

HEIGHT
7m (22ft)

SPREAD
8m (25ft)

Cornaceae	

CORNUS FLORIDA 'Spring Song'

Habit Broadly spreading. *Flowers* Tiny, in dense clusters in late spring or early summer. Green, surrounded by 4 broad, pink bracts. *Leaves* Deciduous, oval to elliptic, pointed. Dark green, often bronzed, turning red and purple in autumn.
• NATIVE HABITAT Garden origin.
• CULTIVATION Unsuitable for shallow, chalky soils. Tolerates dappled shade. Grow in deep, fertile, moisture-retentive soil.
• PROPAGATION By softwood cuttings in summer.

☼ ◊ ❄ ❄ ❄

HEIGHT
6m (20ft)

SPREAD
8m (25ft)

Leguminosae	

CERCIS CANADENSIS 'Forest Pansy' ♉

Habit Broadly spreading, with a rounded crown. *Flowers* Small, pea-like, in clusters in mid-spring, before the leaves. Pale pink, magenta in bud. *Leaves* Deciduous, heart-shaped. Bronze-purple when young, dark red-purple when mature.
• NATIVE HABITAT Species occurs in damp woodland in North America. Garden origin.
• CULTIVATION Tolerates dappled shade. Grow in deep, fertile, moisture-retentive soil. A very attractive foliage specimen for small gardens.
• PROPAGATION By budding in late summer.

☼ ◊ ❄ ❄ ❄

HEIGHT
10m (30ft)

SPREAD
10m (30ft)

Rosaceae

PRUNUS CERASIFERA 'Nigra'

Habit Broadly spreading, round-headed.
Flowers Small, single, 5-petalled, in a profusion of dense clusters in early to mid-spring, with or before the leaves. Rich pink, fading to blush-pink.
Fruits Rounded, plum-like, 3cm (1¼in) across, edible. Dark red.
Leaves Deciduous, oval, toothed, pointed. Dark red-purple.
• NATIVE HABITAT Garden origin.
• CULTIVATION Grow in any but waterlogged soil. May be used for hedging. Trim after flowering.

These trees, and other dark-leaved cherry plums such as *P. cerasifera* 'Pissardii' and *P. cerasifera* 'Rosea', are invaluable in small gardens because of their early spring blooming. They also make a handsome contrast to grey-leaved trees such as *Sorbus aria* 'Lutescens' and *Pyrus salicifolia* 'Pendula'.
• PROPAGATION By softwood cuttings in summer.

HEIGHT
10m (30ft)

SPREAD
10m(30ft)

Boraginaceae (Ehretiaceae)	

EHRETIA DICKSONII

Habit Fast-growing, open, spreading.
Flowers Small, fragrant, star-shaped, in large, flattened heads in mid-summer. White.
Leaves Deciduous, large, oblong-elliptic. Lustrous dark green, roughly hairy above, velvety beneath.
• NATIVE HABITAT China, Japan, and Taiwan.
• CULTIVATION Grow in any fertile soil, in a warm, sunny, sheltered site. Young growth susceptible to frost damage.
• PROPAGATION By softwood cuttings in summer.
• OTHER NAMES *E. macrophylla* of gardens.

HEIGHT 10m (30ft)

SPREAD 10m (30ft)

Rosaceae	WEEPING WILLOW-LEAVED PEAR

PYRUS SALICIFOLIA 'Pendula'

Habit Broadly weeping. **Flowers** 5-petalled, in clusters, opening with the leaves in spring. Creamy-white. **Fruits** Small, hard, pear-shaped.
Leaves Deciduous, narrowly elliptic to lance-shaped. Grey, downy when young.
• NATIVE HABITAT Species occurs in thickets in the Caucasus and N.E. Turkey.
• CULTIVATION Tolerant of urban pollution. Grow in any moderately fertile soil.
• PROPAGATION By budding in summer or by grafting in winter.

HEIGHT 8m (25ft)

SPREAD 6m (20ft)

Araliaceae	TOOTHED LANCEWOOD

PSEUDOPANAX FEROX

Habit Narrowly upright, unbranched when young, becoming rounded with maturity.
Leaves Evergreen, long, narrow, rigid, with hooked marginal teeth, downward-pointing. Deep bronze-green, bloomed white, with an orange midrib.
• NATIVE HABITAT Scrub and lowland forests of New Zealand.
• CULTIVATION Tolerates partial shade. Grow in any fertile soil in a sunny, sheltered site.
• PROPAGATION By semi-ripe cuttings in summer or by seed in autumn or spring.

HEIGHT 5m (15ft)

SPREAD 2m (6ft)

Ulmaceae	CAMPERDOWN ELM

ULMUS 'Camperdownii'

Habit Slow-growing, dense, with a dome-shaped head and pendulous branches. *Leaves* Deciduous, large, broadly oval, pointed, unequal at the base, rough-textured. Dull green.
• NATIVE HABITAT Garden origin.
• CULTIVATION Grow in any fertile, well-drained soil. Susceptible to Dutch elm disease.
• PROPAGATION By softwood cuttings in summer or by suckers in autumn.
• OTHER NAMES *U. glabra* 'Camperdownii', *U. pendula* 'Camperdownii'.

HEIGHT
8m (25ft) or more

SPREAD
8m (25ft)

Juglandaceae	LITTLE WALNUT, TEXAN WALNUT

JUGLANS MICROCARPA

Habit Shrubby, round-headed. *Flowers* Catkins, male and female on same plant, in late spring. Yellow-green. *Leaves* Deciduous, aromatic, with 15–23 slender-pointed, narrowly lance-shaped leaflets. Glossy green, turning yellow in autumn.
• NATIVE HABITAT By stream sides on the plains and in the mountain foothills of Texas and New Mexico.
• CULTIVATION Grow in deep, fertile soil.
• PROPAGATION By seed in autumn.
• OTHER NAMES *J. rupestris.*

HEIGHT
7m (22ft)

SPREAD
7m (22ft)

Rosaceae	

CYDONIA OBLONGA 'Vranja'

Habit Low-branching, broadly spreading. *Flowers* Large, 5-petalled, in late spring. Pink or white. *Fruits* Very fragrant, large, pear-shaped. Yellow when ripe. *Leaves* Deciduous, broadly elliptic-oval. Grey-downy when young, becoming dark green, but remaining downy beneath.
• NATIVE HABITAT Garden origin.
• CULTIVATION Grow in any fertile soil, with the shelter of a south- or west-facing wall to ensure good cropping.
• PROPAGATION By softwood cuttings in summer.

HEIGHT
5m (15ft)

SPREAD
5m (15ft)

Aceraceae	HORNBEAM MAPLE

ACER CARPINIFOLIUM

Habit Broadly conical. *Leaves* Deciduous, oblong, unlobed, taper-pointed, with deeply impressed, parallel veins. Dark green, turning golden-yellow in autumn.
• NATIVE HABITAT Stream banks in deciduous woodlands of Japan.
• CULTIVATION Tolerates dappled shade, but colours best in sun. Grow in deep, fertile, humus-rich soil.
• PROPAGATION By seed in autumn.

HEIGHT
10m (30ft)

SPREAD
7m (22ft)

Betulaceae	YOUNG'S WEEPING BIRCH

BETULA PENDULA 'Youngii' ♈

Habit Weeping, dome-shaped, with slender, elegant branchlets. **Flowers** Catkins. Male, to 6cm (2½in) long; female shorter, on same plant. **Leaves** Deciduous, triangular, serrated. Glossy green, turning golden-yellow in autumn.
Bark White. Rough, black fissures with age.
• NATIVE HABITAT Garden origin.
• CULTIVATION Grow in any moist but well-drained soil in an open, sunny site.
• PROPAGATION By grafting in late winter or softwood cuttings in early summer.

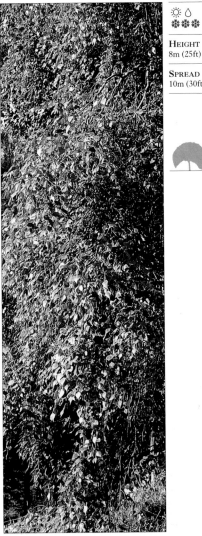

☼ ◊
❀ ❀ ❀

HEIGHT
8m (25ft)

SPREAD
10m (30ft)

Aceraceae	

ACER SHIRASAWANUM f. *AUREUM* ♈

Habit Round-headed, bushy. **Leaves** Deciduous, with 11 pointed, sharply toothed lobes. Soft, pale yellow, turning orange and red in autumn.
• NATIVE HABITAT Species occurs on mountain slopes and in valleys in Japan.
• CULTIVATION Grow in fertile, moisture-retentive, well-drained soil in semi-shade or dappled shade. Leaves may scorch in full sun.
• PROPAGATION By grafting in late winter or early spring or by budding in summer.
• OTHER NAMES *A. japonicum* 'Aureum'.

☼ ◊
❀ ❀ ❀

HEIGHT
To 8m
(25ft)

SPREAD
8m (25ft)

Moraceae	CUT LEAVED WHITE MULBERRY

MORUS ALBA 'Laciniata'

Habit Broadly spreading, with a rounded crown.
Flowers Tiny, male and female on separate plants.
Fruits Small, edible, oval, fleshy clusters. Pink, red, or purple. **Leaves** Deciduous, rounded, deeply lobed. Glossy dark green, turning yellow in autumn.
• NATIVE HABITAT Species occurs on hillsides in N. China. Garden origin.
• CULTIVATION Grow in any fertile soil, in a warm, sunny, sheltered site for good cropping.
• PROPAGATION By softwood cuttings in summer.

☼ ◊
❀ ❀ ❀

HEIGHT
10m (30ft)

SPREAD
10m (30ft)

Leguminosae	

LABURNUM × *WATERERI* 'Vossii' ♈

Habit Broadly spreading. *Flowers* Small, pea-like, in pendent chains, to 50cm (20in) long, in late spring to early summer. Yellow. *Fruits* Small, brown pods, enclosing few seeds.
Leaves Deciduous, divided into 3 elliptic leaflets. Dark green, turning yellow in autumn.
• NATIVE HABITAT Garden origin.
• CULTIVATION Grow in any but waterlogged soil. All parts, especially the seeds, are poisonous and potentially very dangerous to children.⋅
• PROPAGATION By budding in summer.

☼ ◊
❁ ❁ ❁

HEIGHT
10m (30ft)

SPREAD
10m (30ft)

Sapindaceae	GOLDEN RAIN TREE, VARNISH TREE

KOELREUTERIA PANICULATA ♈

Habit Broadly spreading. *Flowers* Small, 4-petalled, in upright panicles in mid- to late summer. Yellow. *Fruits* Papery, bladder-like capsules. Bronze-pink or red, *Leaves* Deciduous, divided, deeply toothed or lobed. Dark green.
• NATIVE HABITAT Hot, dry river valleys in China and Korea.
• CULTIVATION A warm, sunny, sheltered site. Flowers best in hot summers.
• PROPAGATION By seed in autumn or by root cuttings in winter.

☼ ◊
❁ ❁

HEIGHT
10m (30ft)

SPREAD
10m (30ft)

Leguminosae	PLUME ALBIZIA

ALBIZIA LOPHANTHA ♈

Habit Broadly spreading, with a rounded crown. *Flowers* Dense clusters carried in slender spikes in spring and summer. Fine, creamy-yellow stamens. *Leaves* Deciduous, feathery, finely divided, with many small leaflets. Bright green.
• NATIVE HABITAT W. Australia.
• CULTIVATION In mild areas grow on a south- or west-facing wall; otherwise, grow in a cool conservatory.
• PROPAGATION By seed in autumn.
• OTHER NAMES *A. distachya*.

☼ ◊
❁

HEIGHT
8m (25ft)

SPREAD
8m (25ft)

Leguminosae	ALPINE GOLDEN CHAIN

LABURNUM ALPINUM

Habit Open, broadly spreading.
Flowers Fragrant, small, pea-like, in long, slender racemes, to 45cm (18in) long, in early summer. Bright golden-yellow. *Fruits* Brown pods, enclosing shiny, brown seeds. *Leaves* Deciduous, with 3 elliptic, slightly pointed, smooth leaflets. Dark green.
• NATIVE HABITAT Mountains, C. and S. Europe.
• CULTIVATION Grow in any but waterlogged soil. All parts are very poisonous.
• PROPAGATION By seed in autumn.

☼ ◊
❀ ❀ ❀

HEIGHT
8m (25ft)

SPREAD
8m (25ft)

Apocynaceae	YELLOW OLEANDER

THEVETIA PERUVIANA

Habit Upright, with a rounded crown.
Flowers Large, funnel-shaped. Yellow or orange, winter to summer. *Leaves* Evergreen, lance-shaped. Rich, glossy green.
• NATIVE HABITAT Tropical America.
• CULTIVATION Water moderately when in growth, otherwise sparingly. Best grown in a conservatory in cooler climates. Sap is poisonous.
• PROPAGATION By seed in spring or by semi-ripe cuttings in summer.
• OTHER NAMES *T. neriifolia.*

☼ ◊

Min.
13–15°C
(55–59°F)

HEIGHT
10m (30ft)

SPREAD
6m (20ft)

Rosaceae	

SORBUS CASHMIRIANA ♈

Habit Delicate, open, spreading. *Flowers* Small, in broad clusters in late spring. White, pink-flushed. *Fruits* Large, round, in clusters. White, tinted pink at the top at first. *Leaves* Deciduous, with up to 17 sharply toothed leaflets. Deep green above, grey-green beneath. Orange and yellow in autumn.
• NATIVE HABITAT Forests of the W. Himalaya.
• CULTIVATION Tolerates dappled shade. Grow in any fertile, moisture-retentive soil.
• PROPAGATION By softwood cuttings in summer or by seed in autumn.

☼ ◊
❀ ❀ ❀

HEIGHT
8m (25ft)

SPREAD
8m (25ft)

Ericaceae	STRAWBERRY TREE

ARBUTUS UNEDO ♈

Habit Dense, broadly spreading. *Flowers* Small, urn-shaped, in pendent clusters in autumn. White. *Fruits* Small, strawberry-like. Red.
Leaves Evergreen, elliptic to oblong, toothed. Glossy dark green.
• NATIVE HABITAT Thickets and rocky places in S.W. Ireland and the Mediterranean.
• CULTIVATION Tolerates lime, but prefers a deep, fertile, humus-rich soil. Shelter from wind.
• PROPAGATION By seed in autumn or by semi-ripe cuttings in late summer.

☼ ◊
❀ ❀

HEIGHT
8m (25ft)

SPREAD
8m (25ft)

Cornaceae	

CORNUS FLORIDA 'Welchii'

Habit Broadly spreading. ***Flowers*** Tiny, in dense clusters in late spring. Green, surrounded by 4 broad, white bracts. ***Leaves*** Deciduous, oval to elliptic, pointed. Dark green, edged white and pink, turning red and purple in autumn.
• NATIVE HABITAT Garden origin.
• CULTIVATION Unsuitable for shallow, chalky soils. Tolerates dappled shade. Grow in deep, fertile, moisture-retentive soil.
• PROPAGATION By softwood cuttings in summer.

☼ ◊
❁❁❁

HEIGHT
7m (22ft)

SPREAD
8m (25ft)

Rosaceae	

SORBUS VILMORINII

Habit Delicate, open, broadly spreading. ***Flowers*** Small, in broad clusters, from late spring to early summer. White. ***Fruits*** Round. Pink, white flushed with rose when ripe. ***Leaves*** Deciduous, up to 25 oblong leaflets. Deep green, greyish beneath, turning red-purple in autumn.
• NATIVE HABITAT Mountain woods, S.W. China.
• CULTIVATION Tolerates dappled shade. Grow in any fertile, moisture-retentive soil.
• PROPAGATION By softwood cuttings in summer or by seed in autumn.

☼ ◊
❁❁❁

HEIGHT
5m (15ft)

SPREAD
5m (15ft)

Rosaceae	

MALUS 'Veitch's Scarlet'

Habit Spreading, with a rounded crown. ***Flowers*** Large, cup-shaped, in late spring. White. ***Fruits*** Large crab apples. Scarlet, flushed crimson. ***Leaves*** Deciduous, oval. Dark green.
• NATIVE HABITAT Garden origin.
• CULTIVATION Tolerates dappled shade, but flowers and fruits best in sun. Grow in any but waterlogged soil.
• PROPAGATION By budding in summer or by grafting in winter.

☼ ◊
❁❁❁

HEIGHT
9m (28ft)

SPREAD
9m (28ft)

Rosaceae	

CRATAEGUS MACROSPERMA 'Acutiloba'
Habit Spreading, with a domed crown.
Flowers Small, in clusters in late spring. White, with red anthers. **Fruits** Small, rounded haws. Bright red. **Leaves** Deciduous, broad, jaggedly toothed. Dark green.
• NATIVE HABITAT North America.
• CULTIVATION Tolerant of urban pollution, coastal conditions, and exposed sites, and almost any but waterlogged soil.
• PROPAGATION By budding in late summer.

☼ ◌
❄ ❄ ❄

HEIGHT
6m (20ft)

SPREAD
8m (25ft)

Rosaceae	

PHOTINIA DAVIDIANA
Habit Open, spreading. **Flowers** Tiny, in broad clusters in mid-summer. White, with pink anthers.
Fruits Round berries. Bright red.
Leaves Evergreen, elliptic to oblong, taper-pointed at tip. Dark green, then red.
• NATIVE HABITAT Woodlands and thickets in China and Vietnam.
• CULTIVATION Grow in any fertile soil.
• PROPAGATION By seed in autumn or by semi-ripe cuttings in summer.
• OTHER NAMES *Stranvaesia davidiana.*

☼ ◌
❄ ❄ ❄

HEIGHT
8m (25ft)

SPREAD
6m (20ft)

Rosaceae	

MALUS 'Cowichan'
Habit Vigorous, spreading, round-headed.
Flowers Large, cup-shaped, in mid-spring. Red-pink. **Fruits** Large crab apples. Reddish-purple.
Leaves Deciduous, oval. Dark green, red-purple when young.
• NATIVE HABITAT Garden origin.
• CULTIVATION Tolerates dappled shade, but flowers and fruits best in sun. Grow in any but waterlogged soil.
• PROPAGATION By budding in summer or by grafting in winter.

☼ ◌
❄ ❄ ❄

HEIGHT
8m (25ft)

SPREAD
8m (25ft)

Aceraceae	

ACER PALMATUM 'Koreanum'   ♟
Habit Bushy-headed or shrubby. **Flowers** Small, in pendent clusters in spring. Red-purple.
Fruits 2 seeds, fused together, each with a red-tinted wing. **Leaves** Deciduous, with deeply cut lobes. Green, turning brilliant crimson in autumn.
• NATIVE HABITAT Mountain woods of Korea.
• CULTIVATION Grow in fertile, moist but well-drained soil, with shelter from cold winds.
• PROPAGATION By seed in autumn.
• OTHER NAMES *A. palmatum* var. *coreanum.*

☼ ◌
❄ ❄ ❄

HEIGHT
7m (22ft)

SPREAD
7m (22ft)

| Aceraceae | FULL MOON MAPLE |

ACER JAPONICUM 'Vitifolium'

Habit Vigorous, bushy, open, with a rounded crown. **Flowers** Small, in delicate, drooping clusters in spring. Red-purple. **Fruits** 2 seeds, fused together, each with a green wing. **Leaves** Deciduous, with 10–12 sharply toothed lobes. Green, turning rich crimson, orange, and purple in autumn.
• NATIVE HABITAT The species occurs in mountain woodlands, usually in dry, sunny areas, of Japan. Garden origin.
• CULTIVATION *A. japonicum* 'Vitifolium' will thrive in dappled shade. Grow in fertile, moist but well-drained soil. Strong winds and hot sun may scorch the foliage. This tree makes a beautiful specimen for sheltered sites in small or medium-sized gardens.
• PROPAGATION By grafting in late winter or early spring or by budding in summer.

HEIGHT
10m (30ft)

SPREAD
10m (30ft)

Aceraceae	FULL MOON MAPLE

ACER JAPONICUM 'Aconitifolium'   ♥

Habit Bushy, with a rounded crown.
Flowers Small, in drooping clusters in spring. Red.
Fruits 2 seeds, fused together, each with a wing.
Leaves Deciduous, with 7–11 deeply cut, deeply toothed lobes. Green, turning rich crimson in autumn.
• NATIVE HABITAT Garden origin.
• CULTIVATION Grow in fertile, moist but well-drained soil. Strong winds may scorch the foliage.
• PROPAGATION By grafting in late winter or early spring or by budding in summer.

HEIGHT
6m (20ft)

SPREAD
7m (22ft)

Rosaceae	SCARLET HAW

CRATAEGUS PEDICELLATA

Habit Wide-spreading, very thorny.
Flowers Small, in clusters in late spring. White, with red anthers. **Fruits** Bright haws in broad clusters. Scarlet. **Leaves** Deciduous, lobed, sharply toothed. Dark green, then red and orange in autumn.
• NATIVE HABITAT N.E. North America.
• CULTIVATION Tolerant of urban pollution, coastal conditions, exposed sites, and almost any but waterlogged soil.
• PROPAGATION By seed in autumn.
• OTHER NAMES *C. coccinea.*

HEIGHT
5m (15ft)

SPREAD
5m (15ft)

Rosaceae	

MALUS 'John Downie'   ♥

Habit Vigorous, narrowly upright when young, conical with age. **Flowers** Large, cup-shaped, in late spring. White, opening from pink buds.
Fruits Large, egg-shaped crab apples. Yellow-orange, flushed red. **Leaves** Deciduous, elliptic-oval. Bright green when young, then dark green.
• NATIVE HABITAT Garden origin.
• CULTIVATION Tolerates dappled shade, but flowers and fruits best in sun.
• PROPAGATION By budding in summer or by grafting in winter.

HEIGHT
10m (30ft)

SPREAD
7m (22ft)

Anacardiaceae	

RHUS TRICHOCARPA

Habit Open, broadly spreading. **Flowers** Tiny, in conical panicles in summer. Yellowish.
Fruits Small, pendent, bristly, in clusters on female plants. Yellow-brown. **Leaves** Deciduous, long, up to 17 pointed, downy leaflets. Reddish, later matt green, then orange-red in autumn.
• NATIVE HABITAT China, Japan, and Korea.
• CULTIVATION Grow in any fertile soil.
• PROPAGATION By semi-ripe cuttings in summer, by seed in autumn or by root cuttings in winter.
• OTHER NAMES *Toxicodendron succedaneum.*

HEIGHT
7m (22ft)

SPREAD
7m (22ft)

Rosaceae	

MALUS PRUNIFOLIA

Habit Broadly spreading, with a neatly domed head. *Flowers* Fragrant, large, in large clusters in mid-spring. White, opening from soft pink buds.
Fruits Small, rounded to egg-shaped crab apples, in large, long-persistent clusters. Bright red.
Leaves Deciduous, elliptic, toothed. Dark green.
• NATIVE HABITAT Probably of garden origin.
• CULTIVATION Tolerates dappled shade, but flowers and fruits best in sun.
• PROPAGATION By budding in summer or by grafting in winter.

HEIGHT
9m (28ft)

SPREAD
8m (25ft)

Aceraceae	AMUR MAPLE

ACER GINNALA

Habit Broadly spreading. *Flowers* Small, creamy-white, in erect clusters in late spring.
Fruits 2 seeds, fused together, each with a wing.
Leaves Deciduous, small, 3-lobed, toothed. Glossy dark green above, then red in early autumn.
• NATIVE HABITAT Thickets in mountain valleys of China and Japan.
• CULTIVATION Tolerates semi-shade, but colours best in sun. Grow in any fertile soil.
• PROPAGATION By seed in autumn.
• OTHER NAMES *A. tataricum* subsp. *ginnala.*

HEIGHT
9m (28ft)

SPREAD
9m (28ft)

Rosaceae	

MALUS × *ZUMI* 'Calocarpa'

Habit Spreading, rounded to pyramidal.
Flowers Small, cup-shaped, in late spring. White, pink in bud. *Fruits* Small, cherry-like, long-lasting and in profusion. Red. *Leaves* Deciduous, long-tapered, sometimes deeply lobed. Dark green.
• NATIVE HABITAT Garden origin.
• CULTIVATION Tolerates dappled shade, but flowers and fruits best in sun. Grow in any but waterlogged soil.
• PROPAGATION By budding in summer or by grafting in winter.

HEIGHT
9m (28ft)

SPREAD
7m (22ft)

Aceraceae	THREE-FLOWERED MAPLE

ACER TRIFLORUM

Habit Slow-growing, broadly spreading, with an irregularly rounded crown. **Flowers** Tiny, in pendent clusters of 3, in spring, with the new leaves. Yellow. **Fruits** 2 seeds, fused together, enclosed in small, downward-pointing wings. Yellow-green. **Leaves** Deciduous, with 3 leaflets. Pale green, turning brilliant orange and crimson in autumn. **Bark** Peeling, in vertical strips. Pale brown to grey-brown.
• NATIVE HABITAT Mountain woods of N.E. China and Korea.

• CULTIVATION Tolerates semi-shade, but colours best in sun. This is one of the most reliable of species for good autumn colour. Grow in any fertile, moisture-retentive soil. It makes an attractive and elegant specimen tree for medium-sized gardens.
• PROPAGATION By seed in autumn.

☼ ◊
❀ ❀ ❀

HEIGHT
9m (28ft)

SPREAD
9m (28ft)

Cornaceae	

CORNUS 'Eddie's White Wonder' ♔

Habit Dense, upright, broadly conical.
Flowers Tiny, in dense clusters in late spring, with the young leaves. Green, surrounded by 4 large, white, pink-tinted bracts, **Leaves** Deciduous, broadly elliptic, pointed, slightly glossy. Dark green, turning brilliant orange, red, and purple in autumn.
• NATIVE HABITAT Garden origin.
• CULTIVATION Unsuitable for shallow, chalky soils. Tolerates dappled shade. Grow in deep, fertile, moisture-retentive soil.
• PROPAGATION By softwood cuttings in summer.

☼ ◌
✿ ✿ ✿

HEIGHT
6m (20ft)

SPREAD
5m (15ft)

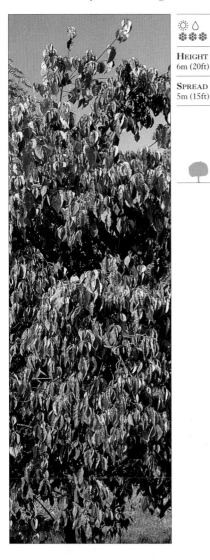

Rosaceae	

MALUS 'Marshall Oyama'

Habit Upright, broadly conical. **Flowers** Large, cup-shaped, in late spring. White, flushed pink.
Fruits Large, rounded crab apples, in profusion. Crimson and yellow. **Leaves** Deciduous, broadly oval, pointed at the tip. Dark green.
• NATIVE HABITAT Garden origin.
• CULTIVATION Tolerates dappled shade, but flowers and fruits best in sun. Grow in any but waterlogged soil.
• PROPAGATION By budding in summer or by grafting in winter.

☼ ◌
✿ ✿ ✿

HEIGHT
9m (28ft)

SPREAD
5m (15ft)

Rosaceae	

CRATAEGUS PERSIMILIS 'Prunifolia' ♔

Habit Broadly spreading, thorny. **Flowers** 5-petals, to 1.5cm (⅝in) across, in rounded clusters in early summer. White. **Fruits** Rounded haws. Bright red.
Leaves Deciduous, broadly elliptic, sharply toothed. Glossy dark green, turning gold, red, and orange in autumn.
• NATIVE HABITAT Garden origin.
• CULTIVATION Tolerant of urban pollution, coastal exposure, and any but waterlogged soil.
• PROPAGATION By budding in late summer.
• OTHER NAMES *C. x prunifolia.*

☼ ◌
✿ ✿ ✿

HEIGHT
6m (20ft)

SPREAD
6m (20ft)

Rosaceae	

MALUS YUNNANENSIS var. *VEITCHII*

Habit Broadly columnar. *Flowers* Small, in flattened heads in late spring. White. *Fruits* Small, hard, round, in clusters in autumn. Red.
Leaves Deciduous, lobed, heart-shaped at the base. Matt green above, grey-downy beneath, turning crimson and orange in autumn.
• NATIVE HABITAT Mountain woods of C. China.
• CULTIVATION Tolerates dappled shade. Grow in any but waterlogged soil.
• PROPAGATION By budding in late summer or by grafting in winter. Seed may not come true.

☼ ◊
❀ ❀ ❀

HEIGHT
8m (25ft)

SPREAD
6m (20ft)

Apocynaceae	FRANGIPANI

PLUMERIA RUBRA

Habit Wide-spreading, sparingly branched.
Flowers Intensely fragrant, large, salver-shaped in summer to autumn. Shades of yellow, orange, pink, red, or white. *Leaves* Deciduous, broadly elliptic or oblong to lance-shaped. Mid-green.
• NATIVE HABITAT Mexico to Panama.
• CULTIVATION Best grown in a conservatory in cooler climates. Grow in very free-draining soil or compost. Keep dry in winter when leafless.
• PROPAGATION By seed or leafless stem-tip cuttings in late spring.

☼ ◊

Min. 10°C
(50°F)

HEIGHT
5m (15ft)

SPREAD
7m (22ft)

Rosaceae	

MALUS 'Professor Sprenger'

Habit Dense, round-headed. *Flowers* Small, cup-shaped, in great profusion from mid- to late spring. White, pink in bud. *Fruits* Small, rounded crab apples. Amber-gold. *Leaves* Deciduous, broadly oval. Dark green, turning yellow in autumn.
• NATIVE HABITAT Garden origin.
• CULTIVATION Tolerates dappled shade, but flowers and fruits best in sun. Grow in any but waterlogged soil.
• PROPAGATION By budding in summer or by grafting in winter.

☼ ◊
❀ ❀ ❀

HEIGHT
7m (22ft)

SPREAD
7m (22ft)

Bignoniaceae	YELLOW BELLS

TECOMA STANS

Habit Upright, rounded, sometimes shrubby.
Flowers Funnel-shaped, in clusters, from spring to autumn. Bright yellow. *Leaves* Evergreen, with 5–13 lance-shaped leaflets. Dark green.
• NATIVE HABITAT Mexico, N. Venezuela, and Argentina.
• CULTIVATION Best grown in a conservatory in cooler climates. Grow in soil or compost.
• PROPAGATION By seed in spring or by semi-ripe cuttings in summer.
• OTHER NAMES *Bignonia stans, Stenolobium stans.*

☼ ◊

Min. 13°C
(55°F)

HEIGHT
6m (20ft)

SPREAD
3m (10ft)

Simaroubaceae	QUASSIA		Leguminosae	

PICRASMA AILANTHOIDES

Habit Spreading. **Flowers** Insignificant.
Fruits Small, pea-like, in early summer. Red.
Leaves Deciduous, with 9–13 sharply toothed
leaflets. Glossy bright green, turning brilliant
yellow, orange, and red in autumn.
• NATIVE HABITAT Japan, N. China, and Korea.
• CULTIVATION Tolerates semi-shade and lime-
rich soil, but grows best in fertile, moisture-
retentive, neutral to acid, loamy soils.
• PROPAGATION By seed in autumn.
• OTHER NAMES P. quassioides.

BAUHINIA VARIEGATA 'Candida'

Habit Dense, rounded, spreading with age.
Flowers Fragrant, large, in short, few-flowered
racemes from winter to early summer. Pure white.
Leaves Deciduous, broadly oval, deeply notched.
Dark green.
• NATIVE HABITAT Garden origin.
• CULTIVATION Best grown in a conservatory in
cooler climates. Grow in fertile soil or compost.
Water freely in growth, then moderately.
• PROPAGATION By leafless cuttings of semi-ripe
wood in summer.

HEIGHT 10m (30ft)
SPREAD 7m (22ft)

Min. 10–13°C (50–55°F)
HEIGHT 8m (25ft)
SPREAD 10m (30ft)

Rosaceae			Leguminosae	ORCHID TREE, MOUNTAIN EBONY

MALUS 'Golden Hornet'

Habit Broadly pyramidal. **Flowers** Large, cup-
shaped, in profusion in late spring. White, flushed
pink, deep pink in bud. **Fruits** Small, rounded
crab apples. Golden-yellow. **Leaves** Deciduous,
broadly oval. Dark green, then yellow in autumn.
• NATIVE HABITAT Garden origin.
• CULTIVATION Tolerates dappled shade, but
flowers and fruits best in sun. Grow in any but
waterlogged soil.
• PROPAGATION By budding in summer or by
grafting in winter.

BAUHINIA VARIEGATA

Habit Dense, rounded, spreading with age.
Flowers Fragrant, large, in short, few-flowered
racemes from winter to early summer. Magenta to
lavender. **Leaves** Deciduous, broadly oval, deeply
notched. Dark green.
• NATIVE HABITAT Tropical mountain forests of
E. Asia.
• CULTIVATION Best grown in a conservatory in
cooler climates. Water freely when in growth.
• PROPAGATION By seed in spring.
• OTHER NAMES B. purpurea of gardens.

HEIGHT 10m (30ft)
SPREAD 8m (25ft)

Min. 10–13°C (50–55°F)
HEIGHT 8m (25ft)
SPREAD 10m (30ft)

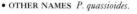

Bignoniaceae	GOLDEN TRUMPET TREE

TABEBUIA CHRYSOTRICHA

Habit Round-headed. *Flowers* Large, trumpet-shaped, in late winter or early spring. Rich yellow. *Leaves* Deciduous, divided into 3–5 oblong-elliptic leaflets. Dark green.
• NATIVE HABITAT Colombia and Brazil.
• CULTIVATION Grow in fertile, free-draining soil or compost. Water moderately when in growth, but very sparingly in winter. Prune when young, but only to shape. Does best grown in the conservatory.
• PROPAGATION By seed or air-layering in spring or by semi-ripe cuttings in summer.

Min.
10–15°C
(50–59°F)

HEIGHT
10m (30ft)

SPREAD
8m (25ft)

Pittosporaceae	VARIEGATED KARO

PITTOSPORUM CRASSIFOLIUM 'Variegatum'

Habit Bushy-headed, dense. *Flowers* Tiny, fragrant, in clusters in spring. Deep red-purple. *Leaves* Evergreen, oval-elliptic. Grey-green, irregularly edged creamy-white.
• NATIVE HABITAT Species occurs in lowland and coastal forest of New Zealand. Garden origin.
• CULTIVATION Thrives in mild, coastal areas. In cold areas, site against a south- or west-facing wall. Protect from cold winds. Will not survive long frosts.
• PROPAGATION By semi-ripe cuttings in summer.

HEIGHT
8m (25ft)

SPREAD
5m (15ft)

Pittosporaceae	

PITTOSPORUM EUGENIOIDES 'Variegatum'

Habit Bushy, columnar, dense. *Flowers* Honey-scented, tiny, star-shaped, in clusters in spring. Pale yellow. *Leaves* Evergreen, narrowly oval, wavy-edged. Glossy dark green, with creamy-white edges.
• NATIVE HABITAT Species occurs in lowland and coastal forests of New Zealand. Garden origin.
• CULTIVATION Thrives in mild areas, especially on the coast. In cold areas, site against a south- or west-facing wall. Protect from cold winds.
• PROPAGATION By semi-ripe cuttings in summer.

HEIGHT
5m (15ft)

SPREAD
3m (10ft)

Aceraceae	

ACER LAXIFLORUM

Habit Spreading. **Flowers** Small, in clusters in spring. Yellow-green. **Fruits** 2 seeds, fused together, each with a pale red wing.
Leaves Deciduous, pointed, shallowly lobed, red-stalked. Dark green, turning orange in autumn.
Bark Streaked white and pale green.
• NATIVE HABITAT Mountain woods in W. China.
• CULTIVATION Dislikes lime-rich soils. Grow in fertile, moisture-retentive, neutral to acid soil.
• PROPAGATION By seed in autumn.
• OTHER NAMES *A. pectinatum* subsp. *laxiflorum.*

☼ ◊
❀ ❀ ❀

HEIGHT
10m (30ft)

SPREAD
10m (30ft)

Agavaceae (Dracaenaceae)	

DRACAENA CINCTA 'Tricolor'

Habit Slow-growing, upright. **Leaves** Evergreen, narrow, strap-shaped. Rich green, striped cream and prominently margined with red.
• NATIVE HABITAT Garden origin.
• CULTIVATION Tolerates partial shade. Grow in well-drained soil or compost. Water moderately when in growth, otherwise sparingly. A beautiful specimen for the home or conservatory.
• PROPAGATION By air-layering in spring or by stem-tip cuttings in summer.
• OTHER NAMES *D. marginata* 'Tricolor'.

☼ ◊

Min. 13°C
(55°F)

HEIGHT
To 3m
(10ft)

SPREAD
1–2m
(3–6ft)

Proteaceae	

GREVILLEA BANKSII

Habit Rounded, loosely branched.
Flowers Tubular, with protruding, recurved styles, in dense racemes, at intervals from early spring to late summer. Crimson. **Leaves** Evergreen, divided into 5–11 slender leaflets. Dark green, silky beneath.
• NATIVE HABITAT E. Australia.
• CULTIVATION Suitable for growing in a conservatory. Grow in neutral to acid soil or compost. Needs protection in hard winters or exposed areas.
• PROPAGATION By seed in spring or by semi-ripe cuttings in summer.

☼ ◊

Min. 7°C
(45°F)

HEIGHT
5m (15ft)

SPREAD
3m (10ft)

Agavaceae	

CORDYLINE AUSTRALIS 'Atropurpurea'

Habit Slow-growing, upright, sparsely branched.
Flowers Scented, small, in sprays in summer. White. **Fruits** Small, round berries in autumn. White. **Leaves** Evergreen, long, linear, arching, in rosettes at stem tips. Purplish-green.
• NATIVE HABITAT Garden origin.
• CULTIVATION Suitable for growing in a conservatory. Grow in well-drained soil or compost. Needs protection in hard winters or exposed areas.
• PROPAGATION By suckers in spring or by stem cuttings in summer.

☼ ◊

Min. 3°C
(37°F)

HEIGHT
To 10m
(30ft)

SPREAD
8m (25ft)

HOLLIES

Hollies belong to the genus *Ilex* and are evergreen or deciduous trees and shrubs that naturally occur in woodland, forest, and hedgerow, in both temperate and tropical regions of the world.

Much valued for its glossy, light-reflecting qualities, holly foliage varies considerably, from smooth and undulating to densely spiny, and from shiny and glossy to a flat, matt texture. Leaf colours range from rich, deep greens to creamy, golden, or silvery-grey variegation.

Hollies are also grown for their mainly spherical berries, which range in colour from red to yellow to orange and black in autumn and follow the insignificant flowers of spring. Most hollies are unisexual (bear flowers of only one sex), so to ensure a good crop of fruits on female plants, males must also be grown. Many hollies make handsome specimen plants, and their stems may be used for floral arrangements.

Most are tolerant of urban pollution and coastal conditions, while the tallest and most vigorous cultivars of *Ilex aquifolium* and *I.* x *altaclerensis* make fine, wind-resistant hedging. Hollies are usually easy to grow in any moderately fertile, well-drained soil, in sun or shade; however, they resent transplanting. Deciduous species and variegated cultivars will do best in sun or semi-shade. Some deciduous varieties of holly shed large numbers of hard, spiny leaves that may present a threat to playing children, so care should be taken when siting the holly tree. Hollies respond well to hard pruning; prune in late spring. Propagate holly species by seed in spring or by taking semi-ripe cuttings in late summer or early autumn. Hollies can also be propagated by grafting, although cultivars are more usually grown by cuttings. Watch out for holly leaf miner and holly aphids, and treat as necessary.

I. MACROCARPA
Habit Upright, spreading, with spur-like branches. **Fruits** Very large, rounded, cherry-like berries. Black. **Leaves** Deciduous, oval-elliptic, saw-toothed, to 11cm (4in) long. Mid-green.
• CULTIVATION Needs a warm, sheltered site.
• HEIGHT 10m (30ft).
• SPREAD 6m (20ft).

I. macrocarpa

☼ ◊ ❋❋

I. OPACA
Habit Upright.
Fruits Rounded berries. Crimson, orange, or yellow. **Leaves** Oblong to elliptic, spiny or spineless, leathery. Matt green above, yellow-green beneath.
• CULTIVATION Does not thrive in chalky soils. Prefers a warmer climate.
• HEIGHT 14m (46ft).
• SPREAD 10m (30ft).

I. opaca
American holly

☼ ◊ ❋❋❋

I. x *ALTACLERENSIS*
'Belgica'
Habit Dense, upright, free-fruiting.
Fruits Large, rounded, berries. Orange-red.
Leaves Lance-shaped to oblong, spiny or spineless. Glossy mid-green. **Stems** Young growth green to yellow-green.
• HEIGHT 12m (40ft).
• SPREAD 5m (15ft).

I. x *altaclerensis*
'Belgica'
FEMALE

☼ ◊ ❋❋

I. x *ALTACLERENSIS*
'N. N. Barnes'
Habit Dense, shrubby.
Fruits Berries. Red.
Leaves Oval, mainly spineless but spine-tipped. Glossy dark green. **Stems** Young stems purple.
• HEIGHT 5.5m (18ft).
• SPREAD 4m (12ft).

I. x *altaclerensis*
'N. N. Barnes'
FEMALE

☼ ◊ ❋❋

I. x *ALTACLERENSIS* 'Balearica'

Habit Vigorous, upright, conical when young. Free-fruiting.
Fruits Large, round, berries. Bright red.
Leaves Large, broadly oval, spiny or spineless. Glossy dark green.
• HEIGHT 12m (40ft).
• SPREAD 5m (15ft).

I. x *altaclerensis* 'Balearica'
FEMALE

☼ ◊ ❀ ❀

I. x *ALTACLERENSIS* 'Camelliifolia'

Habit Pyramidal. Free-fruiting. An excellent specimen tree.
Fruits Large berries. Scarlet. *Leaves* Large, oblong, mainly spineless. Glossy dark green. Red-purple when young.
Stems Young stems purple.
• HEIGHT 14m (46ft).
• SPREAD 3m (10ft).

I. x *altaclerensis* 'Camelliifolia'
FEMALE

☼ ◊ ❀ ❀

I. AQUIFOLIUM 'Pyramidalis'

Habit Conical, dense, broadening with age. Free-fruiting.
Fruits Round, self-fertile berries. Scarlet.
Leaves Narrowly elliptic, slightly spiny. Glossy mid-green.
Stems Young stems green.
• HEIGHT 6m (20ft).
• SPREAD 5m (15ft).

I. aquifolium 'Pyramidalis'
FEMALE

☼ ◊ ❀ ❀ ❀

I. AQUIFOLIUM 'Scotica'

Habit Compact, stiffly upright. *Fruits* Round berries. Red.
Leaves Oval, thick, leathery, usually spineless, slightly undulated. Very dark green.
• HEIGHT 5m (15ft).
• SPREAD 3m (10ft).

I. aquifolium 'Scotica'
FEMALE

☼ ◊ ❀ ❀ ❀

I. AQUIFOLIUM

Habit Upright, much-branched. Often shrubby and multi-stemmed.
Fruits Globose berries. Red. *Leaves* Variable, elliptic or oval, wavy-margined or spiny. Glossy dark green.
• CULTIVATION Tolerates industrial pollution and coastal conditions. Excellent for hedging.
• HEIGHT Up to 18m (60ft).
• SPREAD 6m (20ft).

I. aquifolium
Common holly, English holly

☼ ◊ ❀ ❀ ❀

I. AQUIFOLIUM 'Silver Milkmaid'

Habit Dense, shrubby. Free-fruiting.
Fruits Round berries. Scarlet. *Leaves* Elliptic, wavy-edged, very spiny. Bright green, centrally blotched creamy-white. Shrimp pink when young.
• CULTIVATION Tends to revert. Cut out shoots that are green only.
• HEIGHT 5.5m (18ft).
• SPREAD 4m (12ft).

I. aquifolium 'Silver Milkmaid'
FEMALE

☼ ◊ ❀ ❀ ❀

I. AQUIFOLIUM 'Argentea Marginata Pendula'
Habit Compact, domed, weeping. **Fruits** Round berries. Red.
Leaves Elliptic, spiny. Mottled grey-green, broadly margined creamy-white. Pink when young. **Stems** Young stems purple.
• HEIGHT 6m (20ft).
• SPREAD 5m (15ft).

I. aquifolium 'Argentea Marginata Pendula'
Perry's weeping silver
FEMALE
☼ ◊ ❄❄❄

I. AQUIFOLIUM 'Argentea Marginata'
Habit Columnar. Free-fruiting. **Fruits** Round berries. Red.
Leaves Broadly oval, spiny. Green, broadly margined creamy-white. Shrimp-pink when young. **Stems** Young stems green, streaked cream.
• HEIGHT 14m (46ft).
• SPREAD 5m (15ft).

I. aquifolium 'Argentea Marginata'
Silver-margined holly
FEMALE
☼ ◊ ❄❄❄

I. × ALTACLERENSIS 'Lawsoniana'
Habit Dense, bushy. **Fruits** Not freely produced. **Leaves** Large, oblong to oval, usually spineless. Bright green, irregularly splashed with gold; paler green in the centre.
• CULTIVATION Tends to revert. Cut out shoots that are green only.
• HEIGHT 6m (20ft).
• SPREAD 5m (15ft).

I. × altaclerensis 'Lawsoniana'
FEMALE
☼ ◊ ❄❄

I. AQUIFOLIUM 'Silver Queen'
Habit Dense, shrubby. **Leaves** Elliptic, spiny. Very dark green, broadly margined cream. Shrimp-pink when young. **Stems** Young shoots very dark purple.
• OTHER NAMES
I. aquifolium 'Argentea Regina'.
• HEIGHT 5m (15ft).
• SPREAD 4m (12ft).

I. aquifolium 'Silver Queen'
MALE
☼ ◊ ❄❄❄

I. AQUIFOLIUM 'Elegantissima'
Habit Compact, dense, shrubby. **Leaves** Small, oval, wavy-margined, spiny. Bright green, margined, and faintly marbled creamy-white. Pink when young. **Stems** Young stems green, streaked yellow.
• HEIGHT To 6m (20ft).
• SPREAD 5m (15ft).

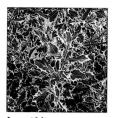

I. aquifolium 'Elegantissima'
MALE
☼ ◊ ❄❄❄

I. × ALTACLERENSIS 'Belgica Aurea'
Habit Dense, upright. **Fruits** Berries. Red.
Leaves Large, lance-shaped, slightly spiny or spineless. Dark green, mottled grey-green, and irregularly margined yellow.
• OTHER NAMES *I. × altaclerensis* 'Silver Sentinel', *I. perado* 'Aurea'.
• HEIGHT 8m (25ft).
• SPREAD 3m (10ft).

I. × altaclerensis 'Belgica Aurea'
FEMALE
☼ ◊ ❄❄

I. AQUIFOLIUM 'Madame Briot'
Habit Vigorous, bushy. **Fruits** Round berries. Bright scarlet.
Leaves Large, broadly oval, spiny. Dark green, mottled and margined golden-yellow.
Stems Young stems purplish.
• HEIGHT 10m (30ft).
• SPREAD 6m (20ft).

I. aquifolium 'Madame Briot'
FEMALE
☼ ◊ ❄❄❄

I. AQUIFOLIUM 'Aurifodina'

Habit Erect, dense, shrubby. Free-fruiting. *Fruits* Round berries. Deep scarlet. *Leaves* Elliptic, spiny. Olive green, golden margins tawny-yellow in winter. *Stems* Young stems purplish.
• OTHER NAMES *I. aquifolium* 'Muricata'.
• HEIGHT 6m (20ft).
• SPREAD 3m (10ft).

I. aquifolium 'Aurifodina'
FEMALE

☼ ◊ ❀ ❀ ❀

I. x *ALTACLERENSIS* 'Camelliifolia Variegata'

Habit Slow-growing, pyramidal. *Fruits* Rarely produced. *Leaves* Large, oblong. Glossy dark green, marbled pale green, broadly margined golden-yellow.
• HEIGHT 5m (15ft).
• SPREAD 3m (10ft).

I. x *altaclerensis* 'Camelliifolia Variegata'
FEMALE

☼ ◊ ❀ ❀

I. AQUIFOLIUM 'Pyramidalis Aurea Marginata'

Habit Vigorous, upright, pyramidal. Free-fruiting. *Fruits* Round berries. Red. *Leaves* Narrowly elliptic, spiny on upper half. Glossy mid-green, irregularly margined golden-yellow. *Stems* Young stems green.
• HEIGHT 6m (20ft).
• SPREAD 5m (15ft).

I. aquifolium 'Pyramidalis Aurea Marginata'
FEMALE

☼ ◊ ❀ ❀ ❀

I. AQUIFOLIUM 'Ovata Aurea'

Habit Dense, shrubby. One of the most brightly variegated cultivars. *Leaves* Oval, thick, regularly short-spined. Dark green, margined bright golden yellow. *Stems* Young stems deep purple.
• HEIGHT 5m (15ft).
• SPREAD 4m (12ft).

I. aquifolium 'Ovata Aurea'
MALE

☼ ◊ ❀ ❀ ❀

I. AQUIFOLIUM 'Crispa Aurea Picta'

Habit Upright, open. *Leaves* Narrowly oval, twisted, sparsely spiny. Very dark green, with central splash of pale green and yellow.
• CULTIVATION Tends to revert.
• HEIGHT 10m (30ft).
• SPREAD 6m (20ft).

I. aquifolium 'Crispa Aurea Picta'
MALE

☼ ◊ ❀ ❀ ❀

I. PURPUREA

Habit Upright. *Flowers* Small. Red or lavender. *Fruits* Oval. Scarlet. *Leaves* Oblong-elliptic, tapered, rounded teeth. Dark green. Bright pink when young.
• CULTIVATION Tender. Needs protection as may defoliate in harsh winters.
• OTHER NAMES *I. chinensis*.
• HEIGHT 3–5m (10–15ft).
• SPREAD 3–5m (10–15ft).

I. purpurea

☼ ◊ ❀

I. AQUIFOLIUM 'Watereriana'

Habit Slow-growing, dense, compact. An excellent specimen plant. *Leaves* Oval, spiny or almost spineless. Grey-green, mottled, and irregularly and broadly margined golden-yellow. *Stems* Young stems green, streaked yellow.
• HEIGHT 5m (15ft).
• SPREAD 5m (15ft).

I. aquifolium 'Watereriana'
Waterer's gold holly
MALE
☼ ◊ ❀ ❀ ❀

I. PEDUNCULOSA

Habit Upright, often shrubby. *Fruits* Rounded, on very long stalks. Bright red. *Leaves* Oval, pointed, spineless, wavy-edged. Glossy dark green.
• CULTIVATION Unsuitable for chalky soils.
• HEIGHT 10m (30ft).
• SPREAD 6m (20ft).

I. pedunculosa

☼ ◊ ❀ ❀ ❀

Proteaceae	SILVER TREE

LEUCADENDRON ARGENTEUM

Habit Conical to columnar, spreading with age.
Flowers Individually tiny, in spherical heads,
surrounded by broadly ovate, silvery, shining bracts,
from autumn to winter. **Leaves** Evergreen, lance-
shaped, clothed in long, silky, white hairs.
• NATIVE HABITAT The Cape, South Africa.
• CULTIVATION Grow in a mix of peat and sand
that is low in phosphates and nitrogen. Water
moderately when in growth, otherwise sparingly.
Makes a handsome plant for home or conservatory.
• PROPAGATION By seed in spring.

☼ ◊

Min. 7°C
(45°F)

HEIGHT
9m (28ft)

SPREAD
2m (6ft)

Agavaceae (Dracaenaceae)	DRAGON TREE

DRACAENA DRACO

Habit Slow-growing, upright, with a wide-branching
head when mature. **Leaves** Evergreen, narrowly
lance-shaped, stiff. Grey-green or blue-green.
• NATIVE HABITAT Canary Islands.
• CULTIVATION Tolerates partial shade. Grow in
well-drained soil or compost. Water moderately
when in growth, otherwise sparingly. Leggy plants
may be cut back almost to soil level in spring.
Makes a handsome plant for home or conservatory.
• PROPAGATION By air-layering in spring or by
stem-tip cuttings in summer.

☼ ◊

Min. 13°C
(55°F)

HEIGHT
To 8m
(25ft)

SPREAD
8m (25ft)

Myrtaceae	SILVER DOLLAR GUM, SPINNING GUM

EUCALYPTUS PERRINIANA

Habit Open, broadly spreading. **Flowers** Small,
in clusters in the leaf axils in late summer. White.
Leaves Evergreen. Juvenile: semi-circular, clasping
each other across the stem, blue-grey. Adult: lance-
shaped, purple, turning deep blue-green.
Bark Peeling. Grey and brown.
• NATIVE HABITAT In moist soils in the
mountains of S.E. Australia and Tasmania.
• CULTIVATION Grow in fertile, well-drained soil
and provide shelter from cold winds.
• PROPAGATION By seed in spring or autumn.

☼ ◊
❀ ❀

HEIGHT
7m (22ft)

SPREAD
5m (15ft)

Palmae	JELLY PALM, YATAY PALM

BUTIA CAPITATA

Habit Slow-growing, unbranched, with a
spreading crown. **Leaves** Evergreen, feather-
shaped, to 2m (6ft) or more in length, strongly
arching, with many leathery leaflets. Blue-green.
• NATIVE HABITAT Woodlands and grasslands of
Argentina.
• CULTIVATION Tolerates partial shade. Grow in
any fertile, well-drained soil or compost. Water
moderately when in growth, less in winter.
• PROPAGATION By seed in spring.
• OTHER NAMES *Cocos capitata*.

☼ ◊

Min. 5°C
(41°F)

HEIGHT
To 6m
(20ft)

SPREAD
3m (10ft)

Araliaceae	PUKA

MERYTA SINCLAIRII

Habit Round-headed, multi-stemmed.
Flowers Small, in dense umbels, sporadically from spring to autumn. Greenish-white. *Fruits* Small, rounded, berry-like. Black. *Leaves* Evergreen, oblong to broadly oval, leathery. Glossy dark green.
• NATIVE HABITAT New Zealand.
• CULTIVATION Grow in the home or conservatory in cooler climates. Grow in humus-rich soil or compost. Water freely in growth, then moderately.
• PROPAGATION By semi-ripe cuttings in summer, or by seed as soon as ripe in autumn.

☼ ◦

Min. 5°C
(41°F)

HEIGHT
To 8m
(25ft)

SPREAD
6m (20ft)

Fagaceae	

LITHOCARPUS HENRYI

Habit Broadly conical. *Flowers* Catkins: slender, upright, in late summer. Creamy-white.
Fruits Acorns, rounded, to 2cm (¾in) long, enclosed in a shallow cup. *Leaves* Evergreen, elliptic to lance-shaped, slender-pointed. Glossy pale green, becoming darker with age.
• NATIVE HABITAT Mountain woodland in China.
• CULTIVATION Tolerates semi-shade. Grow in deep, fertile, neutral to acid soil. Provide shelter from strong, cold winds.
• PROPAGATION By seed in autumn.

☼ ◦
❀❀

HEIGHT
10m (30ft)

SPREAD
10m (30ft)

Betulaceae	

CARPINUS BETULUS 'Fastigiata'   ♀

Habit Very distinctive, pyramidal – narrowly so when young, later spreading. *Leaves* Deciduous, narrowly oval, pointed at the tip, rounded at the base. Neatly and prominently veined. Bright green on emergence, later dark green, turning orange and gold in autumn.
• NATIVE HABITAT Garden origin.
• CULTIVATION Grow in any fertile soils, including clay and chalky ones. An elegant specimen tree, also well suited to avenue plantings.
• PROPAGATION By budding in late summer.

☼ ◦
❀❀❀

HEIGHT
10m (30ft)

SPREAD
12m (40ft)

Pittosporaceae	

PITTOSPORUM DALLII

Habit Round-headed, dense, sometimes shrubby.
Flowers Small, honey-scented, cup-shaped, in clusters in summer. White. *Leaves* Evergreen, oblong-elliptic, sharply toothed, leathery, carried in clusters at stem tips. Dark green.
• NATIVE HABITAT Mountain forests of the South Island of New Zealand.
• CULTIVATION Thrives in sheltered places, especially near the coast. In cold, frosty areas, site against a south- or west-facing wall.
• PROPAGATION By budding in summer.

☼ ◦
❀❀

HEIGHT
5m (15ft)

SPREAD
6m (20ft)

Palmae	GOLDEN-YELLOW PALM, YELLOW PALM

CHRYSALIDOCARPUS LUTESCENS ♟

Habit Upright, suckering, with thick, cane-like stems. **Leaves** Evergreen, arching, feather-shaped, to 2m (6ft) long, with slender leaflets. Yellow-green.
• NATIVE HABITAT Moist, tropical forests of Madagascar.
• CULTIVATION Best grown in a conservatory in cooler climates. Tolerates partial shade. Water moderately when in growth, otherwise very sparingly.
• PROPAGATION By seed or suckers in spring.
• OTHER NAMES *Areca lutescens*.

☀ ◊

Min.
10–15°C
(50–59°F)

HEIGHT
To 10m
(30ft)

SPREAD
1m (3ft)

Cyatheaceae	ROUGH TREE FERN

CYATHEA AUSTRALIS

Habit Upright, with a light, open crown.
Leaves Evergreen fronds, 2–4m (6–12ft) long, in finely divided leaflets. Light green, bluish beneath.
Bark Trunk almost black.
• NATIVE HABITAT Forests of Australia, Tasmania.
• CULTIVATION Best grown in a conservatory in cooler climates. Grow in humus-rich, moisture-retentive but well-drained soil or compost. Water freely when in growth, otherwise moderately.
• PROPAGATION By spores in spring.
• OTHER NAMES *Alsophila australis*.

☀ ◊

Min. 5°C
(41°F)

HEIGHT
8m (25ft) or
more

SPREAD
4m (12ft) or
more

Agavaceae	ELEPHANT'S FOOT, PONY-TAIL

BEAUCARNEA RECURVATA ♟

Habit Slow-growing, with sparsely branched stems and a flask-shaped trunk.
Leaves Evergreen, to 1m (3ft) long, linear, recurved. Persisting after turning brown.
• NATIVE HABITAT Arid areas of S.E. Mexico.
• CULTIVATION Best grown as a house plant in cooler climates. Tolerates drought. Grow in sharply drained soil or compost.
• PROPAGATION By seed or suckers in spring or by stem-tip cuttings in summer.
• OTHER NAMES *Nolina recurvata, N. tuberculata*.

☀ ◊

Min. 7°C
(45°F)

HEIGHT
To 8m
(25ft)

SPREAD
5m (15ft)

Aceraceae	PAPERBARK MAPLE

ACER GRISEUM ♟

Habit Broadly columnar, later spreading.
Flowers Small, pendent clusters in late spring. Greenish. **Fruits** 2 seeds, fused together, each with a wing. **Leaves** Deciduous, with 3 elliptic leaflets. Dark green, paler beneath, turning orange and red.
Bark Peeling. Chestnut to cinnamon-brown.
• NATIVE HABITAT Mountain woods in C. China.
• CULTIVATION Tolerates dappled shade but colours best in sun. Grow in any fertile, moisture-retentive soil.
• PROPAGATION By seed in autumn.

☀ ◊
❀ ❀ ❀

HEIGHT
10m (30ft)
or more

SPREAD
10m (30ft)

| Pinaceae | BLUE ATLAS CEDAR |

CEDRUS LIBANI subsp. *ATLANTICA* Glauca Group

Habit Broadly conical, flat-topped with age, branches ascending or horizontal. *Fruits* Barrel-shaped cones, upright, to 8cm (3in) long, smooth. Green-purple, turning brown when ripe.
Leaves Needle-like, slender, sharp-pointed, to 2cm (¾in) long, in dense whorls. Silver-blue, especially bright in early summer. *Bark* Fissured into scaly plates. Dark grey.
• NATIVE HABITAT Atlas Mountains, N. Africa.
• CULTIVATION Tolerates dry soils, both acid and alkaline, and cool summers. This conifer thrives in well-drained soil in warm, sunny, sheltered sites. It is widely planted as a specimen, but as it eventually reaches a considerable size, it is best suited to larger gardens.
• PROPAGATION By seed in autumn or spring.
• OTHER NAMES *C. atlantica* f. *glauca*.

HEIGHT
25m (80ft)
or more

SPREAD
10m (30ft)
or more

Pinaceae	

ABIES CONCOLOR 'Argentea'

Habit Upright, conical, with branches in whorls.
Fruits Upright, oblong to ovoid cones. Pale blue-green. **Leaves** Linear, blunt-tipped, uppermost needles upswept. Silver-white above and below.
• NATIVE HABITAT Mountains, W. United States.
• CULTIVATION Grow in moist but freely draining soil. Shelter from drying winds.
• PROPAGATION By grafting in late summer, winter or early spring. Seed sown in autumn may not come true.
• OTHER NAMES *A. concolor* 'Candicans'.

HEIGHT
20m (65ft)
or more

SPREAD
8m (25ft) or
more

Pinaceae	

PINUS × HOLFORDIANA

Habit Open, broadly conical. **Fruits** Large, pendent, slightly curved, resinous cones, to 30cm (12in) long. **Leaves** Needle-like, slender, to 18cm (7in) long, pendent and flexible, in clusters of 5. Glaucous blue-grey to silver-green.
• NATIVE HABITAT Garden origin.
• CULTIVATION Tolerant of dry soils, wind, and coastal conditions. Grow in any well-drained soil.
• PROPAGATION By grafting in late summer, winter or early spring.

HEIGHT
To 25m
(80ft)

SPREAD
5m (15ft)

Cupressaceae	KASHMIR CYPRESS

CUPRESSUS CASHMERIANA ♥

Habit Broadly conical, branch tips weeping, spreading with age. **Fruits** Small, rounded cones, scales with hooked point. Blue-grey, ripening to brown. **Leaves** Aromatic, small, scale-like, carried in flattened, pendent sprays. Blue-green.
• NATIVE HABITAT Probably from the Himalaya.
• CULTIVATION Grow in moist but well-drained soil. Susceptible to wind scorch.
• PROPAGATION By seed in autumn or spring or by cuttings of current year's growth from autumn to spring.

HEIGHT
16m (60ft)

SPREAD
10m (30ft)

Cupressaceae	LEYLAND CYPRESS

× CUPRESSOCYPARIS LEYLANDII

Habit Vigorous, fast-growing, upright, columnar.
Leaves Small, scale-like, in flattened sprays. Dark green or grey-green, paler beneath.
• NATIVE HABITAT Garden origin.
• CULTIVATION Tolerant of a wide range of soils and conditions, including chalky soils and coastal exposure. Good for screens and hedges. Clip in summer. Do not cut back into old growth.
• PROPAGATION By cuttings of the current year's growth from autumn to spring.
• OTHER NAMES *Cupressus × leylandii*.

HEIGHT
To 30m
(100ft)

SPREAD
3m (10ft) or
more

| Pinaceae | MACEDONIAN PINE |

PINUS PEUCE

Habit Upright, slender-pyramidal. *Flowers* Male and female on same plant in separate clusters on the young shoots. Males: yellow; females: red. *Fruits* Cylindrical to conical, drooping cones. Green, turning brown when ripe. Covered in white resin. *Leaves* Stiff, needle-like, to 10cm (4in) long, forward-pointing, in dense clusters of 5. Dark blue-green. *Bark* Fissured and cracked into plates. Purple-brown; young shoots bloomed, green.
• NATIVE HABITAT Mountains of S.E. Europe.
• CULTIVATION Tolerant of a wide range of soils and conditions including coastal exposure. The Macedonian pine maintains its dense, pyramidal outline, with branches reaching to ground level, making it an attractive and reliable species for specimen plantings. It grows consistently well in all sites.
• PROPAGATION By seed in autumn or spring.

HEIGHT
To 30m
(100ft)

SPREAD
10m (30ft)

Cupressaceae	

CHAMAECYPARIS LAWSONIANA 'Intertexta' ♇

Habit Elegant, weeping, columnar with age.
Fruits Round cones, to 8mm (¼in) across, at branch tips, carried in lax, flattened, pendulous sprays.
Leaves Aromatic, very small, scale-like. Grey-green.
• NATIVE HABITAT Garden origin.
• CULTIVATION Tolerant of shade, exposure, urban pollution, and dry, alkaline soils. Grow in moist but well-drained, neutral to acid soils.
• PROPAGATION By heeled greenwood cuttings in late summer or by softwood cuttings in summer.

☀ ◑
❀ ❀ ❀

HEIGHT
25m (80ft)

SPREAD
8m (25ft)

Pinaceae	EASTERN WHITE PINE, WEYMOUTH PINE

PINUS STROBUS

Habit Narrowly conical when young, later open, rounded. *Fruits* Curved, cylindrical, pendent cones, to 15cm (6in) or more in length. *Leaves* Slender, needle-like, to 15cm (6in) long, in clusters of 5. Grey green. *Bark* Smooth, fissured with age. Grey.
• NATIVE HABITAT Low altitude woodlands of E. North America.
• CULTIVATION Tolerant of a wide range of soils and conditions including coastal exposure, but intolerant of urban pollution.
• PROPAGATION By seed in autumn or spring.

☀ ◑
❀ ❀ ❀

HEIGHT
To 50m
(160ft)

SPREAD
10m (30ft)

Pinaceae	BIG-CONE PINE

PINUS COULTERI ♇

Habit Fast-growing, broadly spreading.
Fruits Large cones, broadly ovoid, to 35cm (14in) long, resinous, with hook-spined scales.
Leaves Stiff, needle-like, to 30cm (12in) long. Grey-green, in dense clusters of 3, sparsely set on branches. *Bark* Fissured, plated. Red-brown
• NATIVE HABITAT Rocky Mountains of California.
• CULTIVATION Tolerates most soils including heavy clay and very wet soils.
• PROPAGATION By seed in autumn or spring.

☀ ◑
❀ ❀ ❀

HEIGHT
To 25m
(80ft)

SPREAD
15m (50ft)

Pinaceae	EUROPEAN LARCH

LARIX DECIDUA

Habit Narrowly conical. **Flowers** Male: pendent, red; female: upright, yellow, on same plant in spring. **Fruits** Upright, ovoid cones, to 4cm (1½in) long. Brown. **Leaves** Deciduous, soft, needle-like, to 4cm (1½in) long. Emerald green when young, later bright green, turning clear, russet-gold in autumn. **Bark** Fissured, scaly. Red-brown.
• **NATIVE HABITAT** Mountains of Europe.
• **CULTIVATION** Tolerates both chalky and poor, acid soils.
• **PROPAGATION** By seed in autumn or spring.

This, and other species of larch, are best planted in their final location when young and left undisturbed. *L. decidua* is especially suitable for specimen plantings. It is exceptionally beautiful in spring when its new leaves emerge, and again in autumn, when they turn gold before falling.
• **OTHER NAMES** *L. europaea.*

HEIGHT
40m (130ft)

SPREAD
5–15m
(15–50ft)

Pinaceae	VEITCH FIR

ABIES VEITCHII ♀

Habit Fast-growing, narrowly conical.
Fruits Upright, cylindrical cones, to 7.5cm (3in)
long. Violet-blue, brown when ripe. **Leaves** Linear,
notched at the tip, to 3cm (1¼in) long, forward-
pointing on top of shoot, spreading beneath. Glossy
dark green above, with 2 silver-blue bands below.
Bark Smooth, becoming scaly with age. Grey.
• NATIVE HABITAT Forests and mountains, Japan.
• CULTIVATION Quite tolerant of urban pollution
but does not thrive in shallow soils over chalk.
• PROPAGATION By seed in autumn or spring.

HEIGHT
To 25m
(80ft)

SPREAD
5m (15ft) or
more

Cupressaceae	VEITCH FIR

Cupressaceae	INCENSE CEDAR

CALOCEDRUS DECURRENS ♀

Habit Narrowly columnar, but very variable.
Fruits Oblong cones, with overlapping scales.
Leaves Aromatic, scale-like, sharp-pointed in
flattened sprays. Dark green. **Bark** Scaly. Grey,
red-brown beneath.
• NATIVE HABITAT Mountain forests of W. North
America.
• CULTIVATION Grow in moist, well-drained,
preferably neutral to acid soils.
• PROPAGATION By seed in autumn or spring.
• OTHER NAMES *Libocedrus decurrens.*

HEIGHT
30m (100ft)
or more

SPREAD
4m (12ft) or
more

Cupressaceae (Taxodiaceae)	DAWN REDWOOD

METASEQUOIA GLYPTOSTROBOIDES ♀

Habit Fast-growing, narrowly conical. **Fruits** Small,
rounded cones. Green, turning brown when ripe.
Leaves Deciduous, opposite, linear, soft, flattened.
Bright green, then dark green, turning yellow and
red in autumn. **Bark** Fibrous. Red-brown.
• NATIVE HABITAT Riversides and damp soils in
S.W. China.
• CULTIVATION Tolerant of urban pollution and
chalky and waterlogged soils. Best in moist, well-
drained soils.
• PROPAGATION By seed in autumn or spring.

HEIGHT
To 35m
(120ft)

SPREAD
10m (30ft)

Cupressaceae (Taxodiaceae)	SIERRA REDWOOD, WELLINGTONIA, BIG TREE

SEQUOIADENDRON GIGANTEUM ♀

Habit Fast-growing, conical. **Fruits** Barrel-
shaped cones, to 7.5cm (3in) long. Green, turning
brown when ripe. **Leaves** Tiny, spirally arranged,
scale-like, pointed. Blue-green, with a musty scent
when crushed. **Bark** Spongy, fibrous. Red-brown.
• NATIVE HABITAT Rocky Mountains, California.
• CULTIVATION Tolerant of exposure and almost
any soil, except shallow chalk.
• PROPAGATION By seed in autumn or spring.
• OTHER NAMES *Sequoia wellingtonia, S. gigantea.*

HEIGHT
To 80m
(260ft)

SPREAD
20m (65ft)

| Pinaceae | BLUE DOUGLAS FIR, COLORADO DOUGLAS FIR |

PSEUDOTSUGA MENZIESII var. *GLAUCA*

Habit Fast-growing, conical. **Fruits** Pendent cones to 10cm (4in) long. Red-brown, with distinctive, 3-pronged bracts protruding from between the scales. **Leaves** Aromatic – smelling of turpentine when crushed – linear, blunt-tipped, to 3cm (1¼in) long. Glaucous, blue-green.
Bark Thick, grooved, corky. Grey-brown.
• **NATIVE HABITAT** Evergreen forests in the Rocky Mountains, from Montana to New Mexico.
• **CULTIVATION** Unsuitable for shallow, chalky soils but more lime-tolerant than the species. It is a large, stately tree for large or medium-sized gardens, although it may only reach 25m (80ft) in cultivation. Grow in moist, well-drained soils. The tree's common name commemorates David Douglas, the 19th-century Scottish plant hunter.
• **PROPAGATION** By seed in autumn or spring.
• **OTHER NAMES** *P. glauca.*

HEIGHT
To 60m
(200ft) less
in cult.

SPREAD
15m (50ft)

Pinaceae	CEDAR OF LEBANON

CEDRUS LIBANI

Habit Broadly conical, irregular with age, tiered branches horizontal or slightly ascending. **Fruits** Barrel-shaped cones, upright, to 12cm (5in) long. Purple-green, then brown. **Leaves** Needle-like, slender, sharp-pointed, to 3cm (1¼in) long, in dense whorls. Dark grey-green.
• NATIVE HABITAT Mountain forests of Lebanon and S.E. Turkey.
• CULTIVATION Tolerates dry soils, both acid and alkaline, and cool summers.
• PROPAGATION By seed in autumn or spring.

☼ ◐
❀ ❀ ❀

HEIGHT
To 40m
(130ft)

SPREAD
20m (65ft)
or more

Pinaceae	PONDEROSA PINE, WESTERN YELLOW PINE

PINUS PONDEROSA ♈

Habit Upright, or broadly conical. **Fruits** Ovoid cones, with spine-tipped scales. Purple, turning glossy red-brown when ripe. **Leaves** Stiff, needle-like, to 25cm (10in) long, in clusters of 3, forward-pointing. Dark grey-green. **Bark** Thick, scaly, deeply fissured. Yellow-brown to red.
• NATIVE HABITAT Rocky Mountains, W. North America.
• CULTIVATION Tolerates coastal exposure and most soils, including heavy clay.
• PROPAGATION By seed in autumn or spring.

☼ ◐
❀ ❀ ❀

HEIGHT
To 50m
(160ft)

SPREAD
20m (65ft)

Pinaceae	BHUTAN PINE, HIMALAYAN PINE, BLUE PINE

PINUS WALLICHIANA ♈

Habit Broadly conical. **Fruits** Curved, cylindrical cones, to 30cm (12in) long. Green, turning pale brown when ripe. **Leaves** Slender, needle-like, flexible, and drooping, to 20cm (8in) long, in clusters of 5. Blue-green. **Bark** Smooth, fissured with age. Grey.
• NATIVE HABITAT Mountain forests, Himalaya.
• CULTIVATION Tolerant of a range of soils and exposure, but dislikes shallow, chalky soils.
• PROPAGATION By seed in autumn or spring.
• OTHER NAMES *P. chylla, P. excelsa, P. griffithii.*

☼ ◯
❀ ❀ ❀

HEIGHT
To 40m
(130ft)

SPREAD
15m (50ft)

Pinaceae	BISHOP PINE

PINUS MURICATA ♈

Habit Fast-growing, broadly columnar, flat-topped with age. **Fruits** Ovoid cones, to 8cm (3in) long, persisting on branches. Red-brown. **Leaves** Stiff, needle-like, to 15cm (6in) long, in pairs. Blue- to grey-green. **Bark** Deeply ridged. Purple-brown.
• NATIVE HABITAT Low, coastal hills of California.
• CULTIVATION Tolerant of coastal exposure and poor, sandy soil. Dislikes shallow chalk soils. Grow in any well-drained soil.
• PROPAGATION By seed in autumn or spring.

☼ ◯
❀ ❀ ❀

HEIGHT
To 25m
(80ft)

SPREAD
8m (25ft)

Pinaceae	JEFFREY PINE

PINUS JEFFREYI   ♈

Habit Upright, conical or spire-shaped.
Fruits Conical cones, to 30cm (12in) long, scales with a curved spine. **Leaves** Stiff, needle-like, to 25cm (10in) long, in clusters of 3. Blue-green.
Bark Finely fissured. Black; shoots grey-bloomed.
• NATIVE HABITAT Dry mountain slopes in S.W. United States.
• CULTIVATION Dislikes shallow, chalky soils.
• PROPAGATION By seed in autumn or spring.
• OTHER NAMES *P. ponderosa* var. *jeffreyi*.

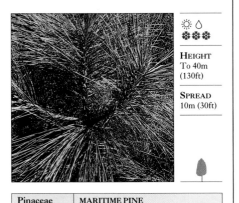

☀ ◊
❀ ❀ ❀

HEIGHT
To 40m
(130ft)

SPREAD
10m (30ft)

Pinaceae	MARITIME PINE

PINUS PINASTER   ♈

Habit Vigorous, with a domed crown.
Fruits Cones, conical, to 20cm (8in) long, in whorls. Glossy brown. **Leaves** Stiff, needle-like, to 20cm (8in) long, sharply pointed, in pairs. Dark grey-green. **Bark** Deeply fissured. Purple-brown.
• NATIVE HABITAT Sandy soils of N. Africa and S.W. Europe.
• CULTIVATION Thrives on dry, sandy soils and tolerates coastal exposure in mild areas.
• PROPAGATION By seed in autumn or spring.
• OTHER NAMES *P. maritima*.

☀ ◊
❀ ❀

HEIGHT
To 35m
(120ft)

SPREAD
12m (40ft)

Pinaceae	SERBIAN SPRUCE

PICEA OMORIKA   ♈

Habit Graceful, narrowly conical, spire-shaped, with pendulous branches that arch slightly outwards at the tips. **Fruits** Narrowly ovoid cones. Violet-purple; brown when ripe. **Leaves** Slender, needle-like, to 2cm (¾in) long. Dark green, with blue-white bands beneath. **Bark** Plated. Purple-brown.
• NATIVE HABITAT On limestone rocks alongside the River Drina, Bosnia-Herzegovina.
• CULTIVATION Tolerates urban pollution and almost any soil, including chalky or wet soils.
• PROPAGATION By seed in autumn or spring.

☀ ◊
❀ ❀ ❀

HEIGHT
To 30m
(100ft)

SPREAD
4–5m
(12–15ft)

Araucariaceae	CHILE PINE, MONKEY PUZZLE

ARAUCARIA ARAUCANA

Habit Open, usually symmetrically domed.
Fruits Large, globose. Green, with golden spines, enclosing shining, brown seeds.
Leaves Triangular, rigid, spine-tipped. Dark green scales overlap around the shoot. **Bark** Wrinkled, with persistent branch scars. Dark grey.
• NATIVE HABITAT Mountains of Argentina and Chile.
• CULTIVATION Tolerates coastal exposure. Grow in any fertile, moisture-retentive soil.
• PROPAGATION By seed in autumn or spring.

☀ ◊
❀ ❀ ❀

HEIGHT
25m (80ft)

SPREAD
To 15m
(50ft)

Pinaceae	WESTERN HEMLOCK

TSUGA HETEROPHYLLA ♈

Habit Narrowly conical. *Fruits* Ovoid, pendent cones, to 2cm (¾in) long. *Leaves* Linear, of mixed sizes, to 2cm (¾in) long. Dark green above, with 2 broad, white bands beneath. *Bark* Ridged, flaking. Purple-brown.
• NATIVE HABITAT Mountain forests of W. North America.
• CULTIVATION Tolerates light, sandy soil and clay soil. Withstands clipping. Avoid exposed sites.
• PROPAGATION By seed in autumn or spring.
• OTHER NAMES *T. albertiana.*

☀ ◐
❄ ❄ ❄

HEIGHT
40m (130ft)
or more

SPREAD
12m (40ft)

Cupressaceae (Taxodiaceae)	CALIFORNIA REDWOOD, COAST REDWOOD

SEQUOIA SEMPERVIRENS ♈

Habit Narrowly conical. *Fruits* Barrel-shaped cones, to 3cm (1¼in) long. Red-brown.
Leaves Linear, to 2cm (¾in) long. Dark green above, with 2 white bands beneath. *Bark* Thick, soft, fibrous. Red-brown.
• NATIVE HABITAT Foothills of coastal mountains in S. Oregon and California.
• CULTIVATION Intolerant of urban pollution. Grow in any fertile soil. Performs best in cool, humid areas.
• PROPAGATION By seed in autumn or spring.

☀ ◐
❄ ❄ ❄

HEIGHT
40m (130ft)
or more

SPREAD
8m (25ft) or more

Pinaceae	JAPANESE LARCH

LARIX KAEMPFERI ♈

Habit Broadly conical. *Flowers* Male: yellow, drooping; female: upright, creamy-pink, on same plant in spring. *Fruits* Upright, ovoid cones, to 3cm (1¼in) long. *Leaves* Deciduous, soft, needle-like, to 4cm (1½in) long, in dense whorls. Grey- to blue-green, turning gold in autumn. *Bark* Scaly. Red-brown.
• NATIVE HABITAT Mountains of C. Japan.
• CULTIVATION Tolerates poor and acid soils.
• PROPAGATION By seed in autumn or spring.
• OTHER NAMES *L. leptolepis.*

☀ ◐
❄ ❄ ❄

HEIGHT
30m (100ft)
or more

SPREAD
5–8m (15–25ft) or more

Cupressaceae	EASTERN WHITE CEDAR, AMERICAN ARBOR-VITAE

THUJA OCCIDENTALIS

Habit Narrowly conical. **Fruits** Oblong, upright cones, to 1cm (½in) long. Yellow-green, brown when ripe. **Leaves** Aromatic, very small, scale-like, on flattened shoots, in flat sprays. Dark green above, paler beneath. **Bark** Peeling in strips. Orange-brown.
• NATIVE HABITAT Mountain slopes and swamps of E. North America.
• CULTIVATION Grow in any but waterlogged soil. Tolerates clipping and may be used for hedging. Plant several for hedging at 60cm (20in) apart.

Clip in spring and early autumn. *T. occidentalis* is slower growing as a hedge than the more commonly used leyland cypress (x *Cupressocyparis leylandii*) but is beautifully scented, with a fresh, apple-like smell.
• PROPAGATION By softwood cuttings in summer or by heeled greenwood cuttings in late summer.

HEIGHT
20m (65ft)

SPREAD
5m (15ft)

Ginkgoaceae	GINKGO, MAIDENHAIR TREE

GINKGO BILOBA

Habit Variable: conical when young, later broadly columnar or spreading; often multi-stemmed.
Flowers Seldom borne: female flowers resemble small acorn; males on separate plants.
Fruits Rounded, smooth, plum-like; flesh smells putrid when ripe. **Leaves** Deciduous, fan-shaped, to 12cm (5in) across, deeply notched at the tip. Bright green, turning yellow in autumn. **Bark** Ridged and fissured. Dull grey.
• NATIVE HABITAT Once thought extinct in the wild, but occurs in Guizhou and Zheijiang, S. China.

Fossil evidence indicates that the tree has remained unchanged for some 200 million years.
• CULTIVATION Grow in any well-drained soil with shelter from cold, dry winds.
• PROPAGATION By seed in autumn, by softwood cuttings in summer, or by hardwood cuttings in winter.

HEIGHT
30m (100ft)

SPREAD
12m (40ft)
or more

Pinaceae	AUSTRIAN PINE

PINUS NIGRA subsp. *NIGRA*

Habit Broadly columnar, sometimes multi-stemmed. *Fruits* Ovoid cones, to 8cm (3in) long. Brown. *Leaves* Stiff, needle-like, to 15cm (6in) long, in pairs. Very dark green, in dense tufts. *Bark* Ridged, scaly. Almost black.
• NATIVE HABITAT Foothills and mountains, often on limestone, in C. and S.E. Europe.
• CULTIVATION Very tolerant of exposure and lime-rich or chalky soils.
• PROPAGATION By seed in autumn or spring.
• OTHER NAMES *P. nigra* var. *austriaca.*

HEIGHT
35m (120ft)

SPREAD
12m (40ft)

Pinaceae	MONTEREY PINE

PINUS RADIATA

Habit Fast-growing, broadly conical, domed when mature. *Fruits* Ovoid cones, asymmetrical at base, persistent, remaining tightly closed for many years. Green; brown when ripe. *Leaves* Slender, needle-like, to 15cm (6in) long, in clusters of 3. Bright green. *Bark* Deeply fissured. Dark grey.
• NATIVE HABITAT Dry, coastal hills of California.
• CULTIVATION Tolerant of dry, sandy soils and exposure.
• PROPAGATION By seed in autumn or spring.
• OTHER NAMES *P. insignis.*

HEIGHT
30m (100ft)
or more

SPREAD
10m (30ft)

Pinaceae	GIANT FIR, GRAND FIR

ABIES GRANDIS

Habit Vigorous, narrowly conical. *Fruits* Upright, cylindrical cones, to 10cm (4in) long. Green, turning brown when ripe. *Leaves* Very aromatic, linear, slender, flattened, to 5cm (2in) long, with a notched tip. Bright green, with 2 silver-white bands beneath. *Bark* Smooth, cracking with age. Grey-brown.
• NATIVE HABITAT Evergreen forests in mountain foothills of W. North America.
• CULTIVATION Dislikes chalky and lime-rich soils. Very shade-tolerant once established.
• PROPAGATION By seed in autumn or spring.

HEIGHT
50m (160ft)

SPREAD
6m (20ft)

Pinaceae	NORWAY SPRUCE

PICEA ABIES

Habit Fast-growing, narrowly conical. *Fruits* Curved, cylindrical, pendent cones to 15cm (6in) long. *Leaves* Rigid, slender, needle-like, to 2cm (¾in) long, 4-sided. Dark green. *Bark* Peeling. Red-brown to grey.
• NATIVE HABITAT Damp mountain forests in Europe.
• CULTIVATION Commonly grown as a Christmas tree. Prefers well-drained, acid soils.
• PROPAGATION By seed in autumn or spring.
• OTHER NAMES *P. excelsa.*

HEIGHT
50m (160ft)

SPREAD
5m (15ft)

Pinaceae	BOSNIAN PINE

PINUS HELDREICHII var. *LEUCODERMIS*

Habit Narrowly conical, or ovoid, with ascending branches. *Fruits* Ovoid cones, to 10cm (4in) long. Deep cobalt-blue, turning yellow-brown when ripe. *Leaves* Rigid, needle-like, to 9cm (3½in) long, densely clustered, forward-pointing. Dark green. *Bark* Cracking into shallow plates with maturity. Grey.
• NATIVE HABITAT Limestone mountains in Bosnia-Herzegovina, Albania, and N. Greece.
• CULTIVATION Tolerates chalky or lime-rich soils and dry or acid soils. The Bosnian pine is a distinctive tree, notable for its dark foliage and slender outline, and is easily identified by its cobalt-blue young cones. As a dense, shapely, and attractive conifer, it is well suited to specimen planting.
• PROPAGATION By seed in autumn or spring.
• OTHER NAMES *P. leucodermis*.

HEIGHT
20m (65ft)

SPREAD
3m (10ft)

Cupressaceae	

x *CUPRESSOCYPARIS LEYLANDII* 'Harlequin'

Habit Vigorous, fast-growing, upright, columnar. *Leaves* Small, scale-like, in flattened, plume-like sprays. Dark green or grey-green, paler beneath, with ivory-white patches.
• NATIVE HABITAT Garden origin.
• CULTIVATION Tolerant of a wide range of soils and conditions, including chalky soils and coastal exposure. Good for screens and hedges.
• PROPAGATION By cuttings of the current year's growth from autumn to spring.

☀ ◊
❀ ❀ ❀

HEIGHT
20m (65ft)
or more

SPREAD
3m (10ft) or
more

Cupressaceae	

x *CUPRESSOCYPARIS LEYLANDII* 'Castlewellan'

Habit Vigorous, upright, columnar, slower-growing than the type. *Leaves* Small, scale-like, in flattened sprays. Bright green, tinted bronze-yellow.
• NATIVE HABITAT Garden origin.
• CULTIVATION Tolerant of a wide range of soils and conditions, including chalky soils and coastal exposure. Good for screens and hedges. Clip in summer; do not cut back into old growth.
• PROPAGATION By cuttings of the current year's growth from autumn to spring.

☀ ◊
❀ ❀ ❀

HEIGHT
25m (80ft)
or more

SPREAD
3m (10ft) or
more

Pinaceae	

PICEA ORIENTALIS 'Skylands'

Habit Slow-growing, dense, conical.
Fruits Cylindrical, slightly curved, pendent cone, to 10cm (4in) long, resinous. Purple, turning brown when ripe. *Flowers* Male flowers brick-red.
Leaves Needle-like, to 8mm (⁵⁄₁₆in) long. Golden-yellow throughout the year.
• NATIVE HABITAT Garden origin.
• CULTIVATION Grow in moist but well-drained neutral to acid soil.
• PROPAGATION By grafting in late summer, winter or early spring.

☀ ◊
❀ ❀ ❀

HEIGHT
25m (80ft)

SPREAD
2–3m
(6–10ft)

Cupressaceae (Taxodiaceae)	BALD CYPRESS, SWAMP CYPRESS

TAXODIUM DISTICHUM ♢

Habit Broadly conical. *Fruits* Small, globose to ovoid cones. Green, turning brown when ripe.
Leaves Deciduous, alternate, linear, soft, flattened. Fresh green, turning gold in late autumn.
Bark Stringy. Pale red-brown.
• NATIVE HABITAT Swamps and stream sides in S.E. United States.
• CULTIVATION Thrives in waterlogged conditions and in deep, moisture-retentive soils.
• PROPAGATION By seed in autumn or spring or by cuttings of current year's growth in late summer.

☀ ●
❀ ❀ ❀

HEIGHT
35m (120ft)

SPREAD
5m (15ft)

Pinaceae	

ABIES PROCERA 'Glauca'

Habit Narrowly conical. **Fruits** Upright,
cylindrical cones, to 25cm (10in) long, with
protruding, down-curved bracts. Purple-brown.
Leaves Linear. Bright silver-blue when young,
turning blue-grey. **Bark** Smooth. Silvery.
• NATIVE HABITAT Mountains, W. United States.
• CULTIVATION Unsuitable for shallow, chalk
soils. Grow in moist but well-drained, neutral to
slightly acid soil.
• PROPAGATION By seed in autumn or spring.
• OTHER NAMES *A. nobilis* 'Glauca'.

☼ ◐
❀ ❀ ❀

HEIGHT
To 40m
(130ft) or
more

SPREAD
5m (15ft)

Pinaceae	ENGELMANN SPRUCE

PICEA ENGELMANNII

Habit Broadly conical. **Fruits** Cylindrical,
slightly curved cones, to 5cm (2in) long. Brown-
purple. **Leaves** Aromatic, soft, flexible, needle-
like, 4-angled. Blue-green. **Bark** Flaking. Orange.
• NATIVE HABITAT Mountains of W. North
America.
• CULTIVATION Tolerates most poor soils, except
shallow soils over chalk.
• PROPAGATION By seed in autumn or spring.

☼ ◐
❀ ❀ ❀

HEIGHT
25m (80ft)
or more

SPREAD
5m (15ft)

Pinaceae	

PICEA PUNGENS 'Koster'   ♈

Habit Upright, conical. **Fruits** Narrowly ovoid,
slightly curved, pendent cones, to 10cm (4in) long.
Pale brown. **Leaves** Rigid, needle-like, spine-
tipped, to 3cm (1¼in) long. Bright silvery-blue,
fading to green with age. **Bark** Scaly. Grey.
• NATIVE HABITAT Species occurs in high
mountains of W. United States. Garden origin.
• CULTIVATION Grows best in fertile, well-
drained, neutral to acid soil.
• PROPAGATION By grafting in late summer,
winter or early spring.

☼ ◐
❀ ❀ ❀

HEIGHT
15m (50ft)
or more

SPREAD
5m (15ft)

Pinaceae	

PICEA GLAUCA 'Coerulea'

Habit Narrowly conical, dense, becoming rounded
with age. **Fruits** Narrowly cylindrical, pendent
cones, to 6cm (2½in) long. Coppery-brown.
Leaves Slender, rigid, needle-like, 4-sided, to
1.5cm (⅝in) long. Blue-green to silver. **Bark** Scaly.
Grey-brown.
• NATIVE HABITAT Species occurs in forests of
Canada and N.E. United States. Garden origin.
• CULTIVATION Tolerates cold, exposed sites.
• PROPAGATION By grafting in late summer,
winter or early spring.

☼ ◐
❀ ❀ ❀

HEIGHT
15m (50ft)
or more

SPREAD
5m (15ft)

Cupressaceae	

CHAMAECYPARIS LAWSONIANA 'Pembury Blue' ♚

Habit Upright, conical. *Fruits* Round cones, to 8mm (¼in) across, at branch tips. *Leaves* Aromatic, very small, scale-like, carried in lax, flattened, pendulous sprays. Bright silver-blue.
• NATIVE HABITAT Garden origin.
• CULTIVATION Tolerant of shade, exposure, urban pollution, and dry, alkaline soils. Grow in moist but well-drained, neutral to acid soils.
• PROPAGATION By softwood cuttings in summer or by heeled greenwood cuttings in late summer.

☀ ◐
❋ ❋ ❋

HEIGHT
15m (50ft)

SPREAD
5m (15ft)

Cupressaceae	ITALIAN CYPRESS

CUPRESSUS SEMPERVIRENS

Habit Narrowly columnar. *Fruits* Ovoid to rounded cones, with overlapping scales.
Leaves Tiny, scale-like, closely pressed to the shoots, in erect, irregular sprays. Very dark grey-green. *Bark* Shallow, spiral ridges. Brown-grey.
• NATIVE HABITAT Rocky areas in the mountains of S.W. Asia and E. Mediterranean.
• CULTIVATION Tolerates lime-rich soils, but best on neutral to slightly acid soils, in a warm, sunny site with shelter from cold, dry winds.
• PROPAGATION By seed in autumn or spring.

☀ ◐
❋ ❋

HEIGHT
15m (50ft)
or more

SPREAD
3m (10ft)

Cupressaceae	

JUNIPERUS CHINENSIS 'Keteleeri'

Habit Slender, narrowly conical to columnar; free-fruiting. *Fruits* Small, berry-like cones, to 8mm (⁵⁄₁₆in) long. Bloomed blue-green.
Leaves Aromatic, tiny, scale-like, closely pressed to the shoot. Bright, shining grey-green.
Bark Peeling. Brown.
• NATIVE HABITAT Species occurs in hills and mountains of China and Japan. Garden origin.
• CULTIVATION Grow in any well-drained soil.
• PROPAGATION By cuttings of the current year's growth from autumn to spring.

☀ ◐
❋ ❋ ❋

HEIGHT
15m (50ft)

SPREAD
4m (12ft)

Pinaceae	BREWER'S SPRUCE

PICEA BREWERIANA ♚

Habit Broadly conical, with spreading branches and pendulous branchlets. *Fruits* Cylindrical, pendent cones, to 12cm (5in) long. Purple; red-brown when ripe. *Leaves* Slender, often curved, flattened, needle-like. Very dark green above, with 2 narrow, white bands beneath. *Bark* Pink-grey, becoming grey-purple and scaly with age.
• NATIVE HABITAT Mountains of Oregon and California.
• CULTIVATION Best grown in slightly acid soil.
• PROPAGATION By seed in autumn or spring.

☀ ◐
❋ ❋ ❋

HEIGHT
12m (40ft)
or more

SPREAD
5m (15ft)

Pinaceae	JAPANESE WHITE PINE

PINUS PARVIFLORA

Habit Slow-growing, broadly columnar to spreading, with level branches. *Flowers* Males and females in separate clusters on the young shoots in early summer. Males: purple-red; females: red. *Fruits* Ovoid cones, to 7cm (3in) long, with leathery scales. Green, turning red-brown when ripe. *Leaves* Slightly twisted, needle-like, to 6cm (2½in) long, in clusters of 5. Blue-green on outer surface, blue-white within. *Bark* Curling scales. Purple-brown.
• NATIVE HABITAT On stony ground in the mountains of Japan.
• CULTIVATION Tolerates coastal exposure and poor soils but dislikes shallow, chalky soils. Makes a picturesque specimen tree, valued for its layered, twisted foliage and much planted in Japanese-style gardens. Suitable for growing as a bonsai.
• PROPAGATION By seed in autumn or spring.

HEIGHT
12m (40ft)
or more

SPREAD
5m (15ft)

Cupressaceae	PATAGONIAN CYPRESS

FITZROYA CUPRESSOIDES

Habit Conical when young; vase-shaped to sprawling with age. **Fruits** Small, rounded cones. Brown. **Leaves** Thick, oblong, in whorls of 3, in pendulous sprays. Blue-green above, white banded beneath. **Bark** Peeling in vertical strips. Red-brown.
• NATIVE HABITAT Mountains of Argentina and Chile.
• CULTIVATION Grow in well-drained, slightly acid soil. Shelter from cold, dry winds.
• PROPAGATION By seed in autumn or spring.
• OTHER NAMES *F. patagonica.*

☼ ◐
❀ ❀ ❀

HEIGHT
12m (40ft)
or more

SPREAD
6m (20ft)

Podocarpaceae	WILLOW PODOCARP

PODOCARPUS SALIGNUS

Habit Upright, often multi-stemmed, irregular. **Fruits** Fleshy, plum-like. Dark red-violet. **Leaves** Slender, narrowly lance-shaped, soft, flexible, to 12cm (5in) long. Glossy, bright grey-green, with yellow-green beneath. **Bark** Fibrous, peeling in strips. Red-brown.
• NATIVE HABITAT Mountains of Chile.
• CULTIVATION Grow in any moist but well-drained soil. Shelter from wind.
• PROPAGATION By seed in autumn or spring.
• OTHER NAMES *P. chilinus.*

☼ ◐
❀ ❀

HEIGHT
12m (40ft)
or more

SPREAD
5m (15ft)

Pinaceae	JAPANESE BLACK PINE

PINUS THUNBERGII

Habit Conical when young, rounded with age. **Fruits** Ovoid cone. Green or purple-tinted, brown when ripe. **Leaves** Rigid, thick, needle-like, to 10cm (4in) long, forward pointing, in pairs. Dark grey-green, emerging from silky white buds. **Bark** Deeply fissured. Dark grey to purplish-pink.
• NATIVE HABITAT Coastal areas of Japan, Korea, and N.E. China.
• CULTIVATION Tolerant of coastal exposure, including sea spray, and of poor, sandy soils.
• PROPAGATION By seed in autumn or spring.

☼ ◐
❀ ❀ ❀

HEIGHT
15m (50ft)
or more

SPREAD
7m (22ft)

Pinaceae	PITCH PINE, NORTHERN PITCH PINE

PINUS RIGIDA

Habit Conical when young, later irregularly and broadly domed. **Fruits** Cylindrical to barrel-shaped cones to 7cm (3in) long. Red-brown. **Leaves** Thick, stiff, twisted, needle-like, to 9cm (3½in) long, in clusters of 3. Grey-green. **Bark** Deeply fissured. Brown.
• NATIVE HABITAT E. North America.
• CULTIVATION Tolerant of coastal conditions, exposure and poor soils. Good for shelter belts in coastal areas.
• PROPAGATION By seed in autumn or spring.

☼ ◐
❀ ❀ ❀

HEIGHT
15m (50ft)
or more

SPREAD
6m (20ft)

Cupressaceae	CHILEAN CEDAR

AUSTROCEDRUS CHILENSIS

Habit Slow-growing, narrowly conical to columnar. *Fruits* Oblong cones, with 4 overlapping scales. Green; brown when ripe. *Leaves* Small, flattened, scale-like, in sprays. Glossy dark green, banded white beneath. *Bark* Scaly. Grey-brown.
• NATIVE HABITAT Mountains of Argentina and Chile.
• CULTIVATION Grow in moisture-retentive, neutral to slightly acid soil. Shelter from winds.
• PROPAGATION By seed in autumn or spring.
• OTHER NAMES *Libocedrus chilensis.*

☀ ◦ ◊
❀ ❀

HEIGHT
15m (50ft)
or more

SPREAD
5m (15ft)

Cupressaceae (Taxodiaceae)	CHINA FIR, CHINESE FIR

CUNNINGHAMIA LANCEOLATA

Habit Open, broadly columnar. *Fruits* Rounded cones, to 4cm (1½in) across. Green; brown when ripe. *Leaves* Lance-shaped, sharply pointed, to 6cm (2½in) long, firm but flexible. Glossy dark green, banded silver-white beneath. *Bark* Finely stringy. Chestnut-brown.
• NATIVE HABITAT Evergreen forests in China.
• CULTIVATION Grow in moisture-retentive, lime-free soils with shelter from cold, dry winds.
• PROPAGATION By seed in autumn or spring.
• OTHER NAMES *C. sinensis.*

☀ ◊
❀ ❀ ❀

HEIGHT
15m (50ft)
or more

SPREAD
6m (20ft)

Phyllocladaceae	TANEKAHA

PHYLLOCLADUS TRICHOMANOIDES

Habit Slow-growing, conical when young, later rounded. *Fruits* Fleshy, berry-like. White. *Leaves* True leaves tiny, scale-like. Bears frond-like, modified, flattened stems, to 15cm (6in) long, with 5–10 lobed, deep green segments.
• NATIVE HABITAT New Zealand.
• CULTIVATION Grow in moisture-retentive, well-drained soil with shelter from cold, dry winds. Suitable for mild, damp climates.
• PROPAGATION By seed in spring.

☀ ◊
❀ ❀

HEIGHT
10m (30ft)
or more

SPREAD
5m (15ft)

Sciadopityaceae	UMBRELLA PINE, JAPANESE UMBRELLA PINE

SCIADOPITYS VERTICILLATA ♀

Habit Narrowly conical. **Fruits** Ovoid cones. Green; red-brown when ripe. **Leaves** Slender, deeply grooved, needle-like, to 12cm (5in) long, in umbrella-like whorls at branch tips. Dark green, yellowish beneath. **Bark** Peeling. Red-brown.
• NATIVE HABITAT Mountains of Japan.
• CULTIVATION Tolerant of very wet and clay soils, but best in neutral to acid, moisture-retentive soils. Shelter from cold, dry winds. Prefers mild climates.
• PROPAGATION By seed in autumn or spring.

HEIGHT 15m (50ft) or more

SPREAD 5m (15ft)

Pinaceae	MONTEZUMA PINE

PINUS MONTEZUMAE

Habit Broadly spreading, with a rounded crown. **Fruits** Conical to egg-shaped cones, to 15cm (6in) long, with prickly scales. Blue-purple, turning red-brown when ripe. **Leaves** Upswept, needle-like, to 30cm (12in) long, in clusters of 5. Blue-grey to grey-green, in dense bunches at shoot tips.
• NATIVE HABITAT Mountains of Guatemala and Mexico.
• CULTIVATION Dislikes shallow, chalky soils and needs shelter from cold, dry winds.
• PROPAGATION By seed in autumn or spring.

HEIGHT To 20m (65ft)

SPREAD 15m (50ft)

Pinaceae	AROLLA PINE, SWISS STONE PINE

PINUS CEMBRA ♀

Habit Narrowly columnar, dense, branching to ground level. **Fruits** Ovoid cones. Blue-purple, red-brown when ripe. Seed 1cm (½in).
Leaves Needle-like, to 9cm (3½in) long, forward-pointing, in dense clusters of 5. Dark green on the outer surface, blue-white within.
• NATIVE HABITAT Mountains of N. Asia and Europe.
• CULTIVATION Tolerant of coastal conditions, exposure, and poor soils.
• PROPAGATION By seed in autumn or spring.

HEIGHT 15m (50ft) or more

SPREAD 5m (15ft)

Pinaceae	LODGEPOLE PINE

PINUS CONTORTA var. LATIFOLIA

Habit Open, conical. **Fruits** Ovoid to conical cones, to 5cm (2in) long. Pink-brown.
Leaves Twisted, needle-like, to 8cm (3in) long, in pairs. Dark green. **Bark** Thick, ridged. Dark red-brown.
• NATIVE HABITAT Mountains of W. North America.
• CULTIVATION Tolerant of poor and wet soils and exposure.
• PROPAGATION By seed in autumn or spring.

HEIGHT 15m (50ft) or more

SPREAD 6m (20ft)

Pinaceae	GOLDEN LARCH

PSEUDOLARIX AMABILIS ♥

Habit Open, broadly conical. **Fruits** Ovoid cones, to 5cm (2in) long. Green; brown when ripe.
Leaves Deciduous, slender, linear, to 5cm (2in) long, soft, flexible, in dense whorls. Fresh bright green, turning orange-gold in autumn.
Bark Plated. Grey-brown.
• NATIVE HABITAT Mountain forests in E. China.
• CULTIVATION Grow in deep, fertile, lime-free soil. Shelter from cold, dry winds.
• PROPAGATION By seed in autumn or spring.
• OTHER NAMES *P. kaempferi*.

☀ ◐
❀ ❀ ❀

HEIGHT
12m (40ft)
or more

SPREAD
5m (15ft)

Pinaceae	JACK PINE

PINUS BANKSIANA

Habit Slender, irregularly conical. **Fruits** Ovoid cones, curved and bumpy, to 6cm (2½in) long, pointing forwards along the shoots. **Leaves** Broad, twisted, needle-like, to 4cm (1½in) long, in pairs. Fresh yellow-green. **Bark** Shallowly fissured. Orange-grey.
• NATIVE HABITAT Forests of North America, almost as far north as the Arctic Circle.
• CULTIVATION Grow in any well-drained soil other than shallow, chalky soil.
• PROPAGATION By seed in autumn or spring.

☀ ◐
❀ ❀ ❀

HEIGHT
15m (50ft)
or more

SPREAD
5m (15ft)

Cupressaceae	

CHAMAECYPARIS LAWSONIANA 'Green Pillar'

Habit Conical, with upright branches.
Leaves Aromatic, very small, scale-like, carried in flattened sprays. Bright green; gold-tinted in spring.
• NATIVE HABITAT Garden origin.
• CULTIVATION Tolerant of shade, exposure, urban pollution, and dry, alkaline soils. Grow in moist but well-drained, preferably neutral to acid soils. Suitable for hedging; requires little clipping.
• PROPAGATION By softwood cuttings in summer or by heeled greenwood cuttings in late summer.

☀ ◐
❀ ❀ ❀

HEIGHT
15m (50ft)

SPREAD
1–2m
(3–6ft)

Cupressaceae	WHITE CYPRESS

CHAMAECYPARIS THYOIDES

Habit Narrowly, often irregularly, columnar.
Fruits Small, rounded cones. Bloomed green;
brown when ripe. **Leaves** Aromatic, tiny, pointed,
scale-like, in flattened, fan-shaped sprays, on shoots.
Green or blue-grey. **Bark** Fibrous. Grey-brown.
• NATIVE HABITAT Swamps and damp soils of
E. United States.
• CULTIVATION Grow in neutral to acid soil.
• PROPAGATION By seed in autumn or spring, by
softwood cuttings in summer, or by heeled
greenwood cuttings in late summer.

HEIGHT
12m (40ft)
or more

SPREAD
3m (10ft)

Pinaceae	BEACH PINE, SHORE PINE

PINUS CONTORTA

Habit Dense, conical or domed. **Fruits** Ovoid
cones, pointing backwards along the shoot. Pale
brown. **Leaves** Twisted, needle-like, to 5cm (2in)
long, densely clustered, in pairs. Dark green or
yellow-green. **Bark** Fissured. Red-brown.
• NATIVE HABITAT Coastal dunes and bogs of
W. North America.
• CULTIVATION Tolerates coastal exposure, stony
or sandy soils, and very wet soils. Unsuitable for
shallow, chalky soil.
• PROPAGATION By seed in autumn or spring.

HEIGHT
To 15m
(50ft)

SPREAD
8m (25ft)

Pinaceae	TAIWAN SPRUCE

PICEA MORRISONICOLA

Habit Open, conical, columnar with age;
pendulous shoots. **Fruits** Oblong-cylindrical cones.
Leaves Slender, needle-like, sharply pointed,
closely pressed and forward-pointing, against the
shoots. Dark green. **Bark** Flaky. Red-brown.
• NATIVE HABITAT Mountains of Taiwan.
• CULTIVATION Grow in fertile, moisture-
retentive but well-drained, neutral to acid soil.
Shelter from cold, dry winds. A very elegant
specimen.
• PROPAGATION By seed in autumn or spring.

HEIGHT
15m (50ft)
or more

SPREAD
6m (20ft)

Taxaceae	

TAXUS BACCATA 'Fastigiata'

Habit Dense, strongly upright, broadly columnar.
Fruits Fleshy, berry-like, to 8mm (¼in) across,
poisonous. Bright red. **Leaves** Evergreen, linear,
pointed at the tip, to 3cm (¼in) long, standing out
all around the shoots. Very dark green.
• NATIVE HABITAT Originated in Eire.
• CULTIVATION Tolerates very dry and shady
conditions, and a wide range of soil types and pH,
including chalky ones.
• PROPAGATION By cuttings of the current year's
growth from autumn to spring.

HEIGHT
10–15m
(30–50ft)

SPREAD
4–5m
(12–15ft)

Pinaceae	ALEPPO PINE

PINUS HALEPENSIS

Habit Conical, open-crowned. **Fruits** Ovoid cones, to 7cm (3in) long. Glossy brown.
Leaves In pairs, slender, sparse, needle-like, to 11cm (4¼in) long, on outer side of shoots, giving a very open appearance. Glossy bright green.
Bark Fissured. Deep purple-brown; terracotta-orange within the fissures.
• **NATIVE HABITAT** Mediterranean.
• **CULTIVATION** Tolerant of maritime exposure and shallow, chalk soils.
• **PROPAGATION** By seed in autumn or spring.

☼ ◊
❄ ❄ ❄

HEIGHT
15m (50ft)

SPREAD
6m (20ft)

Cephalotaxaceae	CALIFORNIA NUTMEG

TORREYA CALIFORNICA

Habit Open, broadly conical, with horizontal branches. **Fruits** Ovoid, fleshy, enclosing a large, single seed. Green, striped purple when ripe.
Leaves Aromatic, narrow, linear, sharp-pointed, to 3cm (1¼in) long. Glossy dark green above, with 2 white bands beneath. **Bark** Ridged. Red-brown.
• **NATIVE HABITAT** Slopes and canyons from the coast to mountains, in California.
• **CULTIVATION** Grow in fertile, moisture-retentive soil. Shelter from cold, dry winds.
• **PROPAGATION** By seed in autumn or spring.

☼ ◊
❄ ❄

HEIGHT
15m (50ft)
or more

SPREAD
7m (22ft)

Cupressaceae	

CHAMAECYPARIS LAWSONIANA 'Lane' ♈

Habit Upright, conical when young, later columnar. **Fruits** Round cones at branch tips.
Leaves Aromatic, small, scale-like, carried in flattened sprays. Bright green, tipped golden-yellow.
• **NATIVE HABITAT** Garden origin.
• **CULTIVATION** Tolerant of shade. Grow in moist but well-drained, preferably neutral to acid soils.
• **PROPAGATION** By softwood cuttings in summer or by heeled greenwood cuttings in late summer.
• **OTHER NAMES** *C. lawsoniana 'Lanei'*, *C. lawsoniana 'Lanei Aurea'*.

☼ ◊
❄ ❄ ❄

HEIGHT
12m (40ft)

SPREAD
4m (12ft)

Pinaceae	VIRGINIA PINE, SCRUB PINE

PINUS VIRGINIANA

Habit Round-headed, untidy. **Fruits** Oblong to conical cones, to 6cm (2½in) long. Red-brown.
Leaves Stiff, twisted, needle-like, to 6cm (2½in) long, in pairs. Grey- to yellow-green. **Bark** Red-brown; young shoots bloomed pinkish-white.
• **NATIVE HABITAT** E. North America.
• **CULTIVATION** Tolerates poor, sandy soils and exposure, but dislikes shallow, chalk soils.
• **PROPAGATION** By seed in autumn or spring.

☼ ◊
❄ ❄ ❄

HEIGHT
15m (50ft)

SPREAD
7m (22ft)

Pinaceae

PICEA MARIANA 'Doumetii'

Habit Slow-growing, densely branched, shrubby and rounded. *Fruits* Ovoid cones, to 4cm (1½in) long, in pendulous clusters. Purplish; red-brown when ripe. *Leaves* Aromatic, slender, soft, needle-like, to 1.5cm (⅝in) long. Dark bluish-green, with 2 silver-blue bands beneath. *Bark* Flaking. Grey-pink, turning purple-grey with age.
• NATIVE HABITAT Species occurs in Canada and N. United States. Garden origin.
• CULTIVATION Grow in moist but well-drained, preferably neutral to acid soil, in an open position.

This very dense, irregularly rounded, shapely specimen is a very slow-growing conifer, taking 15–20 years to reach 3m (10ft) in height, and by as much across, and so is suitable for use as a specimen tree in a small or medium-sized garden.
• PROPAGATION By grafting in late summer, winter or early spring.

HEIGHT
8m (25ft) or more

SPREAD
5m (15ft)

Pinaceae	BRISTLE-CONE PINE

PINUS ARISTATA

Habit Slow-growing, bushy, rounded-conical. *Fruits* Ovoid, spiny cones, to 10cm (4in) long. Dark purple; brown when ripe. *Leaves* Retained for 10–20 years, slender, needle-like, to 4cm (1½in) long, in dense, forward-pointing clusters of 5. Dark green, conspicuously flecked with resin.
• NATIVE HABITAT Rocky Mountains of Colorado, Arizona, and New Mexico.
• CULTIVATION Tolerates poor, dry soils, lime-rich soils, and exposure.
• PROPAGATION By seed in autumn or spring.

☼ ◐
❀ ❀ ❀

HEIGHT
8m (25ft)

SPREAD
4m (12ft)

Cupressaceae	

JUNIPERUS VIRGINIANA 'Burkii'

Habit Slow-growing, dense, columnar. *Fruits* Berry-like cones, to 6mm (¼in) long. Bloomed, grey-green. *Leaves* Aromatic; juvenile: needle-like; adult: tiny, scale-like; in pairs, both on same shoots. Bluish grey-green. *Bark* Peeling. Red-brown.
• NATIVE HABITAT Garden origin.
• CULTIVATION Grow in almost any well-drained soil.
• PROPAGATION By cuttings of the current year's growth from autumn to spring.

☼ ◐
❀ ❀ ❀

HEIGHT
6m (20ft)

SPREAD
2m (6ft)

Cupressaceae	

CHAMAECYPARIS LAWSONIANA 'Columnaris'

Habit Upright, narrowly columnar. *Fruits* Round cones at branch tips. *Leaves* Aromatic, small, scale-like, in flattened sprays. Blue-grey.
• NATIVE HABITAT Garden origin.
• CULTIVATION Tolerant of shade, exposure, urban pollution, and dry, alkaline soils. Grow in moist, but well-drained soils, preferably neutral to acid. Suitable for hedging and as a specimen.
• PROPAGATION By softwood cuttings in summer or by heeled greenwood cuttings in late summer.

◐ ◑
❀ ❀ ❀

HEIGHT
10m (30ft)

SPREAD
1.5m (5ft)

Cupressaceae	

JUNIPERUS VIRGINIANA 'Robusta Green'

Habit Slow-growing, dense, columnar, free-fruiting. **Fruits** Berry-like cones, to 6mm (¼in) long. Bloomed, grey-green. **Leaves** Aromatic, tiny, scale-like. Green. **Bark** Peeling. Red-brown.
• NATIVE HABITAT Garden origin.
• CULTIVATION Will grow in almost any well-drained soil.
• PROPAGATION By cuttings of the current year's growth from autumn to spring.
• OTHER NAMES *J. chinensis* 'Robusta Green'.

Cupressaceae	

JUNIPERUS CHINENSIS 'Obelisk' ♈

Habit Slender, irregularly columnar, with ascending branches. **Leaves** Aromatic, long, prickly, awl-shaped, densely packed. Dark green.
• NATIVE HABITAT Garden origin.
• CULTIVATION Tolerates a wide range of soils and conditions but especially useful on hot, dry sites.
• PROPAGATION By cuttings of the current year's growth from autumn to spring.

☼ ◊
❀ ❀ ❀

HEIGHT
4m (12ft)

SPREAD
1m (3ft)

☼ ◊
❀ ❀ ❀

HEIGHT
5m (15ft)

SPREAD
1m (3ft)

Pinaceae	

PINUS SYLVESTRIS 'Fastigiata'

Habit Upright, narrowly columnar.
Fruits Conical cone, to 7.5cm (3in) long. Brown.
Leaves Twisted, needle-like, in pairs. Dark blue-green. **Bark** Flaky. Red-brown.
• NATIVE HABITAT Garden origin.
• CULTIVATION Grow in any well-drained soil. Ensure protection from cold wind, which may scorch the foliage.
• PROPAGATION By grafting in late summer, winter or early spring.
• OTHER NAMES *P. sylvestris* f. *fastigiata*.

☼ ◊
❀ ❀ ❀

HEIGHT
8m (25ft)

SPREAD
1m (3ft)

Pinaceae	LACE-BARK PINE

PINUS BUNGEANA

Habit Slow-growing, broadly conical, low-branching. **Fruits** Ovoid cones, to 7cm (3in) long. Yellow-brown. **Leaves** Rigid, slender, needle-like, to 7.5cm (3in) long, in clusters of 3. Yellow-green. **Bark** Smooth, flaking. Grey-green and olive green. Creamy-white patches beneath bark eventually darken to pale green and then purple-brown.
• NATIVE HABITAT On shale on the steep slopes of mountains in N. China.
• CULTIVATION Grow in any well-drained soil. It is drought-tolerant and needs full sun. It makes a beautiful specimen tree, especially if sited to give a clear view of its exquisite, flaking bark, which is uniquely attractive amongst the wide range of conifers. As it is relatively small and slow-growing, it is one of the most suitable of the pines for smaller and medium-sized gardens.
• PROPAGATION By seed in autumn or spring.

☼ ◐
❀ ❀ ❀

HEIGHT
10m (30ft)
or more

SPREAD
7m (22ft)

Pinaceae	MEXICAN NUT PINE, PINYON PINE	

PINUS CEMBROIDES

Habit Slow-growing, bushy, domed.
Fruits Globose cones, to 4cm (1½in) across, opening to release edible seeds. Orange to buff-brown. **Leaves** Sparse, needle-like, in clusters of 2–3 at shoot tips. Olive green. **Bark** Scaly. Silver-grey or grey-brown.
• NATIVE HABITAT Mexico.
• CULTIVATION Tolerant of poor, dry soils. Needs a warm, sheltered site.
• PROPAGATION By seed in autumn or spring.

HEIGHT
6–7m
(20–22ft)

SPREAD
5m (15ft)

Pinaceae	KOREAN FIR	

ABIES KOREANA

Habit Broadly conical. **Fruits** Cylindrical, upright cones, to 7.5cm (3in) long, carried even on young plants. Violet-blue. **Leaves** Linear, to 2cm (¾in) long, rounded or notched at the tip. Dark green above, with 2 white bands, or all white, beneath. **Bark** Dark grey-brown.
• NATIVE HABITAT Mountains of S. Korea.
• CULTIVATION Grow in fertile, humus-rich, neutral to acid soils. Thrives in cool, humid, sheltered conditions.
• PROPAGATION By seed in autumn or spring.

HEIGHT
10m (30ft)
or more

SPREAD
5m (15ft)

Cupressaceae (Taxodiaceae)	

CRYPTOMERIA JAPONICA 'Cristata'

Habit Conical, with twisted, curved, 'cockscomb' shoots. **Leaves** Slender, flattened at the base, taper-pointed. Bright green, ageing to brown. **Bark** Soft, fibrous. Orange-brown.
• NATIVE HABITAT Garden origin.
• CULTIVATION Grow in fertile, neutral to acid, moisture-retentive soil. Thrives in cool, humid, sheltered conditions.
• PROPAGATION By cuttings of the current year's growth from autumn to spring.

HEIGHT
To 10m
(30ft)

SPREAD
3m (10ft)

Cupressaceae	

THUJOPSIS DOLABRATA 'Variegata'

Habit Slow-growing, broadly conical.
Leaves Scale-like, thick, broadly triangular, with pointed tips, to 6mm (¼in) long. Glossy bright green, splashed irregularly with cream, neatly and distinctively marked with silver-white beneath.
• NATIVE HABITAT Garden origin.
• CULTIVATION Grow in fertile, neutral to acid, moisture-retentive soil, preferably in a humid, sheltered site.
• PROPAGATION By cuttings of the current year's growth from autumn to spring.

HEIGHT
10m (30ft)
or more

SPREAD
5m (15ft)

Cupressaceae (Taxodiaceae)			Taxaceae	JAPANESE YEW

CRYPTOMERIA JAPONICA 'Pyramidata'

Habit Narrowly columnar. *Leaves* Slender, flattened at the base, taper-pointed. Blue-green when young, later dark green. *Bark* Soft, fibrous. Orange-brown.

• NATIVE HABITAT Garden origin.
• CULTIVATION Grow in fertile, neutral to acid, moisture-retentive soil. Thrives in cool, humid, sheltered conditions.
• PROPAGATION By cuttings of the current year's growth, from autumn to spring.

TAXUS CUSPIDATA

Habit Broad, rounded, bushy. *Fruits* Poisonous. Fleshy, berry-like, to 8mm (¼in) across. Bright red. *Leaves* Hard, linear, short-pointed, to 2.5cm (1in) long, ascending from the shoots. Dark green above, yellow-green beneath.

• NATIVE HABITAT Japan.
• CULTIVATION Tolerates very dry and shady conditions and a wide range of soil types. Performs best in areas with hot, humid summers.
• PROPAGATION By seed in autumn or spring.

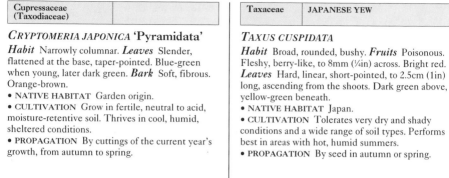

HEIGHT
6m (20ft)

SPREAD
2m (6ft)

HEIGHT
5m (15ft) or more

SPREAD
5m (15ft)

Pinaceae		STONE PINE

PINUS PINEA

Habit Short-trunked, with a rounded, umbrella-shaped crown. *Fruits* Broadly ovoid cones, to 12cm (5in) long. Glossy brown. *Leaves* Stout, needle-like, to 12cm (5in) long, in pairs. Grey-green; the blue-green juvenile foliage is retained on young trees. *Bark* Deeply fissured. Orange-brown.

• NATIVE HABITAT On sandy soils around the Mediterranean coast.
• CULTIVATION Tolerates poor, dry, sandy soils and coastal exposure. It is a useful tree for shelter belt plantings in seaside gardens. When grown as a specimen it becomes increasingly picturesque, especially when grown in exposed, windy sites. When given such growing conditions it frequently branches low and becomes wind-trained, leaning away from the prevailing winds.

• PROPAGATION By seed in autumn or spring.

HEIGHT
10m (30ft)
or more

SPREAD
10m (30ft)

Pinaceae	GOLDEN DEODAR

CEDRUS DEODARA 'Aurea' ♔

Habit Slow-growing, upright, with pendent branch tips. *Leaves* Narrow, needle-like, to 3cm (1¼in) long, in dense whorls. Bright golden-yellow when young, maturing to yellow-green.
• NATIVE HABITAT Garden origin.
• CULTIVATION Grow in any moist but well-drained soils including chalky or lime-rich soils. Excellent specimen for small gardens.
• PROPAGATION By grafting in late summer, winter or early spring.

☼ ◐
❋ ❋ ❋

HEIGHT
5m (15ft)

SPREAD
4m (12ft)

Cupressaceae	

CHAMAECYPARIS OBTUSA 'Crippsii' ♔

Habit Slow-growing, narrowly conical.
Fruits Small, rounded cones, to 12mm (½in) across. Green; brown when ripe. *Leaves* Aromatic, tiny, scale-like, in flattened sprays. Bright golden-yellow on outermost branchlets, dark green within. *Bark* Stringy. Red-brown.
• NATIVE HABITAT Garden origin.
• CULTIVATION Tolerant of alkaline soils but best in moist, well-drained, neutral to acid soils.
• PROPAGATION By softwood cuttings in summer or by heeled greenwood cuttings in late summer.

☼ ◐
❋ ❋ ❋

HEIGHT
10m (30ft)

SPREAD
5m (15ft)

Cupressaceae	MONTEREY CYPRESS

CUPRESSUS MACROCARPA 'Goldcrest' ♔

Habit Fast-growing, conical. *Leaves* Aromatic, tiny, scale-like, with pointed tips, pressed closely to the shoot, in plume-like sprays. Brilliant golden-yellow.
• NATIVE HABITAT Garden origin.
• CULTIVATION Grow in any well-drained soil, except shallow chalk soils. Does not respond well to clipping. Makes a beautiful specimen for small gardens. Foliage is useful in flower arrangements.
• PROPAGATION By softwood cuttings in summer or by heeled greenwood cuttings in late summer.

☼ ◐
❋ ❋

HEIGHT
10m (30ft)

SPREAD
3m (10ft)

| Pinaceae | PYRAMIDAL SCOTS PINE |

PINUS SYLVESTRIS 'Aurea'

Habit Slow-growing, broadly conical, rounded with age. *Leaves* Slender, needle-like, in pairs, carried in twisted bundles. Blue-green, bright golden-yellow in winter and spring.
• NATIVE HABITAT Species occurs on sandy and gravelly soils in the mountains of Asia and Europe. Garden origin.
• CULTIVATION Grow in any well-drained soil. Ensure protection from cold wind which may scorch the foliage. This cultivar produces new growth with a greyish cast during summer that later

assumes a characteristic bright golden coloration during winter. It is very slow-growing and makes an attractive companion plant for winter-flowering heaths and heathers. It may also be grown in collections of dwarf conifers.
• PROPAGATION By grafting in late summer, winter, or early spring.

HEIGHT
10m (30ft)

SPREAD
4m (12ft)

DWARF CONIFERS

Slow-growing and dwarf conifers are invaluable in small gardens, offering year-round interest with an enormous range of colour, form, and habit. The compact cultivars are ideal for rock gardens, while spreading and prostrate forms are invaluable when used as ground cover. Nearly all tolerate a range of growing conditions, thriving on acid to neutral soil, and yew and junipers tolerate lime. Some are not wind-tolerant and need a sheltered site. They may grow to exceed their stated height after 15–20 years but replacement plants can be propagated. *Cupressaceae* root easily with heeled, greenwood, or softwood cuttings, but *Cedrus, Picea, Pseudotsuga*, and *Tsuga* require hardwood cuttings. *Pinus* and *Arbies* are usually grafted.

PICEA PUNGENS
'Montgomery'
Habit Dense, rounded-conical. *Leaves* Rigid, stout, needle-like, sharply spine-tipped, 2cm (¾in) long. Bright grey-blue.
• HEIGHT 1m (3ft).
• SPREAD 1m (3ft).

Picea pungens
'Montgomery'

☼ ◊ ❋ ❋ ❋

ABIES LASIOCARPA
'Arizonica Compacta'
Habit Slow-growing, dense, regular, broadly conical. *Leaves* Linear, forward-pointing on top of the shoots, spreading below. Silvery-blue, with broad, white bands beneath. *Bark* Corky.
• HEIGHT 4–5m (12–15ft).
• SPREAD 1.5–2m (5–6ft).

Abies lasiocarpa
'Arizonica Compacta'

☼ ◊ ❋ ❋ ❋   ♈

JUNIPERUS
SQUAMATA **'Holger'**
Habit Low, prostrate, wide-spreading, with nodding branchlets. *Leaves* Aromatic, needle-like. Steel-blue, turning sulphur-yellow in spring, giving beautiful contrast with older foliage.
• HEIGHT 2m (6ft).
• SPREAD 2m (6ft).

Juniperus squamata
'Holger'

☼ ◊ ❋ ❋ ❋   ♈

PINUS SYLVESTRIS
'Doone Valley'
Habit Irregularly conical, compact, upright. *Leaves* In pairs, straight, or slightly twisted, needle-like, 4–5cm (1½–2in) long. Dark blue-green.
• HEIGHT 1m (3ft).
• SPREAD 1m (3ft).

Pinus sylvestris
'Doone Valley'

☼ ◊ ❋ ❋ ❋

JUNIPERUS
SCOPULORUM
'Springbank'
Habit Narrowly columnar, with drooping branch tips.
Leaves Aromatic, scale-like, pressed closely to shoots. Intense silvery-blue.
• HEIGHT 4m (12ft).
• SPREAD 1m (3ft).

Juniperus scopulorum
'Springbank'

☼ ◊ ❋ ❋

PICEA OMORIKA 'Gnom'
Habit Broadly and irregularly pyramidal. Pendent branches arch out at the tips.
Leaves Slender, needle-like. Dark green, white beneath.
• CULTIVATION Tolerates chalky and limestone soils.
• HEIGHT 1.5m (5ft).
• SPREAD 1–2m (3–6ft).

Picea omorika 'Gnom'

☼ ◊ ❀ ❀ ❀

ABIES CONCOLOR 'Compacta'
Habit Broadly conical.
Leaves Linear, blunt-tipped, upswept. Bright steel-blue.
• OTHER NAMES *A. concolor* 'Glauca Compacta'.
• HEIGHT 2m (6ft).
• SPREAD 2m (6ft).

Abies concolor 'Compacta'

☼ ◊ ❀ ❀ ❀ ♔

JUNIPERUS SQUAMATA 'Blue Star'
Habit Low-growing, dense, compact, bun-shaped.
Leaves Crowded, relatively large, awl-shaped. Bright silvery-blue.
• HEIGHT 50cm (20in).
• SPREAD 60cm (24in).

Juniperus squamata 'Blue Star'

☼ ◊ ❀ ❀ ❀ ♔

JUNIPERUS VIRGINIANA 'Grey Owl'
Habit Vigorous, low, wide-spreading, with ascending branchlets.
Leaves Soft, silver-grey, tips flushed purple in winter.
• HEIGHT 3m (10ft).
• SPREAD 3–5m (10–15ft).

Juniperus virginiana 'Grey Owl'

☼ ◊ ❀ ❀ ❀ ♔

JUNIPERUS HORIZONTALIS 'Douglasii'
Habit Spreading, prostrate, mat-forming.
Leaves Aromatic, with needle- and scale-like leaves. Soft, bright blue-green, tinted plum-purple in winter.
• HEIGHT 30cm (12in).
• SPREAD 2–3m (6–10ft).

Juniperus horizontalis 'Douglasii'
Waukegan juniper

☼ ◊ ❀ ❀ ❀

JUNIPERUS × MEDIA 'Pfitzeriana Glauca'
Habit Spreading, dense. Branches ascending but drooping at the tips.
Leaves Mainly awl-shaped. Grey-blue.
• OTHER NAMES *J. chinensis* 'Pfitzeriana Glauca'.
• HEIGHT 3m (10ft).
• SPREAD 3–5m (10–15ft).

Juniperus × media 'Pfitzeriana Glauca'

☼ ◊ ❀ ❀ ❀

JUNIPERUS SQUAMATA 'Chinese Silver'
Habit Dense, bushy, multi-stemmed, with branch tips nodding.
Leaves Awl-shaped. Intense blue-green, bright silver beneath.
• HEIGHT 3–4m (10–12ft).
• SPREAD 3–4m (10–12ft).

Juniperus squamata 'Chinese Silver'

☼ ◊ ❀ ❀ ❀

JUNIPERUS SABINA 'Mas'
Habit Low-growing, with ascending branches.
Leaves Mainly awl-shaped. Blue above, green below, purple-tinted in winter. Fetid when crushed.
• HEIGHT 60–90cm (24–36in).
• SPREAD 1.5m (5ft).

Juniperus sabina 'Mas'

☼ ◊ ❀ ❀ ❀

JUNIPERUS CHINENSIS 'Stricta'
Habit Compact, conical-columnar, with upright branches. *Leaves* Soft, needle-like. Blue-green.
• HEIGHT 5m (15ft).
• SPREAD 1m (3ft).

Juniperus chinensis 'Stricta'

☼ ◊ ❀❀❀

JUNIPERUS PROCUMBENS
Habit Spreading, prostrate, shrubby.
Fruits Globose, fleshy, berry-like. Brown to black. *Leaves* Aromatic, needle-like. Light green or yellow-green.
• HEIGHT 30–45cm (12–18in).
• SPREAD 2m (6ft).

Juniperus procumbens Creeping juniper

☼ ◊ ❀❀❀

JUNIPERUS PROCUMBENS 'Nana'
Habit Mat-forming, compact.
Fruits Globose, fleshy, berry-like. Brown to black. *Leaves* Aromatic, needle-like. Light green or yellow-green.
• HEIGHT 15–20cm (6–8in).
• SPREAD 75cm (30in).

Juniperus procumbens 'Nana'

☼ ◊ ❀❀❀   ♔

THUJA OCCIDENTALIS 'Caespitosa'
Habit Slow-growing, dense, hummock-forming.
Leaves Congested, irregular, pressed closely to very slender shoots. Dark greyish-green.
• HEIGHT 30cm (12in).
• SPREAD 40cm (16in).

Thuja occidentalis 'Caespitosa'

◑ ◊ ❀❀❀

MICROBIOTA DECUSSATA
Habit Prostrate, shrubby, with wide-spreading branches.
Fruits Small, globose, berry-like cone. Yellow-brown. *Leaves* Small, mostly scale-like, in flat sprays. Yellow-green, bronze in winter.
• HEIGHT 50cm (20in).
• SPREAD 2–3m (6–10ft).

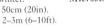

Microbiota decussata

☼ ◊ ❀❀❀   ♔

JUNIPERUS SCOPULORUM 'Skyrocket'
Habit Very narrowly columnar. *Leaves* Tiny, scale-like, closely pressed to slender shoots. Glaucous blue.
• OTHER NAMES *J. virginiana* 'Skyrocket'.
• HEIGHT To 8m (25ft).
• SPREAD 75cm (30in).

Juniperus scopulorum 'Skyrocket'

☼ ◊ ❀❀❀

JUNIPERUS HORIZONTALIS 'Turquoise Spreader'

Habit Vigorous, dense, mat-forming.
Leaves Needle-like, sharp pointed. Rich jade-green.
• CULTIVATION Very tolerant of hot, dry sites.
• HEIGHT 30cm (12in).
• SPREAD 2m (6ft).

Juniperus horizontalis 'Turquoise Spreader'

☀ ◊ ❋ ❋ ❋

ABIES LASIOCARPA 'Roger Watson'

Habit Compact, conical.
Leaves Linear, forward-pointing on top of the shoots, spreading below. Silvery-grey, with broad, white bands beneath.
• HEIGHT 75cm (30in).
• SPREAD 75cm (30in).

Abies lasiocarpa 'Roger Watson'

☀ ◊ ❋ ❋ ❋

ABIES BALSAMEA 'Nana'

Habit Dense, globose.
Leaves Aromatic, linear, flattened. Dark green above, yellow beneath, with 2 white bands.
• OTHER NAMES
A. balsamea var. *nana*.
• HEIGHT 1m (3ft).
• SPREAD 1m (3ft).

Abies balsamea 'Nana'

☀ ◊ ❋ ❋ ❋

PICEA MARIANA 'Nana'

Habit Compact, rounded, mound-forming. **Leaves** Short, soft, slender, needle-like. Blue-grey.
• HEIGHT 50cm (20in).
• SPREAD 50–80cm (20–32in).

Picea mariana 'Nana'

☀ ◊ ❋ ❋ ❋   ♈

ABIES CEPHALONICA 'Meyer's Dwarf'

Habit Slow-growing, spreading, forming a flat-topped mound.
Leaves Sharp, stiff, linear. Dark green above, white beneath.
• OTHER NAMES
A. cephalonica 'Nana'.
• HEIGHT 50cm (20in).
• SPREAD 1.5m (5ft).

Abies cephalonica 'Meyer's Dwarf'

☀ ◊ ❋ ❋ ❋

PODOCARPUS NIVALIS

Habit Rounded, dense, spreading, shrubby.
Leaves Rigid, lance-shaped, leathery. Olive green.
• CULTIVATION Tolerant of chalky soils.
• HEIGHT 2m (6ft).
• SPREAD 3–5m (10–15ft).

Podocarpus nivalis

☀ ◊ ❋ ❋ ❋

PSEUDOTSUGA MENZIESII 'Fretsii'

Habit Slow-growing, broadly conical, with twisted, ascending branches.
Leaves Aromatic, short, needle-like. Dull dark green, with white bands beneath.
• HEIGHT 6m (20ft) or more.
• SPREAD 3–4m (10–12ft).

Pseudotsuga menziesii 'Fretsii'

☀ ◊ ❋ ❋ ❋

JUNIPERUS SABINA 'Cupressifolia'

Habit Spreading, with horizontal or ascending branches. Free-fruiting.
Fruits Rounded, berry-like cones. Blue-black.
Leaves In pairs, mostly scale-like. Dark blue-green.
• HEIGHT 2m (6ft).
• SPREAD 4m (12ft).

Juniperus sabina 'Cupressifolia'

☀ ◊ ❋ ❋ ❋

JUNIPERUS RECURVA 'Densa'

Habit Low, spreading, with drooping branchlets. **Leaves** Aromatic, awl-shaped, in sprays that are erect at the tips. Dark green.
• HEIGHT 30cm (12in).
• SPREAD 1m (3ft).

Juniperus recurva 'Densa'

☼ ◊ ❄❄❄

PINUS SYLVESTRIS 'Nana'

Habit Slow-growing, dense, bushy, broadly conical. **Leaves** In pairs, needle-like, sometimes twisted, widely spaced. Dark blue-green or yellow-green.
• HEIGHT 50cm (20in).
• SPREAD 50cm (20in).

Pinus sylvestris 'Nana'

☼ ◊ ❄❄❄

JUNIPERUS SABINA 'Tamariscifolia'

Habit Low-growing, compact, spreading, with horizontal branches. **Leaves** Mainly needle-like, carried in tiered sprays. Bright green or blue-green.
• OTHER NAMES
J. sabina var. *tamariscifolia*.
• HEIGHT 1m (3ft).
• SPREAD 2m (6ft).

Juniperus sabina 'Tamariscifolia'

☼ ◊ ❄❄❄

PINUS MUGO 'Gnom'

Habit Dense, globose, with stout, twisted branches. **Leaves** In pairs, needle-like, crowded. Dark green.
• HEIGHT 2m (6ft).
• SPREAD 2m (6ft).

Pinus mugo 'Gnom'

☼ ◊ ❄❄❄

PICEA ABIES 'Ohlendorfii'

Habit Slow-growing, dense. Globose when young, later conical. **Leaves** Rigid, slender, needle-like, sharp-pointed. Dark green.
• HEIGHT 1m (3ft).
• SPREAD 1m (3ft).

Picea abies 'Ohlendorfii'

◐ ◕ ❄❄❄

PSEUDOTSUGA MENZIESII 'Oudemansii'

Habit Very slow-growing, broadly conical, with ascending branches. **Leaves** Aromatic, short, needle-like. Glossy dark green above, light green beneath.
• HEIGHT 6m (20ft) or more.
• SPREAD 3–4m (10–12ft).

Pseudotsuga menziesii 'Oudemansii'

◐ ◕ ❄❄❄

PICEA ABIES 'Reflexa'

Habit Prostrate, creeping, dense. **Leaves** Rigid, slender, needle-like, sharp-pointed. Dark green.
• CULTIVATION May be trained up a stake, to form a mound of weeping foliage.
• HEIGHT 30cm (12in).
• SPREAD 5m (15ft).

Picea abies 'Reflexa'

◐ ◕ ❄❄❄

CHAMAECYPARIS LAWSONIANA 'Gnome'

Habit Compact, bun-shaped. **Leaves** Aromatic, very small, scale-like, in flattened sprays. Blue-green.
• HEIGHT 50cm (20in).
• SPREAD 50cm (20in).

Chamaecyparis lawsoniana 'Gnome'

◐ ◕ ❄❄❄

CHAMAECYPARIS LAWSONIANA 'Minima'
Habit Compact, dense, globular.
Leaves Aromatic, very small, scale-like, in flattened sprays. Light green.
• HEIGHT 1m (3ft).
• SPREAD 1m(3ft).

Chamaecyparis lawsoniana 'Minima'

☀ ◐ ❊ ❊ ❊

CHAMAECYPARIS OBTUSA 'Intermedia'
Habit Open, globular.
Leaves Aromatic, tiny, scale-like, in downward-spreading, flattened sprays. Light green.
• HEIGHT 30cm (12in).
• SPREAD 40cm (16in).

Chamaecyparis obtusa 'Intermedia'

☀ ◐ ❊ ❊ ❊

PICEA ABIES 'Gregoryana'
Habit Slow-growing, dense, globose.
Leaves Rigid, slender, needle-like, sharp-pointed. Dark sea-green, arranged radially around the shoot.
• HEIGHT 60cm (24in).
• SPREAD 60cm (24in).

Picea abies 'Gregoryana'

☀ ◐ ❊ ❊ ❊

JUNIPERUS x *MEDIA* 'Pfitzeriana'
Habit Spreading, dense. Branches ascending, drooping at the tips.
Leaves Mainly awl-shaped. Grey-green.
• HEIGHT 3m (10ft).
• SPREAD 3–5m (10–15ft).

Juniperus x *media* 'Pfitzeriana'
Pfitzer juniper

☀ ◐ ❊ ❊ ❊   ♔

CHAMAECYPARIS OBTUSA 'Nana Pyramidalis'
Habit Slow-growing, dense, conical.
Leaves Aromatic, tiny, scale-like, in horizontal, cupped sprays. Dark green.
• HEIGHT 60cm (24in).
• SPREAD 60cm (24in).

Chamaecyparis obtusa 'Nana Pyramidalis'

☀ ◐ ❊ ❊ ❊

PINUS HELDREICHII var. *LEUCODERMIS* 'Schmidtii'
Habit Very slow-growing, dense, ovoid, mound-forming.
Leaves In pairs. Rigid, needle-like, sharp- and forward-pointing. Bright green.
• HEIGHT 50cm (20in).
• SPREAD 50cm (20in).

Pinus heldreichii var. *leucodermis* 'Schmidtii'

☀ ◐ ❊ ❊ ❊   ♔

PICEA GLAUCA var. *ALBERTIANA* 'Conica'
Habit Slow-growing, neat, pyramidal, dense, and firm. **Leaves** Short, slender, rigid, needle-like. Blue-green.
• OTHER NAMES
P. glauca 'Albertiana Conica'.
• HEIGHT 2–5m (6–15ft).
• SPREAD 1–2m (3–6ft).

Picea glauca var. *albertiana* 'Conica'

☀ ◐ ❊ ❊ ❊   ♔

JUNIPERUS COMMUNIS 'Hibernica'
Habit Neatly columnar.
Leaves Aromatic, needle-like. Mid- to yellowish-green.
• OTHER NAMES *J. communis* 'Stricta'.
• HEIGHT 3–5m (10–15ft).
• SPREAD 30–50cm (12–20in).

Juniperus communis **'Hibernica'** Irish juniper

THUJA ORIENTALIS 'Aurea Nana'
Habit Ovoid, round-topped. *Leaves* Small, triangular, blunt-pointed, overlapping, held in vertical sprays. Yellow-green, bronze in winter.
• OTHER NAMES *Biota orientalis* 'Aurea Nana', *Platycladus orientalis* 'Aurea Nana'.
• HEIGHT 60cm (24in).
• SPREAD 60cm (24in).

Thuja orientalis **'Aurea Nana'**

CEDRUS LIBANI subsp. LIBANI 'Sargentii'
Habit Rounded, bushy, with horizontal, then weeping, branches. *Leaves* Slender, needle-like, sharp-pointed, in dense whorls. Grey-green.
• HEIGHT 1–1.5m (3–5ft).
• SPREAD 1–1.5m (3–5ft).

Cedrus libani subsp. *libani* **'Sargentii'**

THUJA ORIENTALIS 'Semperaurea'
Habit Vigorous, ovoid, with a rounded top. *Leaves* Small, triangular, blunt-pointed, overlapping, held in vertical sprays. Golden-yellow.
• OTHER NAMES *Biota orientalis* 'Semperaurea, *Platycladus orientalis* 'Semperaurea'.
• HEIGHT 3m (10ft).
• SPREAD 2m (6ft).

Thuja orientalis **'Semperaurea'**

PINUS HELDREICHII var. LEUCODERMIS 'Compact Gem'
Habit Very slow-growing, dense, broadly conical, with upright branches. *Leaves* In pairs, rigid, needle-like, sharp- and forward-pointing. Very dark green.
• HEIGHT 25–30cm (10–12in).
• SPREAD 25–30cm (10–12in).

Pinus heldreichii var. *leucodermis* **'Compact Gem'**

THUJA OCCIDENTALIS 'Filiformis'
Habit Loose, open, mound-forming. *Leaves* Tiny, scale-like, on very slender, whip-like shoots pendent at the tip. Light green.
• HEIGHT 1.5m (5ft).
• SPREAD 1.5–2m (5–6ft).

Thuja occidentalis **'Filiformis'**

THUJA PLICATA
'Hillieri'
Habit Slow-growing,
dense, rounded.
Leaves Moss-like, in
irregular clusters, on stiff,
stout branchlets. Rich
green.
• CULTIVATION Cut
back any long, untidy, or
protruding branchlets
when young.
• HEIGHT 1m (3ft) or
more.
• SPREAD 1m (3ft).

Thuja plicata 'Hillieri'

☼ ◊ ❀ ❀ ❀

*CRYPTOMERIA
JAPONICA* **'Spiralis'**
Habit Slow-growing,
dense, spreading.
Leaves Slender, needle-
like, incurved, flattened
at the base. Spirally
twisted around the stem.
Bright green.
• HEIGHT 2–3m (6–10ft)
• SPREAD 2–3m (6–10ft)

Cryptomeria japonica
'Spiralis'

☼ ◊ ❀ ❀ ❀

*JUNIPERUS
CHINENSIS* **'Expansa
Variegata'**
Habit Mound-forming,
with horizontal or
ascending branches.
Leaves Aromatic, scale-
and needle-like, in dense
sprays. Bluish-green, with
some sprays creamy-white.
• OTHER NAMES
J. davurica 'Expansa
Albopicta'.
• HEIGHT 75cm (30in).
• SPREAD 1.5–2m (5–6ft).

Juniperus chinensis
'Expansa Variegata'

☼ ◊ ❀ ❀ ❀

JUNIPERUS × MEDIA
'Blue and Gold'
Habit Compact,
spreading, with
ascending branches.
Leaves Mainly scale-
like. Variegated soft sky-
blue and creamy-gold.
• OTHER NAMES
J. 'Blue and Gold'.
• HEIGHT 1m (3ft)
• SPREAD 1m (3ft)

Juniperus × media **'Blue
and Gold'**

☼ ◊ ❀ ❀ ❀

JUNIPERUS × MEDIA
'Pfitzeriana Aurea'
Habit Spreading, dense,
with ascending branches
that droop at the tips.
Leaves Mainly scale-
like. Dark yellow-green.
Shoot tips golden-yellow
in spring.
• OTHER NAMES
J. 'Pfitzeriana Aurea'.
• HEIGHT 3m (10ft).
• SPREAD 3–5m
(10–15ft).

Juniperus × media
'Pfitzeriana Aurea'

☼ ◊ ❀ ❀ ❀

TAXUS BACCATA
'Dovastonii Aurea'
Habit Slow-growing,
wide-spreading, with
horizontally-tiered
branches that weep at the
tips. **Leaves** Linear,
pointed. Dark green,
margined golden-yellow,
on yellow shoots.
• CULTIVATION
Tolerates most acid or
alkaline soils.
• HEIGHT To 6m (20ft).
• SPREAD To 8m (25ft).

Taxus baccata
'Dovastonii Aurea'

☀ ◊ ❀ ❀ ❀   ♈

JUNIPERUS CHINENSIS
'Plumosa Aurea'
Habit Low-growing,
spreading, with
ascending branches that
arch at the tips.
Leaves Tiny, scale-like,
in crowded, plume-like
sprays. Golden-green,
bronzed in winter.
• OTHER NAMES
J. × media 'Plumosa Aurea'.
• HEIGHT 1m (3ft).
• SPREAD 2–3m (6–10ft).

Juniperus chinensis
'Plumosa Aurea'

☼ ◊ ❀ ❀ ❀   ♈

*CHAMAECYPARIS
OBTUSA* **'Nana
Aurea'**
Habit Slow-growing,
flat-topped, broadly and
irregularly columnar.
Leaves Aromatic, tiny,
scale-like, in horizontal,
cupped sprays. Golden-
yellow.
• HEIGHT 2m (6ft).
• SPREAD 2m (6ft).

Chamaecyparis obtusa
'Nana Aurea'

☼ ◊ ❀ ❀ ❀   ♈

CHAMAECYPARIS PISIFERA 'Filifera Aurea'

Habit Broadly conical, with thread-like, pendulous shoots.
Leaves Aromatic, tiny, scale-like, closely pressed to whip-like shoots. Golden-yellow.
• CULTIVATION Foliage will scorch in full sun.
• HEIGHT 4–5m (12–15ft).
• SPREAD 3m (10ft).

Chamaecyparis pisifera 'Filifera Aurea'

☀ ◐ ❋❋❋ ♔

PINUS SYLVESTRIS 'Gold Coin'

Habit Slow-growing, rounded. A dwarf form of *P. sylvestris* 'Aurea'.
Leaves In pairs, slender, stiff, needle-like, carried in dense bundles. Blue-green, turning intense golden-yellow in winter and spring.
• HEIGHT 2m (6ft).
• SPREAD 2m (6ft).

Pinus sylvestris 'Gold Coin'

☀ ◐ ❋❋❋

CRYPTOMERIA JAPONICA 'Sekkan-sugi'

Habit Rounded, broadly pyramidal, with semi-pendulous branchlets.
Leaves Slender, needle-like, flattened at the base. Pale creamy-yellow.
• HEIGHT 10m (30ft).
• SPREAD 3–4m (10–12ft).

Cryptomeria japonica 'Sekkan-sugi'

☀ ◐ ❋❋❋

ABIES NORDMANNIANA 'Golden Spreader'

Habit Slow-growing, flat-topped, spreading.
Leaves Linear, slightly curved, flattened. Bright golden-yellow, intensely so in winter, paler beneath.
• HEIGHT 1m (3ft).
• SPREAD 1m (3ft).

Abies nordmanniana 'Golden Spreader'

☀ ◐ ❋❋❋ ♔

TAXUS BACCATA Aurea Group

Habit Slow-growing, broadly conical, domed with age. **Leaves** Linear, pointed, flattened. Golden-yellow.
• CULTIVATION Withstands close clipping. Tolerates most acid or alkaline soils.
• HEIGHT 6–10m (20–30ft).
• SPREAD 5–8m (15–25ft).

Taxus baccata **Aurea Group**
Golden yew

☀ ◐ ❋❋❋

THUJA PLICATA 'Stoneham Gold'

Habit Slow-growing, dense, conical.
Leaves Aromatic, tiny, scale-like, in flattened sprays. Very dark green within the bush, bright golden-orange at the shoot tips.
• HEIGHT 1–2m (3–6ft).
• SPREAD 1m (3ft).

Thuja plicata 'Stoneham Gold'

☀ ◐ ❋❋❋ ♔

TSUGA CANADENSIS 'Aurea'

Habit Broadly conical, often multi-stemmed.
Leaves Needle-like, flattened, arranged in spirals around the grey shoots. Golden-yellow when young, green with age, with silver bands beneath.
• HEIGHT 5m (15ft) or more.
• SPREAD 2–3m (6–10ft).

Tsuga canadensis 'Aurea'

☀ ◐ ❋❋❋

CRYPTOMERIA JAPONICA 'Elegans Compacta'

Habit Slow-growing, dense, spreading.
Leaves Slender, soft, curved, needle-like, in feathery sprays. Green, turning rich bronze-purple in winter.
• HEIGHT 2–5m (6–15ft).
• SPREAD 2m (6ft).

Cryptomeria japonica 'Elegans Compacta'

☀ ◐ ❋❋❋ ♔

ADDITIONAL SPECIES AND CULTIVARS

Numerous variants of plants exist that differ slightly from the normal form of species. Some of these variants exist in the wild and are termed subspecies (subsp.), varieties (var.), or forms (forma or f.). Others are known as cultivars – a contraction of 'cultivated varieties' – and they exist only in cultivation. The cultivar name is enclosed in inverted commas and follows the botanical name, for example *Alnus incana* 'Aurea'. Below are listed some additional trees to those described in the book. A cross-reference is given to the page number of the species or a close relative.

♀ *Albizia julibrissin* var. *rosea*. A very hardy variety. Similar to the species (p.98) but with bright pink flowers in dense, fluffy heads.

Alnus incana 'Aurea'. Similar to the species (p.23) but with orange shoots in winter, yellow leaves, and red-tinted catkins.

Alnus incana 'Laciniata'. Similar to the species (p.23) but with leaves finely divided into narrow lobes.

♀ *Arbutus unedo* f. *rubra*. A free-fruiting form, similar to the species (p.104) but with pink-flushed flowers.

♀ *Betula ermanii* 'Grayswood Hill'. An exceptionally graceful form of the species (p.41) but with smooth, creamy-white bark, becoming grey-white and peeling with age.

♀ *Betula* 'Jermyns'. Vigorous, broadly conical tree, similar to *B. utilis* var. *jacquemontii* (p.76) but with broader leaves and smooth, unmarked, pure white bark.

♀ *Catalpa* x *erubescens* 'Purpurea'. Deciduous, spreading tree, similar to *C. bignonioides* (p.60). Dark purple, oval or 3-lobed leaves, turn deep green when mature. Has bell-shaped, white flowers, marked with yellow and purple, in mid- to late summer.

♀ *Chamaecyparis lawsoniana* 'Kilmacurragh'. Narrowly columnar tree to 10–15m (30–50ft), with strongly upright branches bearing sprays of dark green foliage. See *C. lawsoniana* 'Columnaris', p.148.

♀ *Chamaecyparis lawsoniana* 'Wisselii'. Fast-growing, slender-conical tree to 15m (50ft), with widely spaced, upright branches bearing fern-like sprays of blue-green foliage. See *C. lawsoniana* 'Green Pillar', p.144.

♀ *Chamaecyparis pisifera* 'Boulevard'. Bushy, slow-growing conical tree to 3m (10ft) or more, with soft, silver-blue foliage, purple-tinged in cold weather. See *C. thyoides*, p.145.

♀ *Crataegus laevigata* 'Rosea Flore Pleno'. Similar to *C. laevigata* 'Paul's Scarlet' (p.98) but with many double pink flowers in late spring and early summer.

Crataegus mollis. Wide-spreading to 12m (40ft) with broadly oval, lobed, dark green leaves that are white-downy beneath when young. Bears clusters of white flowers then short-lived, round, red haws. See *Crataegus flava* p.94 and *C. macrosperma* var. *acutiloba*, p.106.

♀ *Cupressus sempervirens* 'Swane's Gold'. Similar to the species (p.139). Compact, narrowly columnar tree with gold-tinted foliage.

♀ *Davidia involucrata* var. *vilmoriniana*. Very similar to the species (p.59) but leaves are smooth, not silky, beneath, and fruits are more elliptic, and less russeted.

♀ *Eucalyptus globulus*. Fast-growing, half-hardy evergreen with peeling bark and narrow, oval-oblong, silvery-blue leaves, turning glossy mid-green with age. See *E. gunnii*, p.42.

♀ *Eucryphia* x *intermedia* 'Rostrevor'. Similar to *E. lucida* (p.97). Compact, free-flowering, broadly columnar evergreen, with oblong or 3-lobed, glossy dark green leaves, and many single white flowers in late summer.

Fagus sylvatica 'Rohanii'. Similar to *F. sylvatica* var. *heterophylia* 'Aspleniifolia' (see p.38) but with broader leaves that are coloured a greenish-purple with red leaf veins and stalks.

♀ *Fraxinus angustifolia* 'Raywood'. Similar to *F. velutina* (p.65). A vigorous, deciduous, spreading tree of elegant habit. Ash-like leaves have 5–7 narrowly oval leaflets and turn red-purple in autumn.

Halesia carolina. Similar to but smaller than *H. monticola* (p.49). A free-flowering, small tree with masses of white flowers on bare branches in late spring.

Halesia tetraptera. Similar to but smaller than *H. monticola* (p.49). A free-flowering, small tree with masses of pendent, bell-shaped, white flowers on bare branches in late spring.

♀ *Hoheria* 'Glory of Amlwch'. Tree to 7m (22ft). Semi-evergreen, but can be evergreen given mild winters. Similar to *H. angustifolia* (p.95), bearing many snow-white flowers from mid- to late summer.

Juglans cinerea 'Butternut'. Related to *J. nigra* (p.29). A fast-growing, deciduous, spreading tree to 25m (80ft), with large, aromatic leaves divided into 7–19 oval, pointed, bright green leaflets.

♀ *Juniperus chinensis* 'Aurea'. Slow-growing tree to 10–15m (30–50ft), with an oval or conical outline, bearing golden foliage and many yellow, male cones. See *J. chinensis* 'Obelisk', p.149.

♀ *Liquidambar styraciflua* 'Lane Roberts'. Similar to the species (p.36) but produces more reliable autumn colours of deep red-purple.

Liriodendron chinense (Chinese tulip tree). A fast-growing, deciduous tree, similar to *L. tulipifera*, (p.34) but its leaves have a narrower 'waist' at the lobe junction and are more blue-white beneath

♀ *Liriodendron tulipifera* 'Fastigiatum'. Similar to the species (p.34) but a broadly columnar tree with strongly upright branches.

♀ *Malus* 'Red Sentinel'. The pink buds open into white flowers 3cm (1½in) across, which set rounded, long-persitent, glossy deep red frutits 2.5 cm (1in) across. See *M.* 'Profusion', p.53.

♀ *Malus* x *robusta* 'Red Siberian'. Vigorous, deciduous, spreading tree with oval, dark green leaves. Has clusters of white or pink-tinted flowers in spring and bright red crab apples in autumn. See *M. prunifolia*, p.109.

♀ *Malus* x *robusta* 'Yellow Siberian'. Similar to *M.* x *robusta* 'Red Siberian' but with yellow fruits.

Malus 'Van Eseltine'. Deciduous, upright tree to 6m (20ft), bearing clusters of double pink flowers in spring, with small, yellow crab apples in autumn. See *M.* 'John Downie', p.108.

♀ *Picea orientalis* 'Aurea'. Dense, columnar tree to 20m (70ft), with young foliage of creamy-yellow, later becoming golden yellow before turning green. See *P. orientalis* 'Skylands', p.137.

♀ *Picea pungens* 'Hoopsii'. Dense, conical tree to 10–15m (30–50ft), bearing sharp, stout, bright silver-blue needles. See *P. pungens* 'Koster', p.138.

♀ *Populus* x *canadensis* 'Aurea'. A fast-growing tree to 30m (100ft). Similar to *P.* x *canadensis* 'Robusta' (p.22) but with broadly oval leaves that are golden-yellow when young, ageing to yellow-green, and borne on red leaf stalks.

Prunus cerasifera 'Pissardii'. A deciduous, round-headed tree similar to *P. cerasifera* 'Nigra' (p.99) but with white or pale pink flowers, and leaves that are red when young, then darker red, then purple.

♀ *Prunus* 'Kursar'. Deciduous, spreading tree to 8m (25ft), with small, deep pink flowers in early spring, and oval, dark green leaves, turning orange in autumn. See *P.* 'Hokusai', p.87.

♀ *Sorbus aucuparia* 'Sheerwater Seedling'. Similar to the species (p.72), but a narrowly upright tree, to 4m (12ft), with a compact, ovoid crown, and a profusion of orange-red berries in autumn.

♀ *Sorbus commixta* 'Embley'. Similar to the species (see p.71), but with more reliable and longer lasting autumn colours of brilliant red and orange hues. It bears large clusters of bright red fruits in autumn.

Stewartia serrata. Deciduous tree to 10m (30ft) similar to, but smaller than *S. pseudocamellia* (p.60), with good autumn colour and cup-shaped, red-stained white flowers in early summer.

♀ *Taxus baccata* 'Fastigiata Aureomarginata'. Similar to *T. baccata* 'Fastigiata' (p.145) but leaves have a golden yellow margin.

Tsuga canadensis Narrowly conical tree 30m (120ft) high. Has bright green, linear leaves, turning dark green above, with 2 broad, white bands beneath. See *T. canadensis* 'Aurea', p.163.

GUIDE TO TREE CARE

ONCE PLANTED, A TREE will remain in position for many years, so it is essential to provide the best possible growing conditions at the outset. Climate, soil type, and the amount of light and shelter available all affect a tree's growth and must be very carefully considered. Attention to soil preparation, planting, and aftercare are also vital for the successful establishment and healthy

CHOOSING TREES FOR PLANTING

GOOD EXAMPLE

GOOD EXAMPLE

Fibrous 'feeder' roots

Evenly distributed, spreading roots

Well-balanced branch framework

GOOD EXAMPLE

POOR EXAMPLE

Uneven, 'hockey stick' roots

Well-established root framework

POOR EXAMPLE

POOR EXAMPLE

Tightly coiled roots

Congested roots

Container-grown tree
Check that roots are not coiled, overcrowded or protruding from the drainage holes of the pot. It should be easy to remove from the pot and compost should cling to the root ball.

Bare-root tree
A good root system should be well-balanced, spreading evenly in all directions, and with a mass of vigorous, fibrous roots. Avoid those with uneven or tightly coiled roots.

growth of the tree. Before choosing a tree, check that it will thrive within the temperature, rainfall, and humidity ranges that prevail on the planned site. Consider local factors, such as exposure to wind, which may scorch foliage or cause distortion of the tree's canopy. Even within a species, different cultivars may be more suited to certain conditions.

GOOD EXAMPLE

Balanced shape

Firm root ball with covering intact

Root-balled tree
Check that the root ball is firm and has its wrapping and surrounding soil intact. Do not purchase if there are signs of damage or drying-out as it will be less likely to establish well.

In areas with late spring frosts, choose trees that come into leaf late, as young growth, even of otherwise hardy trees, may be damaged by frost.

Within the garden the microclimate may vary considerably. Ensure that the planting site provides appropriate light levels and wind shelter. On sloping sites bear in mind that the bottom of the slope is more likely to form a frost pocket and the top will be more exposed to wind. A position half way up is likely to be warmer and more sheltered.

In coastal gardens shelter from sea-spray and salt-laden winds is vital for some species, although with careful selection certain trees that can withstand these conditions may be used as windbreaks to provide protection for more vulnerable plants.

Avoid planting vigorous species, such as poplars and willows, near to buildings and walls, as their wide-spreading roots may cause damage to foundations or drains as they develop. Similarly, do not plant trees where they may interfere with overhead or underground cables.

Selecting a tree
Trees may be bought container-grown, root-balled or bare-rooted, and in a variety of sizes from seedlings to semi-mature standards. In general, smaller trees establish more quickly while semi-mature specimens lend immediate impact but need greater attention to aftercare. Whatever the size, check that roots and top-growth are healthy, vigorous, well-developed, and evenly balanced around the stem.

Container-grown trees may be planted at any time but do not buy them if they are pot-bound: restricted roots seldom establish well and may result in poor and unstable anchorage at maturity. Bare-root trees, with little or no soil on the roots, and root-balled trees, with roots and surrounding soil wrapped to keep the root ball intact, must be planted when dormant. Check that roots are free from damage and disease, with no sign of dryness caused by exposure to wind.

SOIL PREPARATION AND PLANTING

Trees are best planted as soon as possible after purchase, although if kept moist in frost-free conditions, planting of root-balled and container-grown trees may be delayed until weather conditions are more amenable. Bare-root trees can be heeled in, if necessary, until weather conditions improve.

When to plant

Container-grown plants can be planted out at any time of the year, except during drought and frost. Deciduous bare-root trees should be planted when dormant, between mid-autumn and mid-spring, avoiding frosty weather. Plant hardy evergreens and hardy, deciduous trees with fleshy roots in mid-autumn or mid- to late spring. Half-hardy trees should be planted in mid-spring. Root-balled trees should be planted in early to mid-autumn or in mid-spring; deciduous root-balled specimens can also be planted during mild spells in winter. Autumn planting, while soils retain residual warmth, allows good root establishment. In cold areas, however, spring planting may be more successful.

Prepare the site in advance to allow the soil to settle. Choose a well-drained site and clear all vegetation to at least

1m (3ft) from the base of the tree to eliminate competition for water and nutrients. Double dig the soil and incorporate well-rotted organic matter in the bottom trench.

Once the planting site has been prepared, dig the planting hole and fork over the sides and base of the hole to

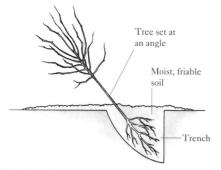

Tree set at an angle

Moist, friable soil

Trench

Heeling in

If planting is delayed, the tree will need to be temporarily heeled in. Prepare a trench and set the tree in it at an angle so that the trunk is supported and the roots well-covered with soil.

PLANTING A CONTAINER-GROWN TREE

1 *Mark out the diameter of the hole at 3–4 times the diameter of the pot. Remove turf and weeds and dig out to 1½ times the depth of the pot.*

2 *Scarify the sides and bottom of the hole with a fork and incorporate well-rotted organic matter into the soil that has been removed from the hole.*

break up the surrounding soil. Mix the removed soil with well-rotted organic matter and, for spring planting, incorporate about 110 g (4oz) of slow-release fertilizer. If you are using a single stake (see p.171), drive it into the hole just off-centre before planting to ensure that the roots are not damaged later.

Container-grown trees need a planting hole 3–4 times the diameter of the root ball. Water thoroughly before removing the tree from the container. Gently tease out the roots by hand and trim away any damaged roots with secateurs. Check the planting depth, adding or removing soil as necessary to ensure the final soil level is the same as it was in the container. Back fill the hole, firming gently in stages to avoid air pockets and to ensure good soil contact with the roots. Lightly prune the top-growth to

3 *Add up to 20 per cent of the mixed organic matter and soil into the hole. Then insert the stake in a slightly off-centre position on the windward side of the tree.*

4 *Place the tree next to the stake and begin back filling the hole. Using a cane, check and adjust the soil level so that it is eventually the same as it was in the pot.*

5 *Back fill in stages, firming gently as you go. Cut back damaged, over-long sideshoots and lower feathers (inset pic). Attach tree to the stake and apply mulch.*

Container trees
Plant at the same depth as in the nursery (using the soil mark on the stem as a guide) with the final soil level at about 5cm (2in) below the rim to permit thorough watering. Support standard trees with a stake inserted before planting.

PLANTING A ROOT-BALLED TREE

Dig a planting hole 2–3 times the diameter of the root ball. Place the tree in the hole, untie the wrapping, and rocking the plant gently to one side, slide out the material. Back fill the hole, firming gently as you go. Water in thoroughly immediately after planting.

balance it with the root system. Attach the tree to its stake with a tree tie, water thoroughly, and apply a deep mulch to conserve moisture and suppress weeds.

Planting of bare-root and root-balled trees is essentially the same as for container-grown specimens, although bare-root trees need a planting hole wide enough to accommodate the roots when fully spread. Root-balled specimens need a planting hole 2–3 times the diameter of the root ball.

Small trees may be planted permanently in containers, which must have adequate drainage, a diameter equal to one-sixth to one-quarter of the tree's height, and a depth equal to one and a half times the tree's root ball. Use clean containers, cover the drainage holes with broken crocks, and add a layer of at least 2.5cm (1in) of crocks or coarse gravel. Use a loam-based potting compost with slow-release fertilizer, and a top-dressing of grit 2.5cm (1in) deep.

Keep all young trees irrigated and weed-free for at least the first 2–3 years after planting.

Staking trees
The root system of newly planted trees may take two or more growing seasons to establish well enough to provide firm anchorage against strong winds.

Transplants (60–120cm /3–4ft tall) and whips (unbranched, single-stemmed young trees 1–2m/3–6ft tall), seldom need staking. However, standards need the initial support of a stake to prevent wind rock at the roots. There is good evidence to show that the movement of a tree's trunk and crown in the wind helps promotes good rooting and encourages the stem to thicken. Stakes are needed to secure the root only, so short stakes are generally preferable. The exception is with slender, flexible-stemmed trees with a densely branched crown, such as crab apples. These are best given the support of a high stake in the first year which is then cut down to a lower level in the second year before removing it in the third. Most trees will

STAKING TREES

LOW ANGLED STAKE

Drive in stake after planting at an angle of about 45°, with it leaning into the prevailing wind.

LOW SINGLE STAKE

Low stakes allow stems to move. Drive in before planting, with 50cm (20in) of stake above the soil.

HIGH SINGLE STAKE

Drive in a long stake before planting and secure with ties positioned at both top and bottom.

LOW DOUBLE STAKES

Drive in two stakes after planting on opposite sides. Secure with heavy-duty rubber ties.

be sufficiently well-established by the end of the second growing season for the stakes to be removed.

Stakes should be driven in to a depth of about 60cm (24in) below soil level to ensure stability. A single low stake is suitable for most standard trees on all but the windiest sites. It is best driven into the planting hole before planting the tree to avoid damage to the roots. Make sure that 50cm (20in) of the stake protrudes above soil level. Site the stake on the windward side so that when the

tree moves in the wind it does not rub against the stake. For container-grown and root-balled trees, especially on windy sites, a short stake, angled into the prevailing wind, is preferable. It can be driven in, clear of the root ball, after planting. Alternatively, two or three short, vertical stakes can be evenly placed around the tree, outside the area of the root ball.

Tree ties

Tree ties should be durable, and adjustable to accommodate the increase in the tree's girth without chafing or cutting into the bark. Proprietary ties of the buckle and spacer type are available. Ties can also be made from nylon webbing or rubber tubing. These are nailed to the stake and formed into a figure of eight to make the spacer. When using two or three stakes, secure the tree to the stakes with strips of heavy duty rubber or plastic.

In many regions it may be necessary to protect young trees from damage caused by rabbits or other animals that strip bark. Enclose the tree trunk in chicken wire, wire netting, or one of the numerous types of plastic or rubber tree guards available from garden centres.

Buckle and spacer tie
Thread tie through spacer and around tree. Buckle so that it is taut but will not damage the bark.

Rubber tie
If using a rubber or plastic tie without a buckle, nail the tie to the stake to prevent bark damage caused by friction.

ROUTINE CARE

The amount of maintenance a tree needs largely depends on the species and its microclimate, soil type, and site. Once established, most trees need little maintenance, but if they are to establish well, young trees need watering, feeding, and most importantly, a clear weed-free area around the base for the first few years after planting.

Trees grown in containers should be regularly top-dressed and re-potted when they have outgrown their existing pot. Controlling pests and diseases, which can be debilitating to young trees, and removal of suckers from grafted specimens, may also be necessary.

Watering

Most trees need plenty of water to grow well, especially on light, sandy soils and for the first two or three years after planting. In the growing season, during periods of dry weather, apply approximately 50–75 litres per sq m (10–15 gallons per sq yd) each week. Established trees seldom need artificial irrigation, except during periods of prolonged drought. During these conditions, however, restrictions are often in place, and measures should be taken to conserve available soil water.

Mulching

Mulching reduces water loss from the soil surface and, in addition, keeps down weeds and reduces the effects of temperature extremes around the roots. Pulverized bark is effective and attractive, but black plastic sheeting or old carpet are also useful where aesthetics are less important. Mulches are best applied in spring, but provided the soil is moist, they can be spread at any time except during frost and drought. Cover an area about 30–45cm (12–18in) larger than the tree's root

TOP DRESSING CONTAINER-GROWN TREES

1 Top dressing should be carried out in spring before the tree starts into growth. Using hands or a trowel, remove any mulch and the top 5cm (2in) of compost.

2 Replenish the top of the container with fresh compost mixed with a slow-release fertilizer. Water thoroughly and add a fresh layer of mulch to the surface.

system, and top-up every other year for young trees. Nutrient-rich, organic mulches may be used when trees also require feeding.

Feeding
Young trees, especially on poor, infertile soils, benefit from feeding, particularly during the first few years after planting. Established trees need only occasional feeding. Apply organic fertilizers such as well-rotted manure or garden compost to a depth of 5–8cm (2–3in) in autumn, or during any frost-free period when the tree is dormant. Leave a clear area immediately around the trunk, and extend the mulch to beneath the outer edge of the canopy. Artificial fertilizers are best applied in spring, according to the manufacturers' recommendations. Trees grown for their flowers and fruit need more potash and phosphate, while those grown for their foliage will need more nitrogen.

Weeding
During the early years of the tree's life, keep the area beneath its canopy free of grass and weeds as these will compete with the tree for any available water and nutrients.

Hand weeding, mulching, or covering the soil with black plastic sheeting, will help to control the weeds. If this does not work adequately, use weedkillers recommended for use around trees and which do not affect the tree roots.

If a tree's growth is too rapid, retaining, or establishing grass around it, will help to slow down its vigorous growth by providing competition for food and water.

Tree problems
Provided trees have been properly planted into well-prepared soil, have been adequately fed, carefully watered, and kept free of competing weeds, they should suffer few problems, as healthy, well-grown trees are far less likely to become infested with pests and diseases. Lack of vigour is a reliable sign

REMOVING SUCKERS

Suckers divert nutrients from the main shoots of the tree. Cut them off close to the base using secateurs, then pare over the cut surface with a sharp knife. Rub out new growth as soon as it appears.

that something is wrong. Make sure that the tree has not been planted too deeply and that the roots or stems have not been damaged.

Check for pests and diseases. Aphids and red spider mites are the most common problems, and on small trees can be treated with appropriate insecticides, preferably before heavy infestations develop. Honey fungus (*Armillaria* spp.) is more serious. White mycelium appears under the bark at the base of the trunk, and black, bootlace-like strands infest the soil around the roots. Yellow or tawny-coloured toadstools appear between mid-summer and mid-winter. Plants will deteriorate over time, and little can be done to treat them. Remove and burn affected plants, stumps and root systems. Large trees should have their stumps chipped or ground out by a contractor.

Trees may be damaged by strong winds and young growth may be badly affected by severe frosts. These problems are best avoided by choosing appropriately hardy species, selecting a suitable site, and providing shelter with windbreaks or screens. Cut back any damaged growth to a suitable bud in spring. Frost may also lift newly planted trees, so check after frosty weather and, if necessary, refirm after thawing.

Suckers and water shoots will divert nutrients from the main shoots of the tree if they are allowed to develop unchecked. Remove them as soon as possible. A tree may produce both stem and root suckers. Stem suckers appear just below the graft union on the understock of a grafted tree. Root suckers develop directly from the roots.

Suckers on grafted plants are frequently more vigorous than the desirable, grafted top-growth and, if left, may eventually outgrow or even replace it. Cut the suckers back to the base with secateurs, check regularly, and rub out any new growth as soon as it emerges.

Vigorous trees or those which have their roots close to the soil surface such as poplars, (*Populus*) and ornamental cherries (*Prunus*) often produce root suckers. Although these may be used for propagation, they can become a nuisance if they invade paths or lawns. Cut or pull off the root suckers as close to their base

as possible, removing the soil to where the sucker joins the root, if necessary. For some genera, such as *Prunus*, painting the wounds on the roots with ammonium sulphamate usually prevents regrowth and in small quantities will not harm the tree. Epicormic or water shoots grow directly out of the trunk and frequently appear around the site of pruning wounds. If allowed to develop, they will grow through and spoil the natural form of the canopy. Cut out at the base with secateurs and rub out any new shoots as they emerge.

Transplanting trees
Careful attention to site and species selection should avoid the need for transplanting, but if it becomes necessary, careful preparation and aftercare will usually enable young trees up to 2.5m (8ft) in height to be transplanted successfully. Mature and larger trees are very difficult to move and so are best left to a specialist firm.

Prepare the young tree in the early autumn of the year before transplanting is to take place. Dig a trench around the area just beyond the root ball, with a

Transplanting a Young Tree

1 *Dig a trench 30cm (1ft) wide, 60cm (2ft) deep, outside the area of the root ball. Undercut the root ball with a sharp spade. Back fill the trench with soil and well-rotted organic matter.*

2 *The following autumn lift the tree gently first to one side, then the other, sliding hessian or plastic sheeting beneath. Carefully tilt the tree the other way and pull the sheeting through underneath the roots.*

diameter about one-third of the tree's height, and undercut to sever any large, coarse roots. Mix the soil taken from the hole with well-rotted organic matter to encourage the production of fibrous feeder roots and then back fill the trench with the soil. Tie the branches to the central stem with soft twine to avoid damage during transit. Transplant in the following early autumn, replanting to the same depth. In the following 2–3 growing seasons, keep well-watered and weed-free. The tree may take several seasons to resume vigorous growth.

Tree felling

Cutting down a tree can be done at any time of year, but trees larger than 5m (15ft) should be tackled by a professional tree surgeon, as felling is a potentially dangerous operation. Also, check that the tree is legally yours and that does not have a Tree Preservation Order on it.

Ensure there is a clear space for the tree to fall and for you to move out of the way. Once felled, remove the stump and large roots by digging a trench, loosening the roots, and winching or digging out. If left, the stump may attract honey fungus.

CUTTING DOWN A TREE

Cut out a wedge of about one-third of the trunk diameter, the lower cut horizontal, the upper at 45°, at 1m (3ft) above ground, on the side where the tree will fall. Make the final cut on the opposite side, just above the base of the wedge. Push gently, if necessary, in the direction of fall. Remove the remaining stump by digging a trench around it, loosening the roots and then winching or digging it out.

3 *Tie the hessian firmly but gently around the root ball and transfer the tree to its new planting hole. Unwrap the root ball and place in the hole by reversing the procedure outlined in Step 2. Replant to the soil mark on the stem.*

4 *Support the newly-planted tree with guy ropes attached to angled stakes. Water thoroughly and apply a deep mulch to conserve water and suppress weeds. Keep well-watered until re-established.*

PRUNING AND TRAINING

Correct pruning and training helps to maintain a tree's health and vigour, regulates its shape, and in some cases improves flowering and fruiting. The formative pruning of young trees is often vital to ensure a well-balanced and structurally sound framework at maturity. Once their form is established, most trees need little further pruning.

The extent of pruning depends on the type of tree and the desired effects. To form a well-shaped tree usually requires little pruning. A pleached hedge or laburnum arch needs more regular work and expertise.

Most deciduous species are pruned when fully dormant, preferably between autumn and mid-winter. Dead wood is removed at any time of year, but is more clearly visible in summer. Most evergreens need little pruning, but if it is necessary, they are best pruned in early spring.

Principles of pruning

First remove any dead, diseased and damaged wood and cut out weak or straggling growth. Then stand back and carefully assess which branches should be removed or shortened in order to produce a well-balanced framework. Hard pruning stimulates vigorous growth while light pruning results in limited replacement growth.

All pruning cuts must be accurate and made with clean, sharp tools to minimize damage to the tree. Cut back to a healthy bud or pair of buds, or to a sideshoot pointing in the required direction of growth. When pruning trees with opposite buds, make a straight cut directly above a pair of buds. Cut back those with alternate leaves using a slanting cut just above the bud so that the base of the cut is level with the top of the bud.

When removing entire branches it is essential to cut just outside the branch collar – a slight swelling at the base of

How to prune
For alternate buds, make a slanting cut 3–5mm (⅛–¹⁄₆in) above the bud (left). For opposite buds, make a straight cut directly above a strong pair of buds (right).

the branch where it joins the trunk. The branch collar constitutes the tree's natural defence against infection and this is where the callus will form to seal the wound and provide protection against wood-rotting organisms.

Branches less than 2.5cm (1in) in diameter can be removed with a pruning saw or secateurs. Larger branches should be removed in sections to avoid tearing the bark on the main trunk.

Formative pruning

The aim of formative pruning is to create trees with a strong, well-balanced framework of evenly spaced branches that are safe and structurally sound when

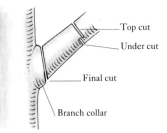

Top cut
Under cut
Final cut
Branch collar

Where to cut
Remove the bulk of the branch with two cuts, as shown. Cut off the stub just outside the branch collar. Do not breach the branch collar when removing a branch.

CUTTING OFF A BRANCH

1 It is much easier – and safer – to remove the branches in sections. Make an undercut with a pruning saw, 30cm (1ft) away from the trunk, to a depth of one-quarter of the branch diameter. This is important to prevent the bark tearing back into the branch collar if the branch should break.

2 Make a top cut, about 2.5cm (1in) further away from the trunk, sawing from above. Gently support the free end of the branch with your free hand, so that the cut does not close on the saw and make sawing movements difficult. This also ensures that the branch does not spring upwards as it falls.

3 Remove the remaining stub, first making a small undercut just outside the branch collar. If the branch collar is not obvious, make this cut at an equal and opposite angle to the ridge of bark which slopes downwards from the crotch into the main trunk. Keep supporting the branch with your free hand.

4 Make the final cut from the top, just outside the branch collar, angling the saw slightly away from the trunk. If the branch angle is acute, it is easier to make the final cut from below. Leave the cut bare (see inset pic). It is unnecessary to apply wound paint or dressing, except in the case of Prunus.

Training a new leader

1 *Replace a broken or damaged leader with a strong upright lateral. Attach a cane firmly to the top of the main stem and tie the new leader to it.*

2 *Prune out the old damaged leader, taking care not to damage its replacement. Once the new leader is growing strongly and is clearly dominant, the support cane can be removed.*

they mature. At its simplest, formative pruning enhances a tree's natural shape, requiring only routine removal of dead, damaged, and diseased wood, along with weak, rubbing, or crossing branches. Ornamental garden trees are often pruned to produce a tree form that displays its features to best effect.

Feathered trees form a central leading shoot and have laterals along the length of the stem. They may be allowed to develop naturally, or may have the lower laterals pruned away to produce a central-leader standard – a tree with a clear length of stem below the crown. A branched-head standard has the lower laterals and the leading shoot removed to create an open crown with widely spreading lateral branches, a form commonly seen in small ornamentals such as the Japanese cherries (*Prunus*).

Feathered trees need little pruning other than to remove weak or poorly placed laterals (feathers) and any shoots that compete with the central leader, ensuring that the remaining laterals are evenly spaced around the central stem. The lower laterals may eventually die back naturally.

To train a central-leader standard, plant a well-feathered young tree and remove any competing leaders and badly placed laterals. Remove laterals from the lowest third of the stem, and reduce the laterals on the middle third by about one half of their length. In the late autumn

or early winter, cut back the pruned laterals to the main stem, and repeat the procedure over 2–3 years until the stem has been cleared to about 1.8m (6ft). If the leader is lost or damaged, it is essential to select and train in a replacement as soon as possible. Dual or multiple leaders form narrow branch angles (crotches) which lead to structural weakness at maturity.

Branched-head standards are trained initially as central-leader standards, until the desired length of clear stem has been achieved. In mid- to late autumn, remove the central leader, cutting back to a strong, healthy bud and leaving a framework of about five strong, evenly spaced branches. Remove any crossed or badly congested laterals. In subsequent years, remove any branches that cause imbalance or congestion in the crown. Take out any vertical, upright branches that may form secondary leaders, and clear the stem of any laterals that develop below the crown. Some branched-head standards are created in the nursery by top-working as for weeping standards.

Weeping standards are created by grafting one or more sections of a weeping cultivar onto a stock plant with a clear stem of about 1.8m (6ft). Pruning is limited to removing crossed, badly placed, or vertical branches. Some semi-upright stems are left to create tiers of weeping branches.

Removing a competing leader

Prune out the competing leader by cutting it back to its base. Make a clean cut with sharp secateurs or loppers, taking care not to damage the remaining leader.

Once the tree is established, it will usually require little further pruning other than the routine removal of dead, damaged, or diseased wood.

Containerized trees need annual pruning to restrict size and spread and to maintain a balanced framework.

Branched-head standards frequently become congested at the centre of the crown, so remove inward-growing shoots and any badly placed branches that spoil the balanced framework. The removal of large branches from mature trees is a potentially dangerous operation that should be performed only by a professional tree surgeon.

Coppicing and pollarding

Coppicing is the regular pruning of a tree to ground level to encourage the production of strong basal shoots, while pollarding is the pruning of a tree back to its main stem or branch framework. These are traditional techniques once used to provide a regular supply of firewood or pliable stems for basket work and fencing, but they are now commonly used for ornamental purposes to enhance leaf colour and size, to produce ornamental stems, or to restrict size. Some trees may be coppiced or pollarded on an annual or biennial basis. Coppice in late winter or early spring. Vigorous trees, such as willows (*Salix*) that are grown for their coloured stems, may be pruned in mid-spring just before, or just as, buds break into new growth.

To coppice, cut back all stems to the base with pruning loppers or sharp secateurs, leaving the swollen basal wood unpruned, as all new growth will form from this point.

HOW TO COPPICE A TREE

Coppicing may be carried out in order to restrict a tree's size, enlarge its leaves, or enhance the stem colour.

Coppicing should be done in late winter or early spring, using tree loppers or a pair of sharp secateurs. Cut back all the stems of the tree to 7cm (3in) above the ground. Take care not to cut into the swollen, woody base of the tree, as all new growth will be produced from this stump.

To produce a pollard, plant a young, branched-head standard and when the clear stem has reached the desired height, cut back branches to within 2.5–5cm (1–2in) of the main stem in late winter or early spring. This results in a proliferation of new shoots from the top of the cut stem, which are cut back annually or every other year. Thin to relieve congestion, and completely remove any new shoots that appear on the clear stem.

To produce a pollard with a main branch framework, allow the tree to produce a well-balanced branch system at the desired height. Then, in late winter or early spring, cut back the branches to about 2m (6ft). Cut back the new shoots every two to five years and, once the pollard is established, prune every or every other year.

Renovating old trees

Mature trees that have outgrown their situation or that have been neglected can sometimes be renovated to restore them to full health and vigour. However, renovation demands considerable care and expertise, and it is advisable to consult a professional tree surgeon. An arboricultural association or a local horticultural college may be able to provide a list of approved contractors and consultants who are properly insured and who comply with safe working practices and up-to-date standards of technical competence.

Before inviting contractors to tender, decide exactly what work is required, including the disposal of any debris – which may be the most expensive part of tree surgery operations. Quotations are normally provided free of charge, but a fee may be charged if there is any advisory work involved.

In some cases, a tree may be too old and full of structural defects to make renovation a viable proposition, and if they are large, renovation will also be potentially dangerous. In these cases it is better to remove and replant.

Renovation may be carried out at any time of the year, except in early spring when the sap is rising, as this commonly

HOW TO POLLARD A TREE

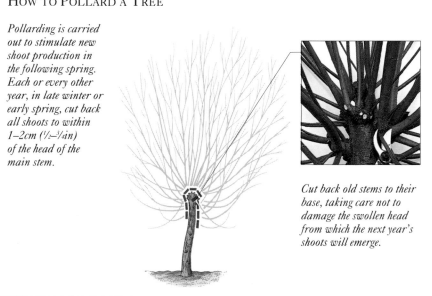

Pollarding is carried out to stimulate new shoot production in the following spring. Each or every other year, in late winter or early spring, cut back all shoots to within 1–2cm (½–¾in) of the head of the main stem.

Cut back old stems to their base, taking care not to damage the swollen head from which the next year's shoots will emerge.

results in excessive bleeding. Usually, renovation is best undertaken in late autumn or winter when the trees are fully dormant and the bare branch framework may be clearly seen. Flowering cherries and other *Prunus* species are best treated in early summer to reduce the risk of silver leaf infection. Where the need for renovation is extensive, the process should be carried out in stages over two or three seasons, as drastic pruning inevitably causes shock that may weaken or even kill a tree in poor health.

To renovate, first remove all dead, diseased, and damaged wood, then take out crossing and congested branches and any that spoil the well-balanced framework. In early spring, feed the tree with a general fertilizer and apply a mulch of well-rotted organic matter. Keep the tree well-fed and mulched for two to three years.

Hard pruning frequently stimulates the production of a mass of epicormic or water shoots. If necessary, select the strongest and best-placed to form replacement framework branches and remove the remainder. Bear in mind, however, that trees renovated in this way are seldom as structurally strong as they would have been if properly trained and pruned when young. The buds of any further water shoots that are produced should be rubbed away before they fully emerge.

Occasionally, you may inherit trees that have been pruned annually, thus producing congested clusters of growth arising from knobbly branches, but without the balanced branch framework of a properly pollarded tree. Such 'haircut' pruning is unsightly and reduces flower and fruit production. Corrective pruning is possible. First thin out the knobbly stumps at the ends of the main branches. Cut out most of the young shoots on the remaining stumps to leave one or two of the strongest, and cut these back by about one-third of their length. This procedure should be repeated over the following three or four seasons, until a more natural habit of growth has been re-established.

RENOVATING A TREE

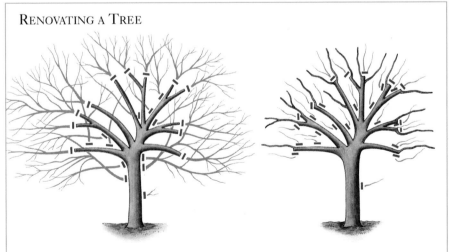

First year
Cut out dead, diseased, and damaged wood. Remove crossing or rubbing branches and any that spoil the balance of the framework.

Second and third year
The following year, thin out new growth from pruning wounds and remove water shoots. If necessary, repeat the following year.

PROPAGATION

Trees may be propagated by seed or vegetatively – by cuttings, layers or grafting. Most species come true from seed, but some, such as birch (*Betula*), hybridize readily and offspring may be variable. Cultivars and hybrids seldom come true when grown from seed and are therefore propagated vegetatively.

Many deciduous trees can be propagated from hardwood cuttings. Fast-rooting species, such as willow, are inserted directly into open ground. Slow-rooting species are tied in small bundles, overwintered in sand in the cold frame, and transferred to trenches in the following spring.

Prepare trenches to receive cuttings in early autumn, in friable, well-drained soil. On clay soils, add sharp sand to the base of the trench. Just after leaf fall, select some vigorous shoots of the current season's growth, cutting just above a bud or pair of buds at the junction between the previous and current season's growth.

Cuttings may sometimes be lifted by frost, so check regularly and refirm if necessary. They should root by the following autumn. Many conifers and broad-leaved evergreens can be propagated by semi-ripe cuttings taken in late summer or autumn from the current season's wood. Root in a equal parts mix of grit and peat, in a closed case at 21°C (70°F).

Take heel cuttings of sideshoots or 10–15cm (4–6in) long cuttings from leading or lateral shoots, trimmed just below a node. Remove the lowest two leaves and reduce the remainder by one half. Wound the base and dip in hormone rooting powder or gel. Insert the bottom third of the cutting into a hole in the compost, spacing so that leaves do not touch. Water with fungicidal solution and label. Keep just moist until rooted, removing fallen leaves regularly to avoid rot. Cuttings with basal heat should root by the spring.

Cuttings can also be inserted into the cold frame, with frost protection in winter. They may not root until the following autumn and therefore are best left in the frame for another winter, before hardening off and potting up in spring. Mist over in summer and shade from strong sun to avoid drying out and foliage scorch.

PLANTING DEPTHS

Multi-stemmed trees
Insert the cuttings with the top 2.5–3cm (1–1½in) above soil level. This enables the buds in the light to break and form several stems. Space cuttings 30–38cm (12–15in) apart outside, or 10cm (4in) apart in a cold frame.

Single-stemmed trees
Insert cuttings so that the top bud is barely covered by the soil. The lack of light on the stem inhibits the growth of all other buds. Space cuttings 30–38cm (12–15in) apart outside, or 10cm (4in) apart in a cold frame.

FAST-ROOTING HARDWOOD CUTTINGS

1 *Prepare a slit trench by driving a sharp spade vertically into the soil. The trench should be about 19cm (7in) deep, with one vertical side and one sloping side.*

2 *Select strong, straight, and healthy stems of about pencil thickness. Remove approximately 30cm (12in) of stem from the parent plant, just above a bud.*

3 *Remove any leaves. Trim cuttings to about 20cm (8in), with a sloping cut just above the top bud and a straight cut just below the bottom bud.*

4 *Insert into the trench at 10–15cm (4–6in) spacings, so that cuttings are positioned upright against the vertical side of the trench.*

5 *Firm the soil around the cuttings. Space further trenches at about 30–38cm (12–15in) apart. Water in thoroughly and label clearly.*

6 *Lift rooted cuttings during the following autumn and either pot them up individually or transplant them to their final location in open ground.*

Softwood cuttings are taken in spring from the tips of fast-growing shoots. They root easily but wilt rapidly, so prepare and insert them immediately after removal from the parent plant. Fill containers with cutting compost and firm gently. Remove the new growth from shoot tips, cutting just above a node with a sharp knife. Place in an opaque plastic bag to conserve moisture. Trim to 6cm (2½in), just below a node. Remove lower leaves, dip the base in hormone rooting powder or gel and insert into the compost. Water, label and place in a mist unit or closed case at 21–24°C (70–75°F). Water weekly with fungicide. Once rooted, harden off and pot up individually.

Raising trees from seed

Many trees are propagated easily from seed. Some seed, for example those of crab apples (*Malus*) or rowans (*Sorbus*), should be cleaned of their fleshy coat before sowing. Hard seed coats, such as those of oaks (*Quercus*), are nicked or rubbed with sandpaper so that they can absorb the water necessary for germination. Leguminous seeds are soaked in hot water for 24 hours.

Many temperate tree seeds exhibit dormancy and must be stored in either warm or cold conditions before they will germinate. Seed sown outside in autumn is chilled naturally during winter, but storing the seed in the refrigerator will produce more reliable results. Mix the seed with moistened vermiculite and place in a clear plastic bag. Store at 0.5–1°C (33–34°F), checking regularly and sowing immediately when signs of germination are seen. Seed chilling requirements vary considerably, from 6–8 weeks for deciduous species, to as little as 3 weeks for conifers. Some seed germinates only after chilling has ceased. Batch sowing over a period – after 4, 8, or 12 weeks of chilling – ensures that at least some seed will germinate.

SLOW-ROOTING HARDWOOD CUTTINGS

For species that do not root easily, tie the cuttings into bundles. Dip the ends of the bundles into a hormone rooting powder or gel. Insert the bundles of cuttings into a sand bed and leave in a cold frame over winter. In spring, insert them individually into a trench at a prepared site outside. The trench should be narrow, with one side vertical, to enable the cuttings to be held securely upright while they take root.

PREPARING SEMI-RIPE CUTTINGS

Cut a shoot 10–15cm (4–6in) long from a leader or sideshoot and trim immediately below a node. Strip off the lower leaves (here of Chamaecyparis obtusa 'Nana Aurea'*) and pinch out the tip if it is soft. Make a shallow wound, about 2.5cm (1in) long, down the side of the cutting and dip it in hormone rooting powder or gel.*

Simple layering

In early spring, cut a 5cm (2in) tongue, 30–45cm (12–18in) behind the growing tip of a vigorous shoot which is still attached to the parent plant. Brush the wound with hormone rooting powder or gel and peg it into a shallow hole. Tie the shoot to a vertical supporting cane and back fill the hole with friable soil mixed together with some leafmould and grit. When it has rooted (after 12 months or so) sever from the parent plant and transplant.

Vigorous shoot

Friable soil

Peg   Tongue

SOWING IN CONTAINERS

1 *Keeping the hand low to prevent the seed (here Sorbus) bouncing on the compost as they drop, sow the fine seed in trays of firmed seed compost, making sure they are scattered thinly and evenly.*

2 *Half-fill a sieve with some seed compost, hold it over the seed tray and tap the sides gently until the seeds are covered to approximately their own depth with seed compost.*

3 *Carefully apply a 5mm (¼in) layer of horticultural grit over the layer of compost. Label the seeds, and then water the tray using a watering can fitted with a fine rose nozzle.*

4 *Once the seedlings are large enough to handle, gently prick them out into individual containers, holding them by the leaves and taking care not to crush their stems and roots. Pot on as necessary.*

GLOSSARY OF TERMS

Italicised words have their own entry.

ACID (of soil). With a pH value of less than 7; see also *alkaline* and *neutral*.

ADVENTITIOUS (of roots). Arising directly from a stem or leaf.

ALKALINE (of soil). With a pH value of more than 7; see also *acid* and *neutral*.

APETALOUS. Having no petals.

APHID. Small, parasitic insect that sucks sap from a tree's bark.

AXIL. The angle between a leaf and stem where an axillary bud develops.

BLOOMED. Covered with a bluish-white deposit.

BOLE. The trunk of a tree from ground level to first major branch.

BRACT. A modified leaf at the base of a flower or flower cluster. It may resemble a normal leaf or be reduced and scale-like in appearance.

BUDDING. Bud-grafting, a form of grafting.

CALYX. The outer part of a flower, usually small and green but sometimes showy and brightly coloured; it is formed from the sepals and encloses the petals in a bud.

CANKER. A fungal infection that causes bark to darken and sink inwards and thus results in a restricted flow of nutrients and water through the tree.

CATKIN. A flower cluster, normally pendulous. Flowers lack petals, are often stalkless, surrounded by scale-like bracts, and are usually unisexual.

CONE. The clustered flowers or woody, seed-bearing structures of a conifer.

COPPICE. To cut back to near ground level each year in order to produce vigorous shoots for ornamental or practical purposes.

COROLLA. The part of a flower formed by the petals.

CROWN. The upper, branched part of a tree above the bole.

CUTTING. A section of a tree which is removed and used for propagation. See *Guide to Tree Care*, pp.182–4.

DECIDUOUS. Losing its leaves annually at the end of the growing season; semi-deciduous trees lose only some leaves.

ELLIPTIC (of leaves). Broadening at the centre and narrowing towards each end.

EPICORMIC. Shoot that grows directly from the trunk of a tree, often round a wound.

EVERGREEN. Retaining its leaves all year round, although losing some older leaves regularly throughout the year. Semi-evergreen trees retain only some leaves or lose older leaves only when the new growth is produced.

FIREBLIGHT. A bacterial infection that attacks blossom first, then stems and foliage.

FISSURED. Bark that is split or cracked due to age or weathering.

FRIABLE (of soil). Of a good, crumbly texture; capable of forming a soil that can be worked easily.

GLAUCOUS. Bluish-white, bluish-green.

GLOBOSE. Spherical.

GRAFTING. A method of propagation by which an artificial union is made between different parts of individual trees.

HABIT. The characteristic growth or general appearance of a tree.

HEEL. The small portion of old wood that is retained at the base of a cutting when it is removed from the stem.

HONEYDEW. Sticky substance found on foliage, the excrement of such pests as aphids, whiteflies and mealybugs.

HONEY FUNGUS. An infection caused by the fungus *Armillaria* which appears as a creamy white mycelium that develops under the bark at the base of the trunk or stem.

HUSK. The rough outer layer of a fruit or seed.

HYBRID. The offspring of genetically different parents, usually produced accidentally or artificially in cultivation, but occasionally arising in the wild.

KEY. A winged seed such as that produced by the sycamore (*Acer pseudoplatanus*).

LANCE-SHAPED (of leaves). Narrow and tapering at both ends.

LATERAL. A side growth that emerges from a shoot or root.

LEADER. The tip of the main stem of a tree.

LEAF MINERS. The larvae of various flies which tunnel into leaves and destroy them.

LEAFLET. A subdivision of a compound leaf.

LINEAR (of leaves). Very narrow with parallel sides.

LIME. Compounds of calcium; the amount of lime in soil determines whether it is alkaline, neutral or acid.

LOAM. Well-structured, fertile soil that is moisture-retentive but free-draining.

LOBE. A rounded projecting segment or part, forming part of a larger structure.

MICROCLIMATE. A small, local climate within a larger climate area, such as a greenhouse or a protected area of a garden.

MONOTYPIC. 1. Of a family: containing one genus that contains one species. 2. Of a genus: containing one species.

MULCH. A layer of organic matter applied to the soil over or around a tree to conserve moisture, protect the roots from frost, reduce the growth of weeds, and enrich the soil.

MYCELIUM. The vegetative part of a fungus, consisting of microscopic, threadlike filaments.

NATIVE. Growing wild naturally in a specific area.

NATURALIZED. Established in the wild and growing as if naturally.

NEUTRAL (of soil). With a pH value of 7, the point at which soil is neither acid nor alkaline.

NODE. The point on a stem from which a leaf or leaves grow.

OPPOSITE (of leaves). Borne two to each node, one opposite the other.

OVATE (of leaves). Egg-shaped in outline, with the broader end at the base, becoming more pointed at the tip.

PALMATE (of leaves). Having four or more leaflets growing from a single point, as in horse chestnut (*Aesculus hippocastanum*).

PANICLE. A compound, branched raceme in which flowers develop on stalks (peduncles) arising from the main stem.

PARASITE. A plant that lives in or on another (the host), from which it obtains nourishment.

PEDUNCLE. The stalk of a flower cluster.

PERFOLIATE (of leaves). Having leaf bases that completely encircle the stem.

PERIANTH. The calyx and corolla, or outer parts of a flower.

PETIOLE. The stalk of a leaf.

PHYLLOCLADE. A flattened stem or branch that functions as a leaf.

PHYLLODE. An expanded leaf stalk, which functions as, and resembles, a leaf blade.

PINNATE (of leaves). A compound leaf in which the leaflets grow in two rows on each side of the midrib.

PLEACHING. A form of training in which branches from a row of trees are interwoven to form a wall or canopy.

POLLARD. To cut back a tree's main branches in order to restrict growth.

PROP ROOTS. Large roots, found above ground at the base of a trunk, which help to support the tree.

PROSTRATE. With stems growing along the ground. Also called procumbent.

RACEME. An unbranched flower cluster with several or many stalked flowers borne singly along a main axis, the youngest at the apex.

RADIALLY ARRANGED (of leaves). Leaves arranged in a ray pattern around the stem.

RED SPIDER MITE. Tiny insects that drain sap from leaves and cause them to fall prematurely.

REVERT. To return to its original state, as when a plain green leaf is produced on a variegated plant.

ROOT. The part of a plant, normally underground, that functions as an anchorage and through which nutrients are absorbed. An aerial root is one

that emerges from the stem at some distance above the soil level. See also *prop root*.

ROOTBALL. The roots and accompanying soil or compost visible when a plant is lifted.

ROSETTE. A group of leaves radiating from approximately the same point, often at ground level at the base of a very short stem.

SCALE. 1. A reduced or modified leaf. 2. Part of the cone of a conifer.

SEPAL. Part of a calyx, usually green. They may be insignificant, but are sometimes showy.

SPIRALLY-ARRANGED (of leaves). Leaves arranged in ascending spiral form around the stem.

STANDARD. A tree with a clear length of bare stem below the lowest branches.

SUCKER. Shoot growing directly from a tree stem, or from below ground level, directly from the root.

TEPAL. A subdivision of the perianth in flowers that have no distinct calyx and corolla.

TOOTH. A small, marginal, often pointed lobe on a leaf.

UPRIGHT (of habit). With vertical or semi-vertical main branches.

VERMICULITE. A lightweight, mica-like mineral added to potting composts to improve moisture retention and aeration.

WATER SHOOT. Shoot growing directly out of a tree stem, frequently around a wound.

WEEPING. With slender branches that hang down.

WHIP. A young tree or grafted seedling without lateral branches.

WINGED (of seeds or fruits). Having a marginal flange or membrane.

P

ACKNOWLEDGMENTS

Key: l = left, r = right, t = top, c = centre, a = above, b = below

Photography by:

A–Z Botanical Collection Ltd 11tr, 192br
Gillian Beckett 72tr
Biofotos/Heather Angel 35bl, 132l
Christopher Brickell 92tr, 120tl
Eric Crichton 11cl, 20tr, 113bl, 150
Michael A. Dirr/The University of Georgia 64br
The Garden Picture Library 34br/John Glover 74br; Robert Estall 133c
Derek Gould 85tr, 111br
Neil Holmes 39br
Oxford Scientific Films/Deni Bown 114l, 154
Photos Horticultural 11tl, 88r, 127c, 159cra, 192tl
Savill Garden, Windsor 153r, 163cla
A. D. Schilling 78
Harry Smith Collection 11c, 11bl, 14t, 14b, 35tl, 51br, 55tr, 69tr, 73br, 74l, 77tr, 77b, 92br, 98br, 101tl, 103l, 103br, 104tr, 104br, 108tr, 113br, 113tr, 126, 132tr, 132br, 135tr, 137bl, 143tl, 148r, 149r, 152b

Additional photographs by:

Christopher Brickell
Eric Crichton
Geoff Dann
Steve Wooster

Picture Research:

Fiona Watson

Every effort has been made to trace the copyright holders. Dorling Kindersley apologizes for any unintentional omissions and would be pleased, in such cases, to add an acknowledgment in future editions.

Abbreviations			
C	centigrade	in	inch, inches
cm	centimetre	m	metre
cv.	cultivar	mm	millimetre
F	fahrenheit	oz	ounce
f.	forma	sp.	species
ft	foot, feet	subsp.	subspecies
g	gram	var.	variant

ill